**Editor**
Emily R. Smith, M.A. Ed.

**Editorial Project Manager**
Elizabeth Morris, Ph.D.

**Editor-in-Chief**
Sharon Coan, M.S. Ed.

**Cover Artist**
Brenda DiAntonis

**Imaging**
Rosa C. See
Alfred Lau

**Product Manager**
Phil Garcia

**Publishers**
Rachelle Cracchiolo, M.S. Ed.
Mary Dupuy Smith, M.S. Ed.

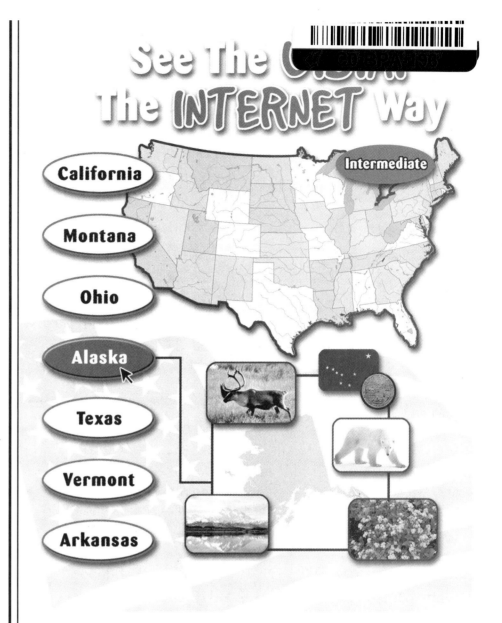

See The USA The INTERNET Way

Intermediate

California
Montana
Ohio
Alaska
Texas
Vermont
Arkansas

**Authors**

*Paula Patton and Karla Neeley Hase, Ed.D.*

Teacher Created Materials

***Teacher Created Materials, Inc.***
6421 Industry Way
Westminster, CA 92683
www.teachercreated.com
*©2002 Teacher Created Materials, Inc.*
Made in U.S.A.
**ISBN 0-7439-3821-6**

# Table of Contents

# How to Use this Book

*See the USA the Internet Way* is an interactive collection of activities for learning about the 50 United States. In the activities throughout the book, the Internet is used to gain knowledge and cultural awareness about each of the states. For each state, there is a fact sheet, a two-page research guide, a map, and a page of interesting trivia with a student activity. A CD-ROM is included with the book. On the CD-ROM, you will find outline maps, outline flags, and general clip art for each state.

The states are arranged by region according to similarities in location, climate, history, and culture. These region names are just labels to make it easier to refer to different parts of the country. The states can easily be rearranged by the teacher to be studied in the order they entered the union, alphabetically, or any other way.

By completing the activities in this book, students will:

- gain a multicultural perspective of the country;

- acquire background knowledge about the country; and

- begin to appreciate the rich diversity of the people who built the United States, helped it develop, and live here now.

The Internet is a vast world of informational resources. Some of them are wonderful and some are useless in the classroom. How do you know which ones are going to work best in your classroom? If you put the phrase *United States* into a search engine, it could return as many as five million websites! Obviously, it is impossible to visit them all. If you try to narrow the search by entering specific states, it can be even more overwhelming (10 million for Arizona, six million for Alaska).

Since teachers never have enough time to spend truly researching websites, this book was developed with the idea of providing teachers with websites specific to the 50 states. There are a wide variety of types of websites. Hopefully you'll find that the book provides enough sites to be useful, but not so many as to be totally daunting.

This book is meant to enhance your regular teaching. It will hopefully be a catalyst— something to spark curiosity and lead to further exploration.

Since typing URLs (Web page addresses) is sometimes difficult to do and is tedious, all of the Web pages are set up through the authors' website:

**http://www.neeleypress.com/usa**

Just make a bookmark (or favorite) pointing to this site. Because of the ever-changing nature of the Internet, there is a problem with "link rot." Websites change addresses, disappear, or just grow old and useless. At the authors' site, the websites can easily be updated for you and your students. If not, please e-mail the authors at the e-mail address found on the website and they will help you.

# How to Use this Book *(cont.)*

## Searching Suggestions

Hopefully, visiting the sites in this book will prompt the students to ask questions about things that are not in this book. When that happens, they can use a search engine to look for information. Some of the best kid-friendly search engines are:

1. **Google**™—Just type your topic and click "Google Search." If you want to narrow your search, go to the bottom of the page and click on "Search within results." Then type your qualifying topic into the new box and get a much more specific group of sites.

   **http://www.google.com**

2. **Yahooligans!**®—This site is specifically designed for kids ages 8–14. You can search by keywords or browse through categories.

   **http://www.yahooligans.com**

3. **AltaVista**—Search by keywords or use the directory. This engine also uses Boolean searches.

   **http://www.altavista.com**

4. **Ask Jeeves for Kids**™—Type your question and click on "ask."

   **http://www.ajkids.com**

A good tutorial on using search engines, called *Seven Steps Toward Better Searching,* can be found at the following website:

**http://edweb.sdsu.edu/WebQuest/searching/sevensteps.html**

There are many places your students can get pen pals or e-pals. Have the students write to a classroom (or individual students) from each state and compare culture, weather, geography, etc. The following websites provide information on obtaining e-mail addresses and/or e-pals.

1. **e-PALS Classroom Exchange**—This is a great place to get free e-mail accounts for the students in your class.

   **http://www.epals.com/**

2. **Teaching.com**—This site is another location where teachers can find e-mail accounts for their students.

   **http://www.teaching.com/keypals/**

# How to Use this Book *(cont.)*

## Teaching Suggestions

It would be beneficial for each child to have a notebook or binder in which to keep all the state papers. The United States map (page 12) could be kept in the front and colored as students study each state.

You might want to have a separate folder for each state if one binder would be too large.

Have the students put items other than those specifically mentioned on their state maps as they discover them.

If the students are familiar with databases, it would be interesting to enter information for each state and then make a comparison of the states. For example, how many states have milk as the official state beverage? If the students are not familiar with databases, a handwritten chart would substitute adequately.

If you have only a short time available, you could choose "experts" on each state and have them make presentations to the class about their states.

Have the students make different types of presentations (paper, posters, notebooks, multimedia slide shows, etc.) and display their work at an open house, board meeting, or other public event.

Greatly enlarge the outline map of each state and assign each to a student. Then, have students from each region arrange themselves according to the states they were assigned.

**Note:** Each state has 20 questions or activities specifically designed for that location. Websites for each of the 20 questions have been located for the students' reference. To access these websites, students should start on the authors' website.

### http://www.neeleypress.com/usa/

Once there, have the students click on the hyperlink for *"Discover" page links*. On that page, students will see links for each state. Within each link is a table with the websites students can use to find responses for the questions and activities.

# TeleTrek Introduction

## Congratulations!

You have just won the TeleTrek Travel Agency's annual sweepstakes. The prize this year is an all-expense paid tour of the United States. The trip will include a visit to each of the 50 states that make up this great country. You will explore the capitals and the capitols. You will discover the symbols and facts that make each state unique. You will be provided a time machine to experience the history of each state. Come prepared to explore this vast and awe-inspiring country. The United States has several of the world's most exciting cities, any kind of climate and landscape you can imagine, many cultures, great history, and wonderful people.

An itinerary will be provided for you or you will get to decide on your own itinerary. During the trip, you will be responsible for keeping a journal to record your findings and impressions. Be sure you keep the United States map handy so that you can color each state as you explore it. You should also label each state with its name and capital city.

Another gift from TeleTrek is a "magic camera" and all the film you want. Take pictures of things that interest you. It will make your journal much more fun to share with your friends and family. To take a picture with your "camera" on a Windows machine, right-click your mouse on the picture, choose *Save image as . . .,* and save it to your disk. To take a picture with your "camera" on a Macintosh machine, click and hold your mouse button on the picture, keep holding it and when the dialog box appears, slide to *Save this image as . . .,* and release the mouse button. You can then insert the pictures into your journals or stories. Be sure you cite your sources (tell where the picture came from) by copying and pasting the URL address into the file with the picture!

Are you packed? Ready? OK, let's go!

# TeleTrek Travel Agency
# Alphabetical Itinerary

| Location | Arrival Date | Departure Date | Location | Arrival Date | Departure Date |
|---|---|---|---|---|---|
| Alabama | | | Nebraska | | |
| Alaska | | | Nevada | | |
| Arizona | | | New Hampshire | | |
| Arkansas | | | New Jersey | | |
| California | | | New Mexico | | |
| Colorado | | | New York | | |
| Connecticut | | | North Carolina | | |
| Delaware | | | North Dakota | | |
| Florida | | | Ohio | | |
| Georgia | | | Oklahoma | | |
| Hawaii | | | Oregon | | |
| Idaho | | | Pennsylvania | | |
| Illinois | | | Rhode Island | | |
| Indiana | | | South Carolina | | |
| Iowa | | | South Dakota | | |
| Kansas | | | Tennessee | | |
| Kentucky | | | Texas | | |
| Louisiana | | | Utah | | |
| Maine | | | Vermont | | |
| Maryland | | | Virginia | | |
| Massachusetts | | | Washington | | |
| Michigan | | | Washington, D.C. | | |
| Minnesota | | | West Virginia | | |
| Mississippi | | | Wisconsin | | |
| Missouri | | | Wyoming | | |
| Montana | | | | | |

# TeleTrek Travel Agency *(cont.)*
# Regional Itinerary

| Location | Arrival Date | Departure Date | Location | Arrival Date | Departure Date |
|---|---|---|---|---|---|
| **New England** | | | Iowa | | |
| Connecticut | | | Michigan | | |
| Maine | | | Minnesota | | |
| Massachusetts | | | Missouri | | |
| New Hampshire | | | Ohio | | |
| Rhode Island | | | Wisconsin | | |
| Vermont | | | **Great Plains** | | |
| **Mid-Atlantic** | | | Kansas | | |
| Delaware | | | Nebraska | | |
| Maryland | | | North Dakota | | |
| New Jersey | | | South Dakota | | |
| New York | | | **Southwest** | | |
| Pennsylvania | | | Arizona | | |
| Washington, D.C. | | | New Mexico | | |
| **South** | | | Oklahoma | | |
| Alabama | | | Texas | | |
| Arkansas | | | **West** | | |
| Florida | | | California | | |
| Georgia | | | Colorado | | |
| Kentucky | | | Hawaii | | |
| Louisiana | | | Idaho | | |
| Mississippi | | | Montana | | |
| North Carolina | | | Nevada | | |
| South Carolina | | | Utah | | |
| Tennessee | | | Wyoming | | |
| Virginia | | | **Pacific Northwest** | | |
| West Virginia | | | Alaska | | |
| **Midwest** | | | Oregon | | |
| Illinois | | | Washington | | |
| Indiana | | | | | |

# TeleTrek Travel Agency *(cont.)*
# Itinerary Based on Admission to the Union

|   | Location | Arrival Date | Departure Date | Date of Admission to US |
|---|----------|--------------|----------------|--------------------------|
| 1 | Delaware | | | December 7, 1787 |
| 2 | Pennsylvania | | | December 12, 1787 |
| 3 | New Jersey | | | December 18, 1787 |
| 4 | Georgia | | | January 2, 1788 |
| 5 | Connecticut | | | January 9, 1788 |
| 6 | Massachusetts | | | February 6, 1788 |
| 7 | Maryland | | | April 28, 1788 |
| 8 | South Carolina | | | May 23, 1788 |
| 9 | New Hampshire | | | June 21, 1788 |
| 10 | Virginia | | | June 25, 1788 |
| 11 | New York | | | July 26, 1788 |
| 12 | North Carolina | | | November 21, 1789 |
| 13 | Rhode Island | | | May 29, 1790 |
| 14 | Vermont | | | March 4, 1791 |
| 15 | Kentucky | | | June 1, 1792 |
| 16 | Tennessee | | | June 1, 1796 |
| 17 | Ohio | | | March 1, 1803 |
| 18 | Louisiana | | | April 30, 1812 |
| 19 | Indiana | | | December 11, 1816 |
| 20 | Mississippi | | | December 10, 1817 |
| 21 | Illinois | | | December 3, 1818 |
| 22 | Alabama | | | December 14, 1819 |
| 23 | Maine | | | March 15, 1820 |
| 24 | Missouri | | | August 10, 1821 |
| 25 | Arkansas | | | June 15, 1836 |

# TeleTrek Travel Agency *(cont.)*
# Itinerary Based on Admission to the Union

| | Location | Arrival Date | Departure Date | Date of Admission to US |
|---|---|---|---|---|
| 26 | Michigan | | | January 26, 1837 |
| 27 | Florida | | | March 3, 1845 |
| 28 | Texas | | | December 29, 1845 |
| 29 | Iowa | | | December 28, 1846 |
| 30 | Wisconsin | | | May 29, 1848 |
| 31 | California | | | September 9, 1850 |
| 32 | Minnesota | | | May 11, 1858 |
| 33 | Oregon | | | February 14, 1859 |
| 34 | Kansas | | | January 29, 1861 |
| 35 | West Virginia | | | June 20, 1863 |
| 36 | Nevada | | | October 31, 1864 |
| 37 | Nebraska | | | March 1, 1867 |
| 38 | Colorado | | | August 1, 1876 |
| 39 | North Dakota | | | November 2, 1889 |
| 40 | South Dakota | | | November 2, 1889 |
| 41 | Montana | | | November 8, 1889 |
| 42 | Washington | | | November 11, 1889 |
| 43 | Idaho | | | July 3, 1890 |
| 44 | Wyoming | | | July 10, 1890 |
| 45 | Utah | | | January 4, 1896 |
| 46 | Oklahoma | | | November 16, 1907 |
| 47 | New Mexico | | | January 6, 1912 |
| 48 | Arizona | | | February 14, 1912 |
| 49 | Alaska | | | January 3, 1959 |
| 50 | Hawaii | | | August 21, 1959 |

# My _____ Journal

(state name)

_____

_____

_____

_____

_____

_____

_____

_____

_____

_____

_____

_____

_____

_____

_____

_____

_____

United States Map

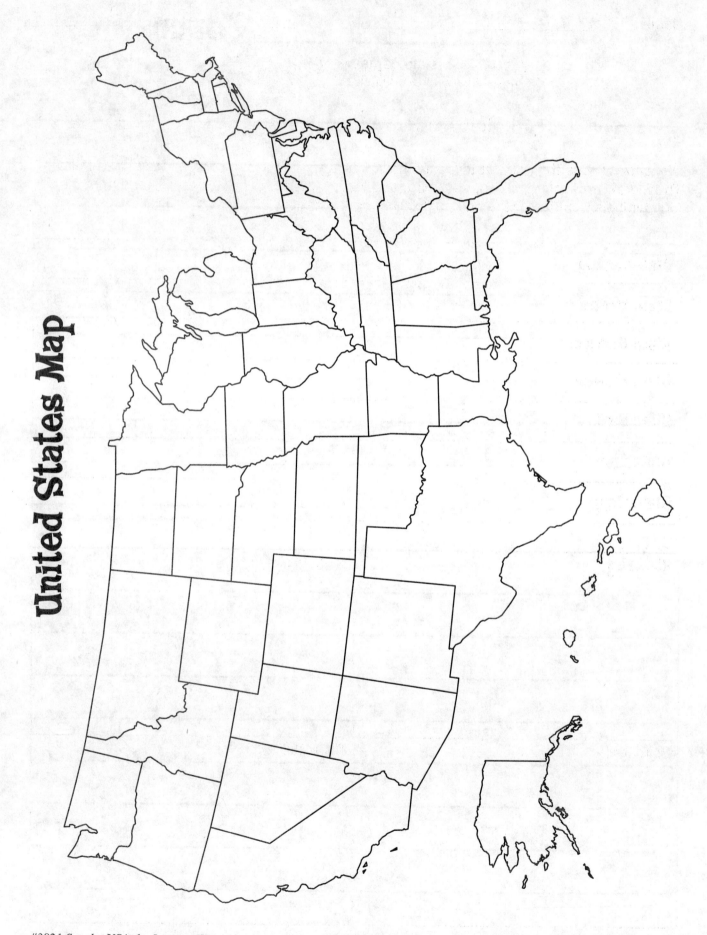

12

Name _____ Date _____

# Connecticut Symbols

## http://www.netstate.com/states/

**Directions:** Use the Internet to locate the symbols of the state to complete the chart below. Then, draw and color the flag, seal, bird, and flower. If you wish, you may instead print the four symbols from a website and paste them on the page.

| | |
|---|---|
| State Capital | |
| State Motto | |
| State Nickname | |
| State Flower | |
| State Bird | |
| State Tree | |
| State Song | |

| | |
|---|---|
| State Flag | State Seal |
| State Bird | State Flower |

Name _____ Date _____

# Discover Connecticut

**Directions:** Research the Internet to find the answers to these questions. Record your answers below in the space provided, on your own paper, or in a word processing document. You should also include any other interesting places you visited, facts you learned, or opinions you developed.

Begin at the authors' website and then click on the correct state. From there, you can choose the corresponding links to answer the questions.

## http://www.neeleypress.com/usa

| | Questions |
|---|---|
| 1 | Where did Connecticut get its name? |
| 2 | How long is the Connecticut River? |
| 3 | What Native Americans lived in the Connecticut area before the Europeans came? |
| 4 | Who was one of the first Europeans to map the area? **Hint:** He was a Dutch trader who traded with the Native Americans. |
| 5 | Let's check out the capital. Who are the governor and the lieutenant governor? |
| 6 | Now that you've met them, go ahead and explore the capitol building. Describe what you see. |
| 7 | Who settled Hartford and how did it get its name? |
| 8 | Many famous inventors lived and worked in Connecticut. One of these is Elias Howe. How did his invention help life in America? |
| 9 | Another famous person from Connecticut is Noah Webster. What did he do? |

# Discover Connecticut *(cont.)*

| | Questions |
|---|---|
| **10** | While you are in Hartford, be sure to stop by the Mark Twain House. What did Mark Twain name his dogs? |
| **11** | Look at some of the Connecticut wildflowers. Have you seen some of these flowers near your home? |
| **12** | Connecticut has an official state hero. Who is it and why was he a hero? |
| **13** | Connecticut has many forms of wildlife. Choose one and write about it in your journal. There are some great pictures to color and more information on the kids' page. |
| **14** | Look at some photographs taken in various places in Connecticut. You may want to cut and paste some into your journal. Describe the photographs. |
| **15** | What are some of the leading agricultural products of Connecticut? |
| **16** | What is a diorama? Visit the Peabody Museum of Natural History to find out. Look around while you are there. |
| **17** | You are just in time for the Wethersfield Festival! Have a good time and learn some history. When the city needed money for the meetinghouse, how did the people pay their taxes? |
| **18** | Yale University is the third oldest institution of its kind in America. Take a tour and find out how much space is under the roof of the Payne Whitney Gymnasium. |
| **19** | Tired of cities and people? Go spend some time with Connecticut's frogs. One of these frogs has been known to live up to 35 years in captivity. Which is it? |
| **20** | Why is the Charter Oak so important to the history of Connecticut? |

**Challenge:** Write a question about the state that isn't addressed above. Then, suggest a website for finding the answer to your question.

**Question 1:** _____

**URL 1:** _____

Name _____ Date _____

# Connecticut State Map

**Directions:** Use the key located below to complete the map of the state. Begin by locating the capital city and at least three other major cities. Then, locate and draw two major rivers and/or mountains in the state. Can you find Bear Mountain and put it on your map? Draw at least two major interstate highways that travel through the state. Finally, label any other states and/or bodies of water that surround the state.

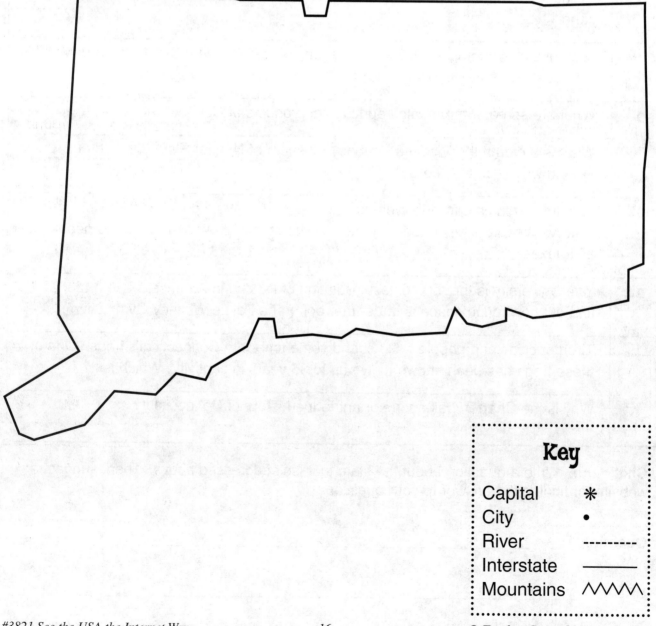

**Key**

| | |
|---|---|
| Capital | ✳ |
| City | • |
| River | - - - - - - |
| Interstate | ———— |
| Mountains | ∧∧∧∧∧ |

16

Name _____ Date _____

# Connecticut Trivia

The only man to have signed all four of our nation's fundamental documents of freedom (the Articles of Association, the Declaration of Independence, the Articles of Confederation, and the Constitution) was Roger Sherman, from Connecticut.

Olympic gold medal figure skater Dorothy Hamil is from Riverside, Connecticut.

There are bronze frogs on the bridge over the Willimantic River in Windham that weigh 2,000 to 3,000 pounds each.

The first telephone book ever issued contained only fifty names. It was published in 1878 by the New Haven District Telephone Company.

Connecticut never ratified the 18th Amendment (Prohibition).

In Hartford, you may not cross the street walking on your hands!

The first automobile law was passed by the state of Connecticut in 1901. The speed limit was set at 12 miles per hour.

The World Wrestling Federation® or the WWF® is headquartered in Stamford.

In colonial New Haven, cut pumpkins were used as guides for haircuts to ensure a round uniform haircut. These New Englanders were nicknamed "pumpkin heads."

In Hartford, Connecticut, it is illegal for a husband to kiss his wife on Sundays.

Connecticut State Law: In order for a pickle to officially be considered a pickle, it must bounce.

A local ordinance in Atwoodville, Connecticut, prohibits people from playing Scrabble® while waiting for a politician to speak.

**Directions:** Use the following substitutions to find the name of the Connecticut State Song.

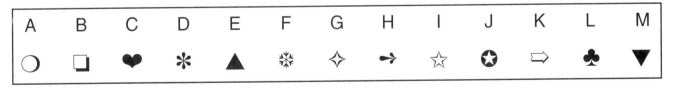

_____  _____  _____  _____  _____  _____    _____  _____  _____  _____  _____  _____

Name _____  Date _____

# Maine Symbols

## http://www.netstate.com/states/

**Directions:** Use the Internet to locate the symbols of the state to complete the chart below. Then, draw and color the flag, seal, bird, and flower. If you wish, you may instead print the four symbols from a website and paste them on the page.

| | |
|---|---|
| **State Capital** | |
| **State Motto** | |
| **State Nickname** | |
| **State Flower** | |
| **State Bird** | |
| **State Tree** | |
| **State Song** | |

| **State Flag** | **State Seal** |
|---|---|
| | |
| **State Bird** | **State Flower** |
| | |

Name _____ Date _____

# Discover Maine

**Directions:** Research the Internet to find the answers to these questions. Record your answers below in the space provided, on your own paper, or in a word processing document. You should also include any other interesting places you visited, facts you learned, or opinions you developed.

Begin at the authors' website and then click on the correct state. From there, you can choose the corresponding links to answer the questions.

## http://www.neeleypress.com/usa

| | Questions |
|---|---|
| 1 | Instead of a capitol building, Maine has a state house. Take a look at this building. When was it built? |
| 2 | In 1873, Chester Greenwood invented earmuffs at the age of 15. What was he doing when he decided he needed to keep his ears warm? |
| 3 | The first colony in America was settled in 1607, thirteen years before the arrival of the Pilgrims. Where was this settlement? Why did they leave? |
| 4 | Louis Cockolexis, a native Penobscot, was one of the first Native Americans to play professional baseball. What two colleges did he attend before playing for the Cleveland Spiders (later named the Indians)? |
| 5 | What exactly is a *Homarus americanus*? Maine harvests over 47 million pounds of them every year. |
| 6 | The Moose Peak Lighthouse on Mistake Island, Maine, is the foggiest place on the east coast. How many consecutive hours did the fog horn have to be sounded in 1916? |
| 7 | The state of Maine produces most of the blueberries in the country. What are three other common names for blueberries? |
| 8 | The state of Maine has 62 lighthouses. The oldest is the Portland Head Light. Which president commissioned this lighthouse? What year was it? |
| 9 | What is the easternmost city in the United States? This small port city is the first place in the United States to receive the rays of the morning sun. |

# Discover Maine *(cont.)*

| | Questions |
|---|---|
| 10 | Eastport is the only United States owned principality that has been under rule by a foreign government. Who ruled it from 1814 to 1818 following the conclusion of the War of 1812? |
| 11 | Joshua L. Chamberlain is credited with turning the tide in the Civil War at Gettysburg. What jobs did he have before and after the war? |
| 12 | Maine's average temperature in the summer is 70 degrees and 20 degrees in the winter. What is the temperature in Bangor, Maine, today? |
| 13 | West Quoddy Head is the easternmost point in the United States. Which president commissioned the construction of this lighthouse? |
| 14 | John B. Curtis and his brother started manufacturing gum in 1848 on top of a Franklin stove. How much did that first gum cost? |
| 15 | Twin brothers, Francis and Freelan Stanley, invented the Stanley Steamer, the first steam motorcar in New England. They also invented a photographic process that they sold to what familiar company? |
| 16 | Henry Wadsworth Longfellow was born in 1807 in Portland, Maine. Read one of his poems at the bottom of this site. Rewrite the poem in your own words. |
| 17 | In 1964, Senator Margaret Chase Smith became the first woman to have her name placed in nomination for the presidency of the United States. How did she initially get into politics? |
| 18 | Former President George Bush has a summer home in Kennebunkport. What was the town's first name? |
| 19 | Fort Knox, Maine, was erected in 1844 from granite from nearby Mount Waldo. Fort Knox was built to thwart an invasion from what country? |
| 20 | Edmund S. Muskie was a governor and United States Senator for Maine. In which branch of the military did he serve? |

**Challenge:** Write a question about the state that isn't addressed above. Then, suggest a website for finding the answer to your question.

**Question 1:** _____

**URL 1:** _____

Name _____   Date _____

# Maine State Map

**Directions:** Use the key located below to complete the map of the state. Begin by locating the capital city and at least three other major cities. Then, locate and draw two major rivers and/or mountains in the state. Draw at least two major interstate highways that travel through the state. Finally, label any other states and/or bodies of water that surround the state. What country, other than the United States, borders Maine? Label it.

**Key**

| | |
|---|---|
| Capital | ✳ |
| City | • |
| River | - - - - - - - - |
| Interstate | ——— |
| Mountains | ∧∧∧∧ |

Name _____     Date _____

# Maine Trivia

Maine is the only state in the United States whose name is just one syllable.

Maine is the only state that shares its border with only one other state.

"M*A*S*H" army surgeon Benjamin Franklin "Hawkeye" Pierce hailed from Crab Apple Cove, Maine.

The state of Maine has at least 28 cities or towns that begin with the word "North," 23 with the word "South," 22 with "West," and 28 with "East."

Maine has 3,500 miles of coastline.

90% of the country's toothpick supply is produced in Maine.

**Directions:** Unscramble these letters to reveal Maine's nickname.

# ipen            erte            taste

_____          _____          _____

Name _____ Date _____

# Massachusetts Symbols

**http://www.netstate.com/states/**

**Directions:** Use the Internet to locate the symbols of the state to complete the chart below. Then, draw and color the flag, seal, bird, and flower. If you wish, you may instead print the four symbols from a website and paste them on the page.

| State Capital | |
|---|---|
| State Motto | |
| State Nickname | |
| State Flower | |
| State Bird | |
| State Tree | |
| State Song | |

| State Flag | State Seal |
|---|---|
| | |
| **State Bird** | **State Flower** |
| | |

Name _____    Date _____

# Discover Massachusetts

**Directions:** Research the Internet to find the answers to these questions. Record your answers below in the space provided, on your own paper, or in a word processing document. You should also include any other interesting places you visited, facts you learned, or opinions you developed.

Begin at the authors' website and then click on the correct state. From there, you can choose the corresponding links to answer the questions.

## http://www.neeleypress.com/usa

| | Questions |
|---|---|
| 1 | Who is the present governor of Massachusetts? |
| 2 | Start your tour of Massachusetts in Plymouth where the Pilgrims started theirs in 1620 and continue to a reconstruction of Plimoth Plantation. Describe the plantation. |
| 3 | What foods were served at the harvest feast of 1621? |
| 4 | Boston is the capital of Massachusetts. The seat of the Massachusetts state government is the State House. Who designed this building? When was the "new" State House built? |
| 5 | The next stop on the Freedom Trail walk is the Boston Common. What is the Boston Common and what are some of the ways it has been used during its long history? |
| 6 | Describe the Boston Massacre in your journal. Does Paul Revere's engraving depict the actual happening? Was the picture an effective tool for stirring up anti-British feeling? |
| 7 | Who was Crispus Attucks? |
| 8 | Where was the battle of Bunker Hill actually fought? |
| 9 | What important document was read from the balcony of the Old State House in Boston? |

# Discover Massachusetts *(cont.)*

| | Questions |
|---|---|
| 10 | What four United States presidents were born in Massachusetts? |
| 11 | Travel over to Cape Cod for a few days. Mark it on your map. Describe what you did and saw on Cape Cod. |
| 12 | The members of the Massachusetts Bay Colony were mostly of what religious group? |
| 13 | What were Samuel Adams and the patriots protesting with the Boston Tea Party? |
| 14 | In 1742, Faneuil Hall was built in Boston. What was it used for then? What is it used for now? |
| 15 | What university was built in Cambridge in 1636? How many students did it have then? How many does it have now? Take a tour and find out this and much more. |
| 16 | For what is the Old North Church famous? |
| 17 | The first governor of Massachusetts was also the first man to sign the Declaration of Independence. Who was he? |
| 18 | What does the name Massachusetts mean and where did it originate? |
| 19 | For what is Danvers, Massachusetts, famous? |
| 20 | What was the event that started the Salem Witch Trials? How long did the era last? |

**Challenge:** Write a question about the state that isn't addressed above. Then, suggest a website for finding the answer to your question.

**Question 1:** _____

**URL 1:** _____

Name _____  Date _____

# Massachusetts State Map

**Directions:** Use the key located below to complete the map of the state. Begin by locating the capital city and at least three other major cities. Then, locate and draw two major rivers and/or mountains in the state. Draw at least two major interstate highways that travel through the state. Finally, label any other states and/or bodies of water that surround the state.

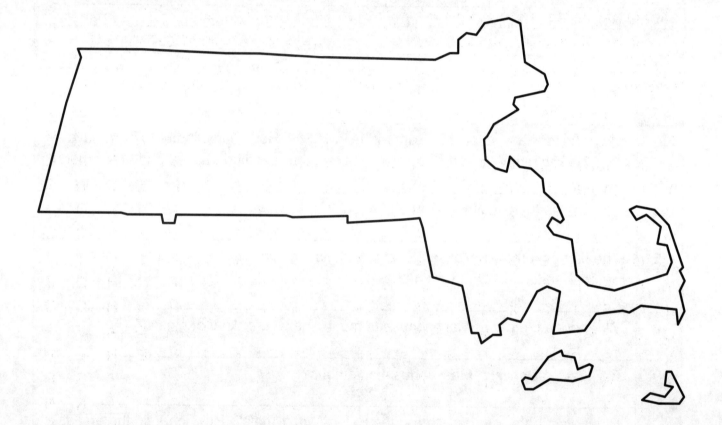

**Key**

| Capital | ✳ |
| City | • |
| River | - - - - - - - |
| Interstate | —————— |
| Mountains | ∧∧∧∧∧∧ |

Name _____   Date _____

# Massachusetts Trivia

Fig Newtons® might have been called Fig Marbleheads. Invented by the Kennedy Biscuit Works in Cambridgeport, Massachusetts, the company wanted a name that used the name of a close town and the word fig to promote local business. In the end, Newton was chosen over the others.

Massachusetts first cultivated its own watermelon in 1629. In those days, nothing was wasted: the rind was pickled, the juice was drunk, the seeds were toasted for snacks, and the flesh was eaten.

If you want to get technical, there are really only 46 states in the United States. The reason: Kentucky, Massachusetts, Pennsylvania, and Virginia are commonwealths.

The official state dessert of Massachusetts is Boston Cream Pie.

The father of the pink flamingo (the plastic lawn ornament) was Don Featherstone of Massachusetts.

**Directions:** Find the names of famous Massachusetts natives in the word search.

```
G S J U F Z V G T T I M C A C R C H P J Y
K S M A D A Y C N I U Q N H O J O Y V D M
Y N I L K N A R F N I M A J N E B T R A E
Y U W F D N Z G J D Q B V E G G H X C W G
Y K Z X C S Y Y R I K U S M A D A N H O J
O L I V E R W E N D E L L H O L M E S O Q
N O S R E M E O D L A W H P L A R I H B B
Y D E N N E K D L A R E G Z T I F N H O J
J O F I Q X Y Y O Z H J E X U N H W H G Q
O S S Y N H W E R E V E R L U A P F A J I
X T S Q C Z V E L I W H I T N E Y E H L M
I S W P F R N H G I H F J C Q N C C O S R
C N Z Q D B A B T V D H O R A C E M A N N
X W S U X C N E Q O K C A V X Y Y X P I N
X K W I L D Q L F S K J W J M V S L N B B
```

## Word Bank

Benjamin Franklin

Horace Mann

John Fitzgerald Kennedy

John Quincy Adams

Paul Revere

Eli Whitney

John Adams

John Hancock

Oliver Wendell Holmes

Ralph Waldo Emerson

Name _____ Date _____

# New Hampshire Symbols

**http://www.netstate.com/states/**

**Directions:** Use the Internet to locate the symbols of the state to complete the chart below. Then, draw and color the flag, seal, bird, and flower. If you wish, you may instead print the four symbols from a website and paste them on the page.

| | |
|---|---|
| **State Capital** | |
| **State Motto** | |
| **State Nickname** | |
| **State Flower** | |
| **State Bird** | |
| **State Tree** | |
| **State Song** | |

| State Flag | State Seal |
|---|---|
| | |
| **State Bird** | **State Flower** |
| | |

Name _____ Date _____

# Discover New Hampshire

**Directions:** Research the Internet to find the answers to these questions. Record your answers below in the space provided, on your own paper, or in a word processing document. You should also include any other interesting places you visited, facts you learned, or opinions you developed.

Begin at the authors' website and then click on the correct state. From there, you can choose the corresponding links to answer the questions.

## http://www.neeleypress.com/usa

| | Questions |
|---|---|
| 1 | What United States president was born in New Hampshire? |
| 2 | When was New Hampshire first settled? By whom was it settled and for what purpose? |
| 3 | In the 1600s, there were two main groups of Native Americans in what is now New Hampshire. What were they? Describe their houses and their lifestyles. |
| 4 | Being leaders in the revolutionary movement, New Hampshire delegates were allowed to be the first to vote on what important document? |
| 5 | In 1816 when the site for the capitol building was chosen, why did the people choose to make the capitol of granite? |
| 6 | Concord was not always called Concord. What were its other names? |
| 7 | What is the "Old Man of the Mountain"? Where is it located? |
| 8 | What is the highest point in New Hampshire? |
| 9 | What place in New Hampshire is rumored to have the world's worst weather? |

# Discover New Hampshire *(cont.)*

| | Questions |
|---|---|
| 10 | Take a tour of the summit of Mount Washington and some of the hiking trails in the White Mountain National Forest. Pretend you won a free trip to stay in the new Tip Top House Hotel. Write a story about your stay. |
| 11 | Name seven mountain peaks in the Presidential Range of the White Mountains that are over one mile high. (How many feet are there in a mile?) |
| 12 | New Hampshire's mountains include five monadnocks. What is a monadnock? Name the New Hampshire monadnocks. |
| 13 | About what percentage of New Hampshire is forest? |
| 14 | What is the salary for New Hampshire legislators? |
| 15 | Who is the present governor of New Hampshire? |
| 16 | What is the longstanding New Hampshire and national political tradition pertaining to presidential elections? |
| 17 | Alan B. Shepard, Jr. was born in East Derry, New Hampshire. For what was he famous? |
| 18 | What sporting event takes place in February in the town of Center Sandwich? |
| 19 | What is the state tree of New Hampshire? By what other names is it known? For what did the Native Americans use the tree? |
| 20 | In what year was the first potato planted in the United States? Where was it planted? |

**Challenge:** Write a question about the state that isn't addressed above. Then, suggest a website for finding the answer to your question.

**Question 1:** _____

**URL 1:** _____

Name _____     Date _____

# New Hampshire State Map

**Directions:** Use the key located below to complete the map of the state. Begin by locating the capital city and at least three other major cities. Then, locate and draw two major rivers and/or mountains in the state. Draw at least two major interstate highways that travel through the state. Finally, label any other states and/or bodies of water that surround the state.

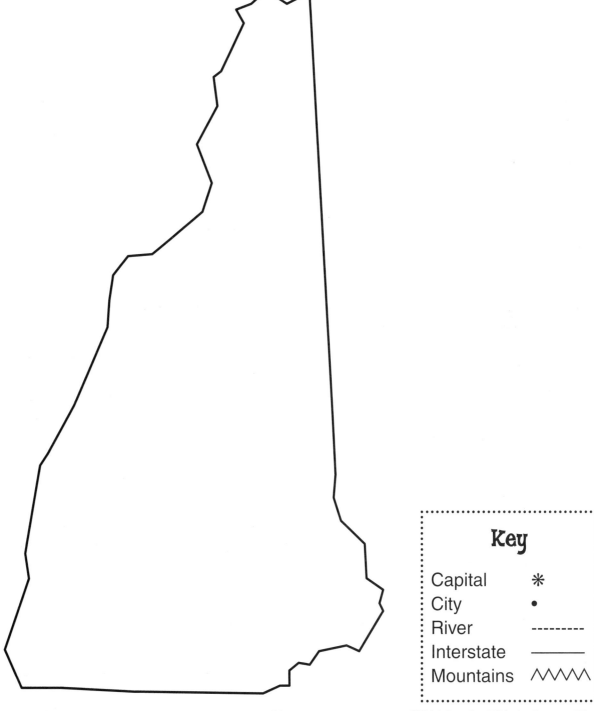

**Key**

| Capital | ✳ |
|---|---|
| City | • |
| River | --------- |
| Interstate | ——— |
| Mountains | ∧∧∧∧∧ |

Name _____   Date _____

# New Hampshire Trivia

Levi Hutchins of Concord invented the first alarm clock in 1787.

The Memorial Bell Tower at Cathedral of the Pines in Rindge has four bronze bas-reliefs designed by Norman Rockwell. The bell tower is specifically dedicated to women—military and civilian—who died serving their country.

It is a state law that you may not tap your feet, nod your head, or in any way keep time to the music in a tavern, restaurant, or cafe.

Sarah Josepha Hale, author and journalist who wrote the poem, "Mary Had a Little Lamb" in 1830, is from Newport, New Hampshire.

The granite profile, "Old Man of the Mountain," is one of the most famous natural landmarks in the state. The Old Man's head measures 40 feet from chin to forehead and is made up of five ledges. Nature carved this profile thousands of years ago. The natural sculpture is 1,200 feet above Echo Lake.

The Pembroke Glass Works produced crown window glass from 1839 until 1850. The process involves gathering molten glass on a blowpipe and blowing the glass into a balloon shape. The blowpipe is removed, a solid "punty" rod is attached, and the glass is spun rapidly until a disc is formed. When the glass cools, the outer portion beyond the central knob is then cut into panes.

It is interesting to note that the New Hampshire state flag is the only state flag that depicts another state on its flag. The illustration of the seal is of the frigate *Raleigh* under construction on a sand bar which at the time the seal was made was part of Massachusetts and is now part of Maine.

**Directions:** Each letter is represented by a number in the puzzle. Figure out which numbers represent which letters to determine the state motto. Some letters have been done for you.
**Hint:** Look for a pattern of even numbers.

| A | B | C | D | E | F | G | H | I | J | K | L | M | N | O | P | Q | R | S | T | U | V | W | X | Y | Z |
|---|---|---|---|---|---|---|---|---|---|---|---|---|---|---|---|---|---|---|---|---|---|---|---|---|---|
| 2 |   |   |   |   |   |   |   |   |   |   |   | 26 | 30 |   |   |   |   |   |   |   |   |   |   |   |   |

M  O        O :                                 O

26  30  40  40  30     24  18  44  10    12  36  10  10    30  36    8  18  10

32

Name _____     Date _____

# Rhode Island Symbols

## http://www.netstate.com/states/

**Directions:** Use the Internet to locate the symbols of the state to complete the chart below. Then, draw and color the flag, seal, bird, and flower.  If you wish, you may instead print the four symbols from a website and paste them on the page.

| | |
|---|---|
| **State Capital** | |
| **State Motto** | |
| **State Nickname** | |
| **State Flower** | |
| **State Bird** | |
| **State Tree** | |
| **State Song** | |

| **State Flag** | **State Seal** |
|---|---|
| **State Bird** | **State Flower** |

Name _____     Date _____

# Discover Rhode Island

**Directions:** Research the Internet to find the answers to these questions. Record your answers below in the space provided, on your own paper, or in a word processing document. You should also include any other interesting places you visited, facts you learned, or opinions you developed.

Begin at the authors' website and then click on the correct state. From there, you can choose the corresponding links to answer the questions.

## http://www.neeleypress.com/usa

| | Questions |
|---|---|
| 1 | What is the official name of Rhode Island? |
| 2 | On May 4, 1776, Rhode Island was the first of the 13 colonies to do what? |
| 3 | On May 29, 1790, Rhode Island was the last of the 13 colonies to do what? |
| 4 | What events led to the founding of Providence by Roger Williams? |
| 5 | Where is the world's largest bug located? How big is it? |
| 6 | The oldest carousel in the United States is in Rhode Island. Where is it and what is its name? |
| 7 | Who is the present governor of Rhode Island, and what are his or her duties? |
| 8 | What is a quahog? How did it get its name? What different uses did the early Native Americans have for it? |
| 9 | What do the stars in the Rhode Island flag represent? |

# Discover Rhode Island *(cont.)*

| | Questions |
|---|---|
| 10 | For what is the state bird famous? |
| 11 | Visit some of the lighthouses on the coast of Rhode Island. Describe your favorite one. |
| 12 | What are some major contributors to the economy in Rhode Island? |
| 13 | What is the name of the Rhode Island state yacht? |
| 14 | Write a short biographical essay about one of the famous Rhode Islanders. |
| 15 | What were the men in General Nathaniel Green's Black Regiment given for fighting in the Revolutionary War? |
| 16 | How many degrees difference are there in the record high temperature and the record low temperature in the state? |
| 17 | Who was the first verifiable European visitor to Rhode Island? For what was he searching? |
| 18 | Describe the State House. |
| 19 | Describe the "Independent Man." |
| 20 | Read the quick facts on the State House. Take the quiz to see how much you learned. |

**Challenge:** Write a question about the state that isn't addressed above. Then, suggest a website for finding the answer to your question.

**Question 1:** _____

**URL 1:** _____

Name _____     Date _____

# Rhode Island State Map

**Directions:** Use the key located below to complete the map of the state. Begin by locating the capital city and at least three other major cities. Then, locate and draw two major rivers and/or mountains in the state. Draw at least two major interstate highways that travel through the state. Finally, label any other states and/or bodies of water that surround the state.

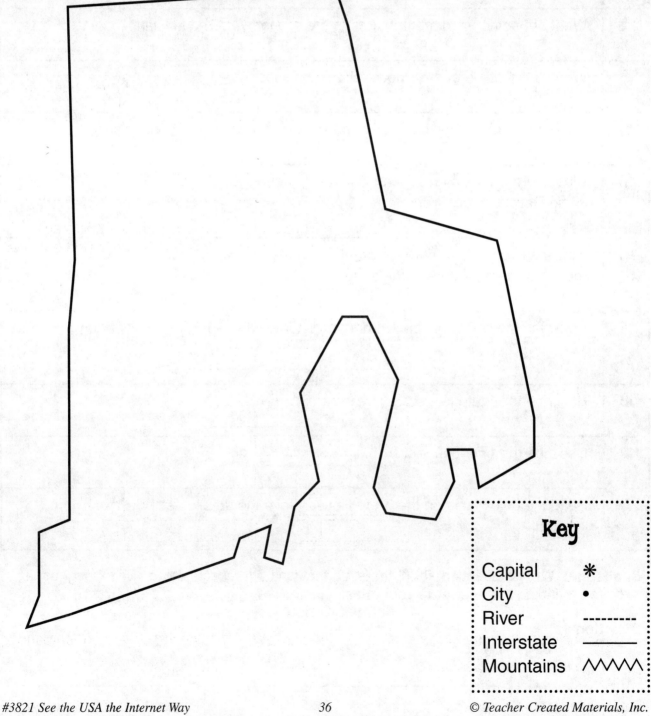

### Key

| | |
|---|---|
| Capital | ✳ |
| City | • |
| River | - - - - - - - - - |
| Interstate | ——— |
| Mountains | ＶＶＶＶＶ |

Name _____     Date _____

# Rhode Island Trivia

Rhode Island never ratified the Eighteenth Amendment: Prohibition.

Rhode Island was the first colony to declare independence from Great Britain— May 4, 1776.

The first toy to be advertised on T.V. was Hasbro's Mr. Potato Head®, born in Pawtucket.

Rhode Island is the smallest state in the United States. It covers 1,214 square miles. North to south it measures 48 miles, and east to west it measures 37 miles.

The oldest schoolhouse in the United States is in Portsmouth. It was built in 1716.

In 1774, Newport, Rhode Island, hosted the first circus in the country.

President John F. Kennedy and Jacqueline Bouvier were married at St. Mary's church in Newport, Rhode Island.

In Rhode Island, it is considered an offense to throw pickle juice on a trolley.

In Newport, you cannot smoke a pipe after sunset.

It is illegal in Providence to wear transparent clothing.

**Directions:** The Wampanoag lived in Eastern Rhode Island. Unscramble the following Wampanoag words, people, and places. Then, unscramble the circled letters to find out what "Wampanoag" means.

1. KEONAOTKP

2. PUTXATE

3. IDNAQAUQEU

4. SUTENA

5. NAMOAGAPW

6. HAOKSWM

7. HANCIMA

8. SIKKOSO

9. WASUSUGSEESTCS

L     F

## Word Bank

| Sokokis | Wessaguscusset | Pokanoket | Mahican | Wampanoag |
|---------|----------------|-----------|---------|-----------|
| Patuxet | Quadequina | Nauset | Mohawks | |

Name _____ Date _____

# Vermont Symbols

## http://www.netstate.com/states/

**Directions:** Use the Internet to locate the symbols of the state to complete the chart below. Then, draw and color the flag, seal, bird, and flower. If you wish, you may instead print the four symbols from a website and paste them on the page.

| State Capital | |
|---|---|
| State Motto | |
| State Nickname | |
| State Flower | |
| State Bird | |
| State Tree | |
| State Song | |

| State Flag | State Seal |
|---|---|
| | |
| **State Bird** | **State Flower** |
| | |

Name _____ Date _____

# Discover Vermont

**Directions:** Research the Internet to find the answers to these questions. Record your answers below in the space provided, on your own paper, or in a word processing document. You should also include any other interesting places you visited, facts you learned, or opinions you developed.

Begin at the authors' website and then click on the correct state. From there, you can choose the corresponding links to answer the questions.

## http://www.neeleypress.com/usa

| | Questions |
|---|---|
| 1 | What three nations of Native Americans were represented in the area that is now Vermont when the first European explorers came? |
| 2 | What does the name Vermont mean? |
| 3 | The capital city of Vermont is the smallest capital city in the United States. What is the capital of Vermont? What is the population? |
| 4 | Take a walk through the State House. What can you find in the marble tiles of the floor in the main lobby? Don't forget to go outside and see the State House as it looks in each season of the year. |
| 5 | Who is the current governor of Vermont? |
| 6 | A couple of friends got together in a renovated gas station in 1978 to do something really sweet. What was the outcome? |
| 7 | How many presidents were born in Vermont? Who were they? |
| 8 | Who is Charlotte? How did she get to Vermont? |
| 9 | Who was Ethan Allen? |

# Discover Vermont *(cont.)*

| | Questions |
|---|---|
| 10 | Where is the highest point in Vermont? |
| 11 | What is sinzibukwud? |
| 12 | How old and how big does a maple tree have to be to be used as a sugar producer? |
| 13 | How many gallons of maple syrup were produced in Vermont in the year 2000? |
| 14 | Wilson Bentley of Jericho, Vermont, had an unusual hobby for his time. What did he do? |
| 15 | Vermont is also the birthplace of Brigham Young. For what is Brigham Young famous? |
| 16 | Look at some other famous people from Vermont. Choose one and write a descriptive paragraph or two about him or her. |
| 17 | Why do you think snow is considered a valuable natural resource in Vermont? |
| 18 | For 14 years, Vermont was an independent republic. How did this come about? |
| 19 | When did Vermont become a state? |
| 20 | Vermont has its own USO (unidentified swimming object). Its name is Champ. Read about it. What do you think? |

**Challenge:** Write a question about the state that isn't addressed above. Then, suggest a website for finding the answer to your question.

**Question 1:** _____

**URL 1:** _____

Name _____    Date _____

# Vermont State Map

**Directions:** Use the key located below to complete the map of the state. Begin by locating the capital city and at least three other major cities. Then, locate and draw two major rivers and/or mountains in the state. Draw at least two major interstate highways that travel through the state. Finally, label any other states and/or bodies of water that surround the state.

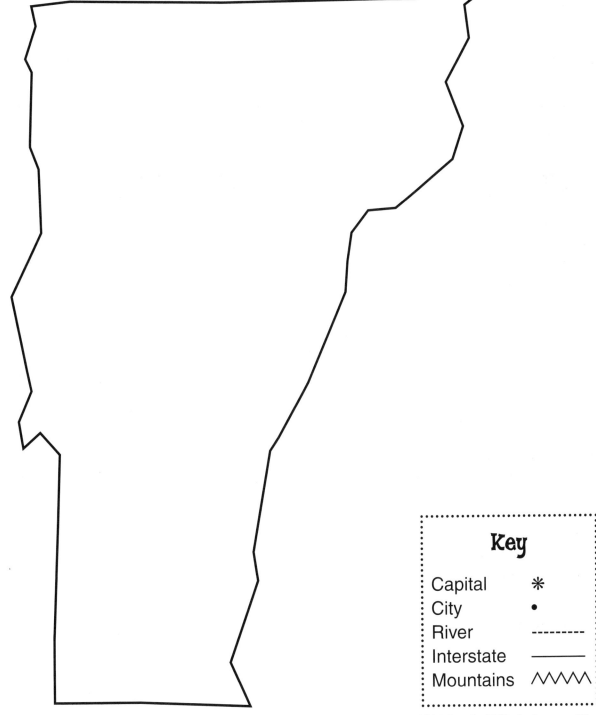

## Key

| | |
|---|---|
| Capital | ✳ |
| City | • |
| River | - - - - - - - - |
| Interstate | —— |
| Mountains | ∧∧∧∧∧ |

Name _____ Date _____

# Vermont Trivia

> Montpelier, Vermont, is the only United States state capital without a McDonald's®.

> Two towns in Vermont claim to be President Chester A. Arthur's birthplace, but recent research supports his opponents' charges that he was born in Canada, and therefore, was not eligible to be president under the United States Constitution.

> Ben & Jerry's® Ice Cream company gives their ice cream waste to local Vermont farmers who use it to feed their hogs. The hogs seem to like all of the flavors except Mint Oreo.

> United States President Calvin Coolidge was the only president born on the fourth of July. He was born in Plymouth, Vermont on July 4, 1872.

**Directions:** Complete the crossword puzzle using the following clues.

**Across**

1. Vermont is the largest producer of this sweet product in the United States (2 words)
6. the capital of Vermont
8. state butterfly
9. a leader of the "Green Mountain Boys" (2 words)
10. Vermont's highest point—Mt. _____

**Down**

2. the second half of Vermont's motto
3. the first half of the motto
4. Vermont was number _____ to become a state.
5. Vermont's state flower (2 words)
7. _____ horse—state animal

Name _____ Date _____

# Delaware Symbols

## http://www.netstate.com/states/

**Directions:** Use the Internet to locate the symbols of the state to complete the chart below. Then, draw and color the flag, seal, bird, and flower. If you wish, you may instead print the four symbols from a website and paste them on the page.

| | |
|---|---|
| **State Capital** | |
| **State Motto** | |
| **State Nickname** | |
| **State Flower** | |
| **State Bird** | |
| **State Tree** | |
| **State Song** | |

| State Flag | State Seal |
|---|---|
| | |
| **State Bird** | **State Flower** |
| | |

Name _____  Date _____

# Discover Delaware

**Directions:** Research the Internet to find the answers to these questions. Record your answers below in the space provided, on your own paper, or in a word processing document. You should also include any other interesting places you visited, facts you learned, or opinions you developed.

Begin at the authors' website and then click on the correct state. From there, you can choose the corresponding links to answer the questions.

## http://www.neeleypress.com/usa

| | Questions |
|---|---|
| 1 | When did Delaware become a state? |
| 2 | Who is the governor of Delaware?  Where was she or he born? |
| 3 | One of Delaware's nicknames is "First State."  Why? |
| 4 | One of Delaware's nicknames is "Diamond State."  Why? |
| 5 | Who were the signers of the Declaration of Independence that hailed from Delaware? |
| 6 | What is the story behind the state bird? |
| 7 | Visit some of the state parks.  Make a flyer describing your favorite one. |
| 8 | What is a water gap? |
| 9 | How did Delaware get its name? |

# Discover Delaware *(cont.)*

| | Questions |
|---|---|
| 10 | What is the state beverage? |
| 11 | What is the leading cash farm product in Delaware? |
| 12 | What does Lenape mean? Who are the Lenape? |
| 13 | Who was Thomas Garrett, and for what was he famous? |
| 14 | What is a tall ship? Why is the Kalmar Nyckel important to Delaware? |
| 15 | In the middle of the Delaware River is an island named Pea Patch Island. What is the legend about its name, and for what two things is it famous? |
| 16 | Take a tour of Lewes' historical buildings. What were the only casualties of a two-day bombardment by the British fleet in 1813? |
| 17 | A famous pirate was also said to have visited Lewes, and he left buried treasure! Who was he? |
| 18 | On Delaware's coastline, there is sometimes stormy weather. In many such times, ships were wrecked. Read about some of the shipwrecks at this website. Besides pirate treasure, what can be gained from exploring ancient shipwrecks? |
| 19 | What family started a gunpowder factory that grew into the world's largest chemical company? |
| 20 | What contest, held at Rehoboth Beach in 1880, was the first of its kind in the United States? What famous inventor was one of its judges? |

**Challenge:** Write a question about the state that isn't addressed above. Then, suggest a website for finding the answer to your question.

**Question 1:** _____

**URL 1:** _____

Name _____    Date _____

# Delaware State Map

**Directions:** Use the key located below to complete the map of the state. Begin by locating the capital city and at least three other major cities. Then, locate and draw two major rivers and/or mountains in the state. Show the Piedmont Plateau and the Coastal Plain. Draw at least two major interstate highways that travel through the state. Finally, label any other states and/or bodies of water that surround the state.

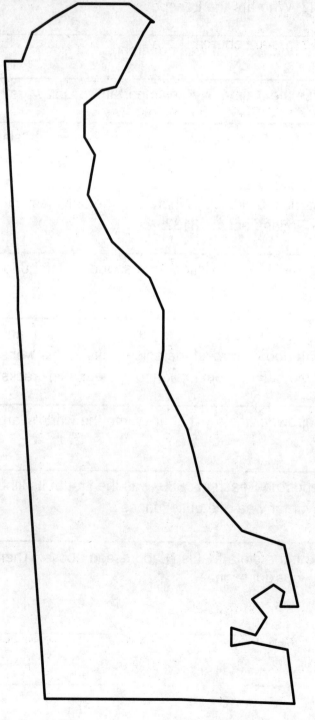

## Key

| | |
|---|---|
| Capital | ✳ |
| City | • |
| River | - - - - - - - |
| Interstate | ——— |
| Mountains | ∧∧∧∧∧ |

Name _____   Date _____

# Delaware Trivia

It is illegal to fly over any body of water in Delaware, unless one is carrying sufficient supplies of food and drink.

Finnish settlers arrived in Delaware in the mid-1600s and brought with them plans for the log cabin, one of the enduring symbols of the American pioneer.

Major league baseball teams buy 182 pounds of special baseball rubbing mud each year from a farmer in Millsboro, Delaware.

Holy Trinity Church, the oldest Protestant church in the United States still in use, is in Wilmington, Delaware.

**Directions:** Find the Delaware-related words in the search below.

```
P   L   O   X   E   D   L   I   B   E   R   T   Y   T   U
N   E   K   C   I   H   C   N   E   H   E   U   L   B   O
F   C   A   F   J   T   V   V   L   I   A   A   L   V   Z
B   N   Z   C   W   J   S   Y   P   P   D   B   O   A   Z
W   E   H   L   H   P   N   H   B   Y   H   Y   H   N   Y
E   D   C   B   K   B   O   X   B   X   F   N   N   G   I
Y   N   N   W   V   V   L   U   F   W   X   Q   A   R   R
X   E   Q   I   A   G   G   O   H   J   U   R   C   I   K
B   P   Y   P   T   G   F   M   S   D   A   I   I   B   W
Q   E   K   O   P   E   V   I   I   S   L   I   R   N   D
M   D   Z   M   P   G   M   O   F   D   O   V   E   R   T
U   N   X   K   G   R   P   T   K   L   I   M   M   H   K
Z   I   A   D   U   Z   N   L   A   F   V   P   A   O   J
Q   X   D   R   Z   F   E   S   E   Q   C   H   L   I   Q
B   B   B   E   T   L   O   Q   W   N   C   E   P   Q   Y
```

## Word Bank

| | | | |
|---|---|---|---|
| American holly | blue hen chicken | Dover | independence |
| ladybug | liberty | milk | peach blossom |

Name _____ Date _____

# Maryland Symbols

**http://www.netstate.com/states/**

**Directions:** Use the Internet to locate the symbols of the state to complete the chart below. Then, draw and color the flag, seal, bird, and flower. If you wish, you may instead print the four symbols from a website and paste them on the page.

| | |
|---|---|
| **State Capital** | |
| **State Motto** | |
| **State Nickname** | |
| **State Flower** | |
| **State Bird** | |
| **State Tree** | |
| **State Song** | |

| **State Flag** | **State Seal** |
|---|---|
| | |
| **State Bird** | **State Flower** |
| | |

Name _____     Date _____

# Discover Maryland

**Directions:** Research the Internet to find the answers to these questions. Record your answers below in the space provided, on your own paper, or in a word processing document. You should also include any other interesting places you visited, facts you learned, or opinions you developed.

Begin at the authors' website and then click on the correct state. From there, you can choose the corresponding links to answer the questions.

## http://www.neeleypress.com/usa

| | Questions |
|---|---|
| 1 | Explore the Maryland Kids' Page website. What's your favorite part? |
| 2 | Who is the present governor of Maryland? |
| 3 | Where did Maryland get its name? |
| 4 | Explore the State House in Annapolis. How old is the State House? |
| 5 | The capital city of Maryland was also the capital of _____ for a short time. |
| 6 | What United States president built a camp/retreat in Maryland? What was it called? |
| 7 | When construction was completed there were 20 cabins at the retreat. A map was drawn giving unique names to the cabins. What were some of these names? |
| 8 | What is the main attraction on Assateague Island? |
| 9 | Proprietary colonies were owned by a single individual. Corporate colonies were owned by a group of investors and run through a corporation. Royal colonies were owned by the king. Which type of colony was Maryland? |

# Discover Maryland *(cont.)*

| | Questions |
|---|---|
| 10 | What were the Ark and the Dove? |
| 11 | Take a virtual tour of the United States Naval Academy in Annapolis to find information. What is a "plebe summer"? |
| 12 | What is the highest point in Maryland? |
| 13 | Who was Mary Pickersgill, and what brought her fame? |
| 14 | Choose one of the famous Marylanders and write a short biography in your journal about him or her. |
| 15 | The blue crab is the official state crusteacean of Maryland. What type of bait would you use if you went line fishing for crab? |
| 16 | Hop aboard the bus and go to Fort McHenry, the birthplace of our National Anthem. For whom was Fort McHenry named? What was its original name? |
| 17 | Oriole Park at Camden Yards, the home of the Baltimore Orioles baseball team, was built within two blocks of the birthplace of what famous baseball player? |
| 18 | While you are in Baltimore, explore the National Aquarium. How many animals are on display at the aquarium? |
| 19 | In the years preceding the American Revolution, Liberty Trees were meeting places for local patriots throughout the colonies. The Maryland Liberty Tree was the last to die. How old did they estimate it to be when it was cut down? What city was home to the Maryland Liberty Tree? |
| 20 | What is the *Pride of Baltimore II*? |

**Challenge:** Write a question about the state that isn't addressed above. Then, suggest a website for finding the answer to your question.

**Question 1:** _____

**URL 1:** _____

Name _____   Date _____

# Maryland State Map

**Directions:** Use the key located below to complete the map of the state. Begin by locating the capital city and at least three other major cities. Then, locate and draw two major rivers and/or mountains in the state. Draw at least two major interstate highways that travel through the state. Finally, label any other states and/or bodies of water that surround the state.

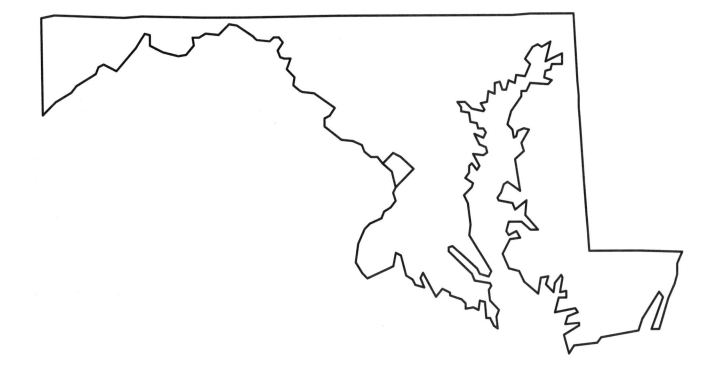

## Key

| | |
|---|---|
| Capital | ✳ |
| City | • |
| River | --------- |
| Interstate | ——— |
| Mountains | ∧∧∧∧ |

Name _____  Date _____

# Maryland Trivia

The first umbrella factory in the United States was founded in 1928 in Baltimore, Maryland.

The United States Naval Academy was founded on October 10, 1845, at Annapolis.

Babe Ruth, the Sultan of Swat, was born in Baltimore and attended Saint Mary's Industrial School.

Dredging and tonging are methods for harvesting oysters.

The Methodist Church of America was formally organized in 1784 at Perry Hall.

Maryland gave up some of its land to form Washington, D.C.

Maryland is a prominent producer and processor of seafood and a national leader in the production of blue crabs and soft clams.

The Bollman Truss Railroad Bridge in Savage is made of both cast iron and wrought iron. It is the only open railroad bridge of its type anywhere in the world.

In Baltimore, it's illegal to take a lion to the movies.

In Baltimore, you may not curse inside the city limits.

Maryland is the only state to boast an official sport—jousting.

The world's first telegraph line was erected between Baltimore and Washington, D.C., in 1844. Baltimore's Mount Clare Station, which was built in 1830 as the first railroad station in the country, was the receiving point of Samuel Morse's famed "What hath God wrought" message.

The army's first Aviation Corps was established at the College Park Airport, the oldest continually operating airport in the country. The most famous instructors at the site were Wilbur and Orville Wright.

The infamous Doc Holliday was a student at the Baltimore College of Dental Surgery, founded in 1840 as the first dental school in the world.

**Directions:** Each letter is represented by a number in the puzzle. Some letters have been done for you. **Hint:** Look for a pattern of odd numbers.

| A | B | C | D | E | F | G | H | I | J | K | L | M | N | O | P | Q | R | S | T | U | V | W | X | Y | Z |
|---|---|---|---|---|---|---|---|---|---|---|---|---|---|---|---|---|---|---|---|---|---|---|---|---|---|
|   | 49 |   |   | 43 |   |   |   |   |   |   |   |   |   |   |   |   |   | 15 |   |   |   |   |   |   | 1 |

\_\_ \_\_ \_\_ \_\_ \_\_ \_\_ \_\_ \_\_ \_\_ 'S     \_\_ \_\_ \_\_ \_\_ \_\_ :     \_\_ \_\_ \_\_ \_\_ \_\_
27 51 17 3 29 51 25 45 15    27 23 13 13 23    27 51 25 29 3

\_\_ E E S \_\_ ,    \_\_ \_\_ \_\_ \_\_ \_\_ \_\_ \_\_    \_\_ \_\_ \_\_ \_\_ S
45 43 43 45 15    7 23 27 51 25 29 3    7 23 17 45 15

Name _____ Date _____

# New Jersey Symbols

## http://www.netstate.com/states/

**Directions:** Use the Internet to locate the symbols of the state to complete the chart below. Then, draw and color the flag, seal, bird, and flower. If you wish, you may instead print the four symbols from a website and paste them on the page.

| | |
|---|---|
| **State Capital** | |
| **State Motto** | |
| **State Nickname** | |
| **State Flower** | |
| **State Bird** | |
| **State Tree** | |
| **State Song** | |

| **State Flag** | **State Seal** |
|---|---|
| | |
| **State Bird** | **State Flower** |
| | |

Name _____     Date _____

# Discover New Jersey

**Directions:** Research the Internet to find the answers to these questions. Record your answers below in the space provided, on your own paper, or in a word processing document. You should also include any other interesting places you visited, facts you learned, or opinions you developed.

Begin at the authors' website and then click on the correct state. From there, you can choose the corresponding links to answer the questions.

## http://www.neeleypress.com/usa

| | Questions |
|---|---|
| 1 | In 1858, some dinosaur bones were found in New Jersey. Where were they found, and what did the scientists find out about them? |
| 2 | Who were New Jersey's first inhabitants? |
| 3 | Who was the first European to explore New Jersey? |
| 4 | What inventor lived and worked in West Orange, New Jersey? |
| 5 | How many patents did the inventor in number four receive for his inventions? |
| 6 | Why was it difficult to put out the fire that damaged the capitol in 1885? |
| 7 | Take a tour of the State House. What is the history behind the chandelier in the Assembly Chamber? |
| 8 | Who is the current governor of New Jersey? Where was he or she born? |
| 9 | Read the story of the Jersey Devil. Why do you think the Pine Barrens was a good area for the Jersey Devil stories to originate? Write your own legend about a certain area in your state. |

# Discover New Jersey *(cont.)*

| | Questions |
|---|---|
| 10 | What are New Jersey's main farm crops? |
| 11 | The Campbell Soup Company was started in New Jersey. Why do you think New Jersey was chosen for this company? |
| 12 | What was the most famous dinosaur fossil found in New Jersey? Where was it found? |
| 13 | Learn about the threatened and endangered animals of New Jersey. What are the three endangered land mammals? |
| 14 | What comedy team hailed from New Jersey? Where were they born? What was the skit that made them famous? Look under "media," then "routines" to find the script. |
| 15 | What famous national landmarks, though owned by the national government, are considered to be in both New York and New Jersey? |
| 16 | What was the importance of Washington's crossing of the Delaware on Christmas night 1776? About how many battles took place in New Jersey during the Revolutionary War? |
| 17 | What is the historical significance of Indian King Tavern? Where is it located? |
| 18 | Play some games with Professor Foulkii and learn some more about New Jersey. What did you learn? |
| 19 | What president was born in New Jersey? How much money did the future president make at his first job (age 14)? |
| 20 | What health or chemical related nickname belongs to New Jersey? Why do you think New Jersey is called this? |

**Challenge:** Write a question about the state that isn't addressed above. Then, suggest a website for finding the answer to your question.

**Question 1:** _____

**URL 1:** _____

Name _____    Date _____

# New Jersey State Map

**Directions:** Use the key located below to complete the map of the state. Begin by locating the capital city and at least three other major cities. Then, locate and draw two major rivers and/or mountains in the state. Draw at least two major interstate highways that travel through the state. Finally, label any other states and/or bodies of water that surround the state.

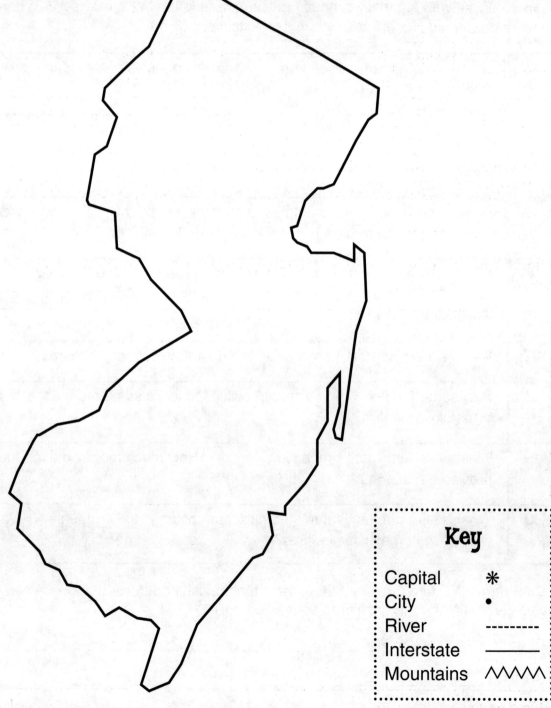

**Key**

| | |
|---|---|
| Capital | * |
| City | • |
| River | - - - - - |
| Interstate | —— |
| Mountains | ∧∧∧∧ |

Name _____ Date _____

# New Jersey Trivia

When Mrs. New Jersey heard her name announced as Mrs. America 1952, she passed out cold on-stage. It took panicked pageant officials several minutes to revive her.

The first Native American reservation in America was established at Indian Mills, New Jersey, on August 29, 1758.

The most densely populated state in the United States is New Jersey.

In 1935, the police in Atlantic City, New Jersey, arrested 42 men on the beach. They were cracking down on topless bathing suits worn by men.

You cannot pump your own gas in New Jersey. All gas stations are full service only.

It is against the law for a man to knit during the fishing season.

You may not slurp your soup.

It is against the law to "frown" at a police officer.

In Manville, it is illegal to offer whiskey or cigarettes to animals at the local zoo.

It is illegal to sell ice cream after 6 P.M. in Newark, unless the customer has a note from his doctor.

**Directions:** How do you picture the Jersey Devil in your imagination? Draw and color it below.

Name _____ Date _____

# New York Symbols

## http://www.netstate.com/states/

**Directions:** Use the Internet to locate the symbols of the state to complete the chart below. Then, draw and color the flag, seal, bird, and flower. If you wish, you may instead print the four symbols from a website and paste them on the page.

| | |
|---|---|
| **State Capital** | |
| **State Motto** | |
| **State Nickname** | |
| **State Flower** | |
| **State Bird** | |
| **State Tree** | |
| **State Song** | |

| State Flag | State Seal |
|---|---|
| | |
| **State Bird** | **State Flower** |
| | |

Name _____ Date _____

# Discover New York

**Directions:** Research the Internet to find the answers to these questions. Record your answers below in the space provided, on your own paper, or in a word processing document. You should also include any other interesting places you visited, facts you learned, or opinions you developed.

Begin at the authors' website and then click on the correct state. From there, you can choose the corresponding links to answer the questions.

## http://www.neeleypress.com/usa

| | Questions |
|---|---|
| 1 | How long did it take to build the New York capitol? |
| 2 | How wide is Niagara Falls?  What is the drop?  How much water goes over in one hour? |
| 3 | How many people crossed the Brooklyn Bridge between 2:00 P.M and 7:00 P.M. on May 24, 1883?  How much did it cost to cross the bridge? |
| 4 | Take a tour of the capitol building.  In a fire in 1911, what saved the building from total destruction? |
| 5 | On September 11, 2001, the worst terrorist attack ever on United States soil occurred in New York.  What was it? |
| 6 | What are the Adirondacks?  Explore and then create a travel brochure advertising an area of the Adirondacks, or plan a vacation for you and your family.  Tell what you will visit and do while vacationing in the Adirondacks. |
| 7 | Learn some facts about the Statue of Liberty.  What is her official title? |
| 8 | What is inscribed on a bronze plaque at the base of the Statue of Liberty? |
| 9 | When was the United Nations established?  How many nations belonged at the outset?  How many nations belong now? |

# Discover New York *(cont.)*

| | Questions |
|---|---|
| 10 | How many New Yorkers have been president of the United States?  Who were they? |
| 11 | Choose one of these presidents and write about him in your journal. |
| 12 | Visit the Empire State Building.  Look through the live cams.  Describe the sights of New York today as seen from the top of the Empire State Building. |
| 13 | Why was the Empire State Building built?  Take a wonderful tour or two by choosing "virtual tour" from the menu. |
| 14 | Name three social and economic changes brought about by the opening of the Erie Canal.  Why were these changes so great? |
| 15 | Why is New York City called the "Big Apple"?  Which theory do you like best? |
| 16 | What are the eleven regions of New York?  Where did the Leatherstocking Region get its name? |
| 17 | Visit the Catskills.  What are the Catskills, and where are they located? |
| 18 | Washington Irving was born in New York.  Who was Washington Irving, and what were some of his contributions? |
| 19 | Take the "Kids Day Out" tour through Central Park in New York City.  Decide which part you like best and write about it. |
| 20 | To end your stay in New York, go to the Bronx Zoo. Take a virtual tour and describe what you see. |

**Challenge:** Write a question about the state that isn't addressed above.  Then, suggest a website for finding the answer to your question.

**Question 1:** _____

**URL 1:** _____

Name _____ Date _____

# New York State Map

**Directions:** Use the key located below to complete the map of the state. Begin by locating the capital city and at least three other major cities. Then, locate and draw two major rivers and/or mountains in the state. Draw at least two major interstate highways that travel through the state. Finally, label any other states and/or bodies of water that surround the state.

### Key

| | |
|---|---|
| Capital | ✳ |
| City | • |
| River | - - - - - - - - - |
| Interstate | ———— |
| Mountains | ∧∧∧∧∧ |

Name _____ Date _____

# New York Trivia

Jason Robards, nominated for more Tony Awards than any other actor, made his New York City acting debut in 1947 as the rear end of a cow in a production of "Jack and the Beanstalk."

New York City became the first capital of the new nation, where President George Washington was inaugurated on April 30, 1789.

New York was the first state to require license plates on automobiles.

In 1892, Ellis Island opened in New York Harbor as the primary immigration depot in the United States.

A rhinoceros was exhibited for the first time in New York City in 1826.

New York City boasts the largest population of peregrine falcons of any place in the world.

Pigs are exceedingly loud creatures. A University of Illinois study measured average pig squeals that ranged from 100 to 115 decibels. The supersonic Concorde jet, by comparison, was originally banned from New York when its engines exceeded 112 decibels at takeoff.

Madcap comedienne Lucille Ball was kicked out of drama school in New York City when she was 15 because she was too quiet and shy.

Three hundred and fourteen acres of trees are used to make the newsprint for the average Sunday edition of the *New York Times*. There are nearly 63,000 trees in the 314 acres.

**Directions:** Circle the New York city names that you find in the puzzle. When you finish, some of the letters that are left uncircled will spell a New York landmark.

```
A  E  M  P  A  A  T  I  R  E  S  P  T  O  A  A
L  A  S  A  C  C  R  T  E  B  O  W  M  L  C  U
L  C  R  R  I  A  O  I  L  U  O  A  W  A  I  D
A  I  E  R  T  H  Y  I  G  L  R  N  A  F  T  H
H  A  K  M  T  T  G  H  L  G  A  T  R  F  U  C
L  M  N  L  A  I  K  O  A  G  H  Q  S  U  R  I
A  A  O  E  D  E  H  R  A  H  O  U  A  B  K  W
V  J  Y  O  E  Y  E  W  Y  I  R  E  W  S  R  N
E  C  T  P  P  T  O  H  N  B  S  E  K  D  A  E
H  E  S  E  V  T  T  F  A  E  E  N  C  K  M  E
W  I  E  I  K  Z  X  B  R  H  S  I  R  R  N  R
E  L  L  E  Y  E  O  E  L  T  E  B  R  O  E  G
S  L  L  X  N  O  R  B  A  Y  A  U  E  Y  D  G
E  H  L  L  I  K  H  S  I  F  D  R  M  W  D  G
C  R  O  C  H  E  S  T  E  R  S  Y  I  E  G  W
N  O  S  K  N  O  H  R  E  K  Y  E  L  N  M  J
```

## Word Bank

| | | | | |
|---|---|---|---|---|
| Albany | Attica | Bronx | Buffalo | Cheektowaga |
| Denmark | Elmira | Fishkill | Greenwich | Horseheads |
| Ithaca | Jamaica | Kerhonkson | Liberty | Limerick |
| Margaretville | New York | Otto | Poughkeepsie | Queensbury |
| Rochester | Sleepy Hollow | Troy | Utica | Valhalla |
| Warsaw | Yonkers | | | |

**New York Landmark:** _____

Name _____  Date _____

# Pennsylvania Symbols

**http://www.netstate.com/states/**

**Directions:** Use the Internet to locate the symbols of the state to complete the chart below. Then, draw and color the flag, seal, bird, and flower. If you wish, you may instead print the four symbols from a website and paste them on the page.

| State Capital | |
|---|---|
| State Motto | |
| State Nickname | |
| State Flower | |
| State Bird | |
| State Tree | |
| State Song | |

| State Flag | State Seal |
|---|---|
| **State Bird** | **State Flower** |

Name _____ Date _____

# Discover Pennsylvania

**Directions:** Research the Internet to find the answers to these questions. Record your answers below in the space provided, on your own paper, or in a word processing document. You should also include any other interesting places you visited, facts you learned, or opinions you developed.

Begin at the authors' website and then click on the correct state. From there, you can choose the corresponding links to answer the questions.

## http://www.neeleypress.com/usa

| | Questions |
|---|---|
| 1 | Sixty percent of Pennsylvania is covered with forests. Where did the state get its name? |
| 2 | Meadowcroft Rock Shelter is the earliest documented place of human habitation in the Western Hemisphere. How was the original discovery made? |
| 3 | The Liberty Bell cracked the first time it was rung. What note does it play when it is struck? |
| 4 | The North and the South disagreed over taxation, commerce, and slavery. The bloodiest battle in the Civil War was at Gettysburg. Who served as president for the North? Who was president of the South? |
| 5 | The Groundhog Day tradition comes from the ancestors of the Pennsylvania Dutch. Tell the story of Punxsutawney Phil. |
| 6 | The Leap-The-Dips roller coaster is the oldest roller coaster in the world. It was built in 1902 and is the only side-friction, figure-eight roller coaster in the United States. What material was used to build the roller coaster? |
| 7 | Rebecca Webb Pennock ran the family iron business after the death of her husband. She was the first woman to do what? |
| 8 | Philadelphia is filled with historic sites that played key roles in the formation of the United States. Click "Next Stop" to begin your tour. What is your favorite place? |
| 9 | Benjamin Franklin lived many years in Philadelphia. While he lived there, he made many significant inventions and discoveries. What was the Union Fire Company? |

# Discover Pennsylvania *(cont.)*

| | Questions |
|---|---|
| 10 | Where was Benjamin Franklin buried?  Who else is buried there? |
| 11 | In December 1957, the first full-scale nuclear power plant in the United States started operating.  Where was the plant located? |
| 12 | Professional baseball was played on the site of Exposition Park in 1891.  Three Rivers Stadium sat in this spot.  Where did it get its name? |
| 13 | You might think that Robert Fulton invented the steamboat, but he didn't.  He made it practical.  How did Robert Fulton think he would make his fortune? |
| 14 | Bill Cosby is a famous comedian, television star, and producer.  Did you know that he has a doctorate in education?  Where did he get his doctorate? |
| 15 | "Independence Hall is, by every estimate, the birthplace of the United States."  What two documents were signed in this historic building? |
| 16 | Milton S. Hershey became interested in German chocolate machines that were exhibited at the 1893 World's Exposition.  What is the name of his famous candy? |
| 17 | Betsy Ross, a seamstress, was asked by General Washington to make the first American flag in Philadelphia.  What are some rules for handling the American flag? |
| 18 | The Franklin Institute quotes Benjamin Franklin with his saying, "The doors of wisdom are never shut."  Take a look around the museum.  What is one of the new exhibits? |
| 19 | Actor Jimmy Stewart was born in Indiana, Pennsylvania.  He starred in the film "It's a Wonderful Life" as well as others.  What was his father's business? |
| 20 | The oldest stone railroad bridge in use in Pennsylvania is the Starrucca Viaduct.  Who uses the viaduct?  Is it still in use today? |

**Challenge:** Write a question about the state that isn't addressed above.  Then, suggest a website for finding the answer to your question.

**Question 1:** _____

**URL 1:** _____

Name _____   Date _____

# Pennsylvania State Map

**Directions:** Use the key located below to complete the map of the state. Begin by locating the capital city and at least three other major cities. Then, locate and draw two major rivers and/or mountains in the state. Draw at least two major interstate highways that travel through the state. Finally, label any other states and/or bodies of water that surround the state.

## Key

| | |
|---|---|
| Capital | ✳ |
| City | • |
| River | - - - - - - - - - |
| Interstate | ——— |
| Mountains | ∧∧∧∧∧ |

Name _____ Date _____

# Pennsylvania Trivia

Technically, there are really only 46 states in the United States. Kentucky, Massachusetts, Pennsylvania, and Virginia are commonwealths.

In Hazelton, Pennsylvania, there is a law on the books that prohibits a person from sipping a carbonated drink while lecturing students in a school auditorium.

Pennsylvania law mandates that all counties provide veterans' graves each year with a flag.

Philadelphia was once the United States capital city.

Pennsylvania is the only original colony not bordered by the Atlantic Ocean.

Pennsylvania received its nickname "The Keystone State" because it was in the middle of the 13 original colonies. Six are to the north and six are to the south.

In 1784, *The Pennsylvania Packet & General Advertiser* was the first successful regular daily newspaper in the United States.

**Directions:** In which documents are the following phrases written? Both of these documents were written in Pennsylvania.

1. *"When in the Course of human events, it becomes necessary for one people to dissolve . . . ."*

   *Document 1:* _____

2. *"We the People of the United States, in Order to form a more perfect Union, establish Justice, insure domestic Tranquility . . . ."*

   *Document 2:* _____

Name _____   Date _____

# Washington, D.C. Symbols

**http://www.enchantedlearning.com/usa/states/dc/**

**Directions:** Use the Internet to locate the symbols of Washington, D.C. to complete the chart below. Then, draw and color the flag, seal, bird, and flower. If you wish, you may instead print the four symbols from a website and paste them on the page.

| Motto | |
| --- | --- |
| Nickname | |
| Flower | |
| Bird | |
| Tree | |
| Song | |

| Flag | Seal |
| --- | --- |
| **Bird** | **Flower** |

Name _____ Date _____

# Discover Washington, D.C.

**Directions:** Research the Internet to find the answers to these questions. Record your answers below in the space provided, on your own paper, or in a word processing document. You should also include any other interesting places you visited, facts you learned, or opinions you developed.

Begin at the authors' website and then click on the correct state. From there, you can choose the corresponding links to answer the questions.

## http://www.neeleypress.com/usa

| | Questions |
|---|---|
| **1** | The United States Capitol houses the Senate and the House of Representatives and serves as the center of government for the United States. Who selected the location for the United States Capitol? |
| **2** | Washington, D.C. is a city. Who is the current mayor of the nation's capital? |
| **3** | The original Smithsonian Institution Building was built in 1855 and looks like a castle. What are the names of the other museums that are a part of the Smithsonian? |
| **4** | Visit the Virtual Wall of the Vietnam Memorial. Look at one panel and select one name from the wall. What year was this person born? |
| **5** | The Iwo Jima Memorial honors Marines who have given their lives to defend this country since 1775. What is this monument's other name? |
| **6** | The Lincoln Memorial honors our 16th president. Mr. Lincoln's famous speech, the Gettysburg Address, is on the south wall. What is the first sentence of this speech? |
| **7** | Thomas Jefferson was the third president of the United States. He was the main author of what document in 1776? |
| **8** | The Washington Monument stands tall at the end of the Reflecting Pool. What shape is this monument? How tall is it? |
| **9** | Take a tour of the White House. Who lives here? What shape is the Blue Room? |

# Discover Washington, D.C. *(cont.)*

| | Questions |
|---|---|
| **10** | The Franklin Delano Roosevelt Memorial celebrates the president and his contributions to the United States. During what years was he president? |
| **11** | The Library of Congress is the world's largest library. How many miles of bookshelves are in the library? |
| **12** | Twenty-three thousand civilians and military personnel work in the Pentagon. What is the Pentagon's main purpose? |
| **13** | The United States Memorial Holocaust Museum helps you understand the effects of prejudice, racism, and stereotyping in any society. What was the Holocaust? |
| **14** | The Old Executive Office Building is often referred to as the "nerve center" of the government. What was this building originally called? |
| **15** | The Supreme Court is the top court in the United States. Who are the current justices on the Supreme Court? |
| **16** | The National Mall stretches from the Washington Monument to the United States Capitol building. What museums are located on the Mall? |
| **17** | Why was Washington, D.C. founded? Who was its first designer? What was its first name, at least during the planning? |
| **18** | The National Cherry Blossom Festival celebrates the beautiful cherry trees that line the Potomac River. Who gave the trees to the people of Washington, D.C.? |
| **19** | Countries from all over the world have their embassies in Washington, D.C. Where is the French Embassy located? |
| **20** | To help prevent counterfeiting of United States dollars, the United States Bureau of Printing and Engraving began issuing new $5, $10, $20, $50, and $100 dollar bills. What are the differences between the old and new five-dollar bills? |

**Challenge:** Write a question about the state that isn't addressed above. Then, suggest a website for finding the answer to your question.

**Question 1:** _____

**URL 1:** _____

Name _____     Date _____

# Washington, D.C. Map

**Directions:** Use the key located below to complete the map of the city. What river runs through Washington, D.C.? Draw the river on your map. Where is the capitol building? Where is the National Mall? Where is the Washington Memorial? Draw at least two major interstate highways that travel through or around the city. Finally, label any states and/or bodies of water that surround the city.

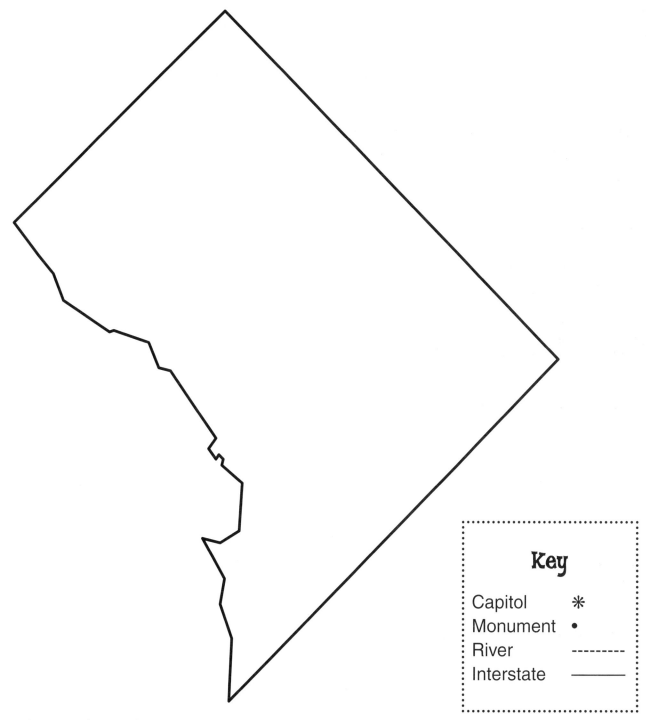

**Key**

| | |
|---|---|
| Capitol | ✳ |
| Monument | • |
| River | -------- |
| Interstate | ———— |

Name _____     Date _____

# Washington, D.C. Trivia

Over a half million people live in Washington, D.C.

The District is named after Christopher Columbus.

Washington, D.C. entered the Union on February 21, 1871, as a municipal corporation.

Washington, D.C. was designed by Major Pierre Charles L'Enfant around 1791. The city is the first American city planned for a specific purpose. It was designed to be a beautiful city with wide streets and many trees.

**Directions:** Find the famous places in the word search.

```
M  E  M  L  K  R  W  Z  L  I  H  O  P  M  Q  L  J  K  W  R
D  W  A  S  H  I  N  G  T  O  N  M  O  N  U  M  E  N  T  S
T  E  I  X  A  S  A  A  L  S  L  D  K  J  F  G  F  H  M  O
E  L  R  W  J  G  T  H  K  L  D  K  M  E  N  O  F  P  L  F
K  L  A  M  S  M  I  T  H  S  O  N  I  A  N  A  E  F  E  L
U  N  N  I  T  E  O  D  S  T  A  T  E  S  O  F  R  E  E  R
Z  X  D  M  C  N  N  B  Q  P  W  O  E  I  R  U  S  T  Y  E
A  L  S  S  L  D  A  K  F  J  H  G  A  M  I  J  O  W  I  N
A  N  P  T  I  D  L  O  T  I  P  A  C  E  S  T  N  A  B  W
L  I  A  S  H  M  M  E  N  T  A  R  I  A  N  I  M  S  M  I
S  U  C  P  E  R  A  C  A  L  I  F  R  A  G  I  E  L  I  C
S  T  E  I  H  O  L  O  C  A  U  S  T  C  E  X  M  P  E  K
A  L  M  I  D  O  L  S  C  H  P  E  N  T  A  G  O  N  A  T
E  X  U  L  O  O  P  N  O  I  T  C  E  L  F  E  R  A  S  T
E  C  S  H  U  N  I  V  E  E  S  U  O  H  E  T  I  H  W  R
V  I  E  T  N  A  M  M  E  M  O  R  I  A  L  S  A  I  T  Y
O  F  U  S  P  U  R  A  R  L  I  N  G  T  O  N  L  A  M  A
R  I  M  L  A  I  R  O  M  E  M  T  L  E  V  E  S  O  O  R
```

## Word Bank

| | | |
|---|---|---|
| Washington Monument | Jefferson Memorial | Roosevelt Memorial |
| Vietnam Memorial | Capitol | White House |
| Pentagon | Smithsonian | Holocaust |
| Air and Space Museum | Iwo Jima | Freer |
| Renwick | National Mall | Reflection Pool |

Name _____  Date _____

# Alabama Symbols

## http://www.netstate.com/states/

**Directions:** Use the Internet to locate the symbols of the state to complete the chart below. Then, draw and color the flag, seal, bird, and flower. If you wish, you may instead print the four symbols from a website and paste them on the page.

| | |
|---|---|
| **State Capital** | |
| **State Motto** | |
| **State Nickname** | |
| **State Flower** | |
| **State Bird** | |
| **State Tree** | |
| **State Song** | |

| State Flag | State Seal |
|---|---|
| | |

| State Bird | State Flower |
|---|---|
| | |

Name _____  Date _____

# Discover Alabama

**Directions:** Research the Internet to find the answers to these questions. Record your answers below in the space provided, on your own paper, or in a word processing document. You should also include any other interesting places you visited, facts you learned, or opinions you developed.

Begin at the authors' website and then click on the correct state. From there, you can choose the corresponding links to answer the questions.

### http://www.neeleypress.com/usa

| | Questions |
|---|---|
| 1 | What is the capital of Alabama? |
| 2 | What does the Creek word *Cheaha* mean? What is Cheaha's claim to fame? |
| 3 | Read about the state seal. Why do you think it was changed after the Civil War (also known as the War Between the States)? |
| 4 | Who is the governor of Alabama? |
| 5 | What is the state insect and in what year was it made official by the legislature? |
| 6 | Research some famous people from Alabama. Who is your favorite? Write a paragraph (or more) about your favorite person. |
| 7 | Describe the climate in Alabama. |
| 8 | What are Alabama's major crops? |
| 9 | Are these crops the main agricultural export? If yes, how much is exported each year? If no, what is the major export? |

# Discover Alabama *(cont.)*

| | Questions |
|---|---|
| 10 | Why was Russell Cave a good place for prehistoric people to live? |
| 11 | What is an *atlatl*? |
| 12 | There are murals beneath the dome in the capitol building. Who painted them, and what do they depict? |
| 13 | What flags have flown over Alabama? |
| 14 | Write the words to the first verse of the state song. |
| 15 | Who is Joseph Zoettel, and what did he do? |
| 16 | Alabama has a memorial to an insect. What insect and why is there a memorial? |
| 17 | How did the South, especially Alabama, become known as "Dixie"? |
| 18 | What is the state quilt of Alabama? |
| 19 | Read the story of the Freedom Quilting Bee. Design a quilt block for your own state. |
| 20 | Visit one (or more) of the sites at "Wacky Alabama" and write about what you discover. |

**Challenge:** Write a question about the state that isn't addressed above. Then, suggest a website for finding the answer to your question.

**Question 1:** _____

**URL 1:** _____

Name _____  Date _____

# Alabama State Map

**Directions:** Use the key located below to complete the map of the state. Begin by locating the capital city and at least three other major cities. Then, locate and draw two major rivers and/or mountains in the state. Draw at least two major interstate highways that travel through the state. Finally, label any other states and/or bodies of water that surround the state.

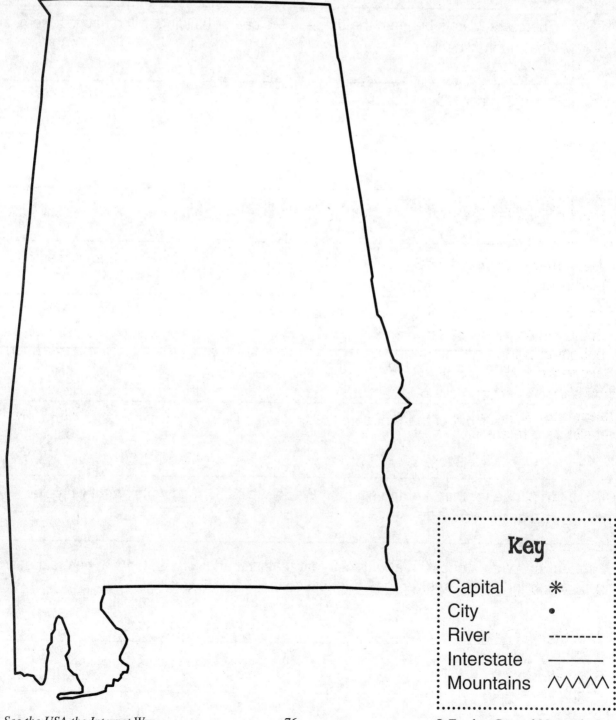

**Key**

| | |
|---|---|
| Capital | ✳ |
| City | • |
| River | - - - - - - - |
| Interstate | ——— |
| Mountains | /\/\/\/\ |

Name _____     Date _____

# Alabama Trivia

The first electric trolley streetcars in the United States began operating in Montgomery, Alabama, in 1866.

Alabama introduced Mardi Gras to the western world. The celebration is held on Shrove Tuesday, the day before Lent begins.

Montgomery was the capital and birthplace of the Confederate States of America.

Baseball player Henry Louis (Hank) Aaron was born in Mobile, Alabama, in 1934.

Huntsville is known as the rocket capital of the world.

Adolf Hitler's typewriter was recovered from his mountain retreat and is exhibited at the Hall of History in Bessemer, Alabama.

Alabama resident Sequoyah devised the phonetic, written alphabet of the Cherokee language.

In the 1880s, Alabama scientist George Washington Carver discovered 300 uses for the peanut and 175 uses for the sweet potato. These discoveries revitalized Alabama's farm economy.

**Directions:** Unscramble the following names to find famous people from Alabama. Use the website as a reference to help you as you unscramble.

## http://www.50states.com/bio/alabama.htm

1. oknnhaaar _____

2. prarelehe _____

3. useiljoo _____

4. etatotitrgoncccks _____

5. smalliiwey _____

6. eekneelrlhl _____

7. rawselilc _____

8. eggrollaeaecw _____

9. samemyruroilh _____

10. esesesnowj _____

Name _____ Date _____

# Arkansas Symbols

### http://www.netstate.com/states/

**Directions:** Use the Internet to locate the symbols of the state to complete the chart below. Then, draw and color the flag, seal, bird, and flower. If you wish, you may instead print the four symbols from a website and paste them on the page.

| | |
|---|---|
| **State Capital** | |
| **State Motto** | |
| **State Nickname** | |
| **State Flower** | |
| **State Bird** | |
| **State Tree** | |
| **State Song** | |

| **State Flag** | **State Seal** |
|---|---|
| | |
| **State Bird** | **State Flower** |
| | |

Name _____    Date _____

# Discover Arkansas

**Directions:** Research the Internet to find the answers to these questions. Record your answers below in the space provided, on your own paper, or in a word processing document. You should also include any other interesting places you visited, facts you learned, or opinions you developed.

Begin at the authors' website and then click on the correct state. From there, you can choose the corresponding links to answer the questions.

## http://www.neeleypress.com/usa

| | Questions |
|---|---|
| **1** | Who is the governor of Arkansas? Tell a few interesting facts about the current governor. |
| **2** | This state park offers you the chance to hunt for something you can't find anywhere else in America. What is it? |
| **3** | Who designed the Arkansas state flag? |
| **4** | What do the 25 stars on the Arkansas state flag represent? |
| **5** | What is the state beverage? Why was this chosen for the honor? |
| **6** | Choose one famous person from Arkansas and write a three-paragraph essay on him or her. |
| **7** | What are some of the ways Arkansas was spelled throughout history? What does the name mean? |
| **8** | How does the water in Hot Springs, Arkansas, get so hot? |
| **9** | Want to be a spelunker? Visit some of the many show caves in Arkansas. Which one of these is your favorite? |

# Discover Arkansas *(cont.)*

| | Questions |
|---|---|
| 10 | What Native Americans originally inhabited the area that is now Arkansas? |
| 11 | What is the Arkansas Creed? |
| 12 | Choose an endangered or threatened animal that lives in Arkansas. Tell what steps are being taken to protect it. |
| 13 | What is the highest point in Arkansas? The lowest point? |
| 14 | The 42nd president of the United States was born in Arkansas. Who was he and what are some interesting facts about his life before he was president? |
| 15 | Visit one of the best preserved Civil War battlefields in the nation. Where is it located? What was the result of the battle? |
| 16 | What is Magnet Cove's claim to fame? Where is it located? |
| 17 | Arkansas is the number one producer of what two American agricultural products? |
| 18 | Take the full tour of the Arkansas capitol building. Describe the part that you like the best. |
| 19 | While you are in Little Rock, the capital city, go to the zoo. Who was "Kitty Cat"? |
| 20 | For your last stop on your tour of Arkansas, visit the Ozark Folk Center. Listen to some music, watch quilts being made, learn some history, and learn some traditional dances. After your visit, describe some of the places you visited in Arkansas, some of the things you learned, and some of the thoughts you have about the state. |

**Challenge:** Write a question about the state that isn't addressed above. Then, suggest a website for finding the answer to your question.


**Question 1:** _____


**URL 1:** _____

Name _____ Date _____

# Arkansas State Map

**Directions:** Use the key located below to complete the map of the state. Begin by locating the capital city and at least three other major cities. Then, locate and draw two major rivers and/or mountains in the state. Label the diamond mine and the birthplace of former President William Clinton. Draw at least two major interstate highways that travel through the state. Finally, label any other states and/or bodies of water that surround the state.

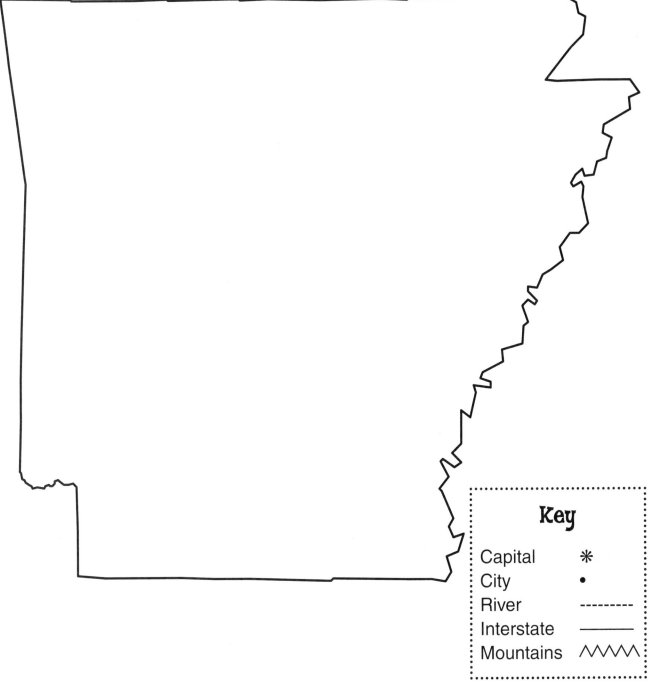

**Key**

| | |
|---|---|
| Capital | ✳ |
| City | • |
| River | - - - - - - - - |
| Interstate | ——— |
| Mountains | ∧∧∧∧∧ |

Name _____    Date _____

# Arkansas Trivia

Mountain View is home to one of the largest producers of handmade dulcimers in the world.

The Magnet Cove region claims to contain 102 varieties of minerals.

Besides being the birthplace of President William Clinton, Hope is famous for its watermelons.

The Basin Park Hotel has eight floors and every one of them is a "ground floor."

During the last year of the Civil War, Arkansas had a Union state government in Little Rock and a Confederate state government at Washington in Hempstead County.

In 1830, the original Bowie Knife was made by James Black, a blacksmith in Washington, Arkansas.

**Directions:** Find and circle the Arkansas town names in the word search below.

```
N  T  D  N  A  D  Y  E  L  L  V  I  L  L  E
P  E  E  L  L  I  V  S  S  A  G  I  V  G  L
N  D  C  X  N  Z  H  G  E  N  T  Z  L  K  L
R  Y  R  R  A  S  I  P  L  T  R  J  G  H  I
B  M  D  N  P  R  Z  S  L  Q  R  S  P  T  V
M  Z  H  H  Y  E  K  E  I  E  A  A  W  I  E
R  Z  S  U  E  G  R  A  V  T  D  U  P  M  T
L  Y  A  W  N  O  C  P  N  H  N  A  O  S  T
D  X  X  V  C  R  J  O  O  A  E  E  K  T  E
Y  Q  Z  K  I  E  H  P  T  B  S  P  H  R  Y
L  O  A  H  W  A  E  K  N  O  Q  X  B  O  A
G  R  U  Y  C  P  I  N  E  B  L  U  F  F  F
A  I  L  O  N  G  A  M  B  P  D  E  P  I  E
T  Y  P  H  L  Q  L  T  N  G  N  V  K  L  O
C  Q  T  S  R  I  B  F  G  L  H  Z  U  Q  Q
```

## Word Bank

| | | | |
|---|---|---|---|
| Arkadelphia | Bentonville | Conway | Fayetteville |
| Fortsmith | Gassville | Hope | Little Rock |
| Magnolia | Pinebluff | Pocahontas | Rogers |
| Texarkana | Yellville | | |

Name _____  Date _____

# Florida Symbols

## http://www.netstate.com/states/

**Directions:** Use the Internet to locate the symbols of the state to complete the chart below. Then, draw and color the flag, seal, bird, and flower. If you wish, you may instead print the four symbols from a website and paste them on the page.

| | |
|---|---|
| **State Capital** | |
| **State Motto** | |
| **State Nickname** | |
| **State Flower** | |
| **State Bird** | |
| **State Tree** | |
| **State Song** | |

| State Flag | State Seal |
|---|---|
| | |
| **State Bird** | **State Flower** |
| | |

Name _____     Date _____

# Discover Florida

**Directions:** Research the Internet to find the answers to these questions. Record your answers below in the space provided, on your own paper, or in a word processing document. You should also include any other interesting places you visited, facts you learned, or opinions you developed.

Begin at the authors' website and then click on the correct state. From there, you can choose the corresponding links to answer the questions.

**http://www.neeleypress.com/usa**

| | Questions |
|---|---|
| 1 | Three log cabins served as Florida's first capitol. What does the current capitol look like? |
| 2 | Where was the first permanent European settlement? |
| 3 | Florida manatees are slow swimmers. How big can they get? |
| 4 | On February 14, 1940, a porpoise was born in captivity for the first time. Is the porpoise a cousin of the dolphin? |
| 5 | Walt Disney World® in Florida was opened to the public in 1971. It is twice the size of Manhattan, New York. Send a postcard to a friend from the Disney site. |
| 6 | In America, Florida is the state struck most often by lightning. See where lightning is striking now. |
| 7 | Greater Miami is the only metropolitan area in the United States whose borders encompass two national parks. Which parks are they? |
| 8 | The Castillo de San Marcos, which served as an outpost to protect Saint Augustine, is the oldest European settlement in North America. What year was it made a national monument? |
| 9 | The Kennedy Space Center is located at Cape Canaveral and is America's launch pad for space flights. Read the latest news from NASA. |

# Discover Florida *(cont.)*

| | Questions |
|---|---|
| **10** | The Benwood was built in England in 1912 and sunk in 1942. Where is the wreckage located? |
| **11** | Aviator Tony Jannus made history on January 1, 1914, by flying the world's first scheduled passenger service airline flight from St. Petersburg's downtown yacht basin to Tampa. What year was Jannus born? |
| **12** | What year did Dr. John Gorrie of Apalachicola invent mechanical refrigeration? |
| **13** | Miami Beach pharmacist Benjamin Green invented the first suntan cream in 1944. What did he use? |
| **14** | Fort Lauderdale is known as the Venice of America because the city has 185 miles of local waterways. What else is interesting about the city? |
| **15** | When first completed in 1989, the Dame Point Bridge became the longest cable-stayed span in the United States. What other name is used for this bridge? |
| **16** | Venice is known as the Shark Tooth Capital of the World. Draw and label the different types of shark teeth in your journal. |
| **17** | What exactly are the Florida Keys? |
| **18** | Take a field trip through the Everglades with the Duke University Wetland Center. Describe what you find. |
| **19** | Before you go to the Everglades, you better learn all that you can about alligators. List your new knowledge. |
| **20** | Key West is the southernmost point of the continental United States. Key West is closer to Cuba than it is to any other state. How many miles is it to Cuba? |

**Challenge:** Write a question about the state that isn't addressed above. Then, suggest a website for finding the answer to your question.

**Question 1:** _____

**URL 1:** _____

Name _____  Date _____

# Florida State Map

**Directions:** Use the key located below to complete the map of the state. Begin by locating the capital city and Miami, Key West, Tampa, and Orlando. Then, locate and draw two major rivers and/or mountains in the state. Can you find Everglades National Park? Draw at least two major interstate highways that travel through the state. Finally, label any other states and/or bodies of water that surround the state.

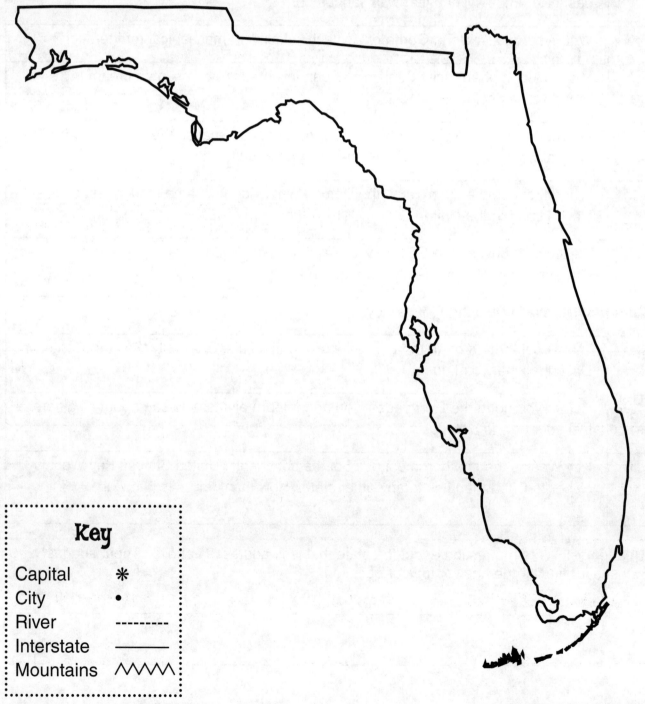

**Key**

| | |
|---|---|
| Capital | * |
| City | • |
| River | - - - - - - |
| Interstate | ——— |
| Mountains | ∧∧∧∧∧ |

Name _____  Date _____

# Florida Trivia

Miami installed the first bank automated teller machine especially for rollerbladers.

Florida is the only state that has two rivers both with the same name. There is a Withlacoochee in north central Florida and a Withlacoochee in central Florida.

Florida is the number one producer of tomatoes in the United States.

Gatorade® got its name after the Gators, the University of Florida football team, tested it.

Safety Harbor is the home of the historic Espiritu Santo Springs. It was given this name in 1539 by the Spanish explorer Hernando de Soto. He was searching for the legendary Fountain of Youth and thought the natural springs might be the Fountain of Youth.

**Directions:** Decode the words below using this key:

| A | B | C | D | E | F | G | H | I | J | K | L | M |
|---|---|---|---|---|---|---|---|---|---|---|---|---|
| ○ | ❑ | ♥ | ✳ | ▲ | ❄ | ✧ | ➜ | ☆ | ✪ | ⇨ | ♣ | ▼ |

| N | O | P | Q | R | S | T | U | V | W | X | Y | Z |
|---|---|---|---|---|---|---|---|---|---|---|---|---|
| 🐚 | ☞ | ✂ | ✈ | ❖ | ◗ | ■ | ✐ | ✍ | ✚ | ★ | ☣ | ❀ |

_____  _____  _____  _____.

Name _____  Date _____

# Georgia Symbols

**http://www.netstate.com/states/**

**Directions:** Use the Internet to locate the symbols of the state to complete the chart below. Then, draw and color the flag, seal, bird, and flower. If you wish, you may instead print the four symbols from a website and paste them on the page.

| | |
|---|---|
| **State Capital** | |
| **State Motto** | |
| **State Nickname** | |
| **State Flower** | |
| **State Bird** | |
| **State Tree** | |
| **State Song** | |

| **State Flag** | **State Seal** |
|---|---|
| | |
| **State Bird** | **State Flower** |
| | |

Name _____  Date _____

# Discover Georgia

**Directions:** Research the Internet to find the answers to these questions. Record your answers below in the space provided, on your own paper, or in a word processing document. You should also include any other interesting places you visited, facts you learned, or opinions you developed.

Begin at the authors' website and then click on the correct state. From there, you can choose the corresponding links to answer the questions.

## http://www.neeleypress.com/usa

| | Questions |
|---|---|
| **1** | The Etowah Indian Mounds are representative of what culture? |
| **2** | What Native American groups lived in Georgia when the European settlers arrived? Choose one group about which to write a short history. |
| **3** | What popular soft drink was "born" in Atlanta? When was it founded? |
| **4** | Now, go to Georgia's oldest city. Who started this city? Click here to start a scenic tour. Write about your favorite part of the tour. |
| **5** | The capital of Georgia has been moved several times. Read about it at this website. When was Atlanta officially voted on as capital? |
| **6** | What are some of the things considered mysterious about the statue on top of the capitol's dome? |
| **7** | Who are the governor and first lady of Georgia? |
| **8** | Georgia has many state parks. Choose several to visit from this site. Describe your favorite one. |
| **9** | One of the state parks is the Little White House. Who built it and why? What is unique about the walkway that leads to the museum? |

# Discover Georgia *(cont.)*

| | Questions |
|---|---|
| 10 | The small town of Plains was the birthplace and home to the 39th president of the United States. Who is he? Visit his boyhood home and school. |
| 11 | What Georgia native won the Nobel Peace Prize in 1964? |
| 12 | While you are in Atlanta, visit the animals at the zoo. Describe the most interesting animal there. |
| 13 | Why did James Oglethorpe decide to come to America? |
| 14 | Take a slow trip through the Okefenokee Swamp area of South Georgia and North Florida. Make up a story about a camping trip you and your best friend took to this area. What wildlife did you see? What sounds did you hear? Were there any unusual plants? Did anything exciting or scary happen? |
| 15 | Take a look at some of the other symbols and facts about Georgia. How did the state marine mammal get its name? |
| 16 | When was the current state flag of Georgia adopted? |
| 17 | Test your knowledge of Georgia facts. Play the game and see how well you do. |
| 18 | What is the Golden Crescent? Check the cultural history to find out what the major crops were in the colonial period. |
| 19 | What is the state butterfly? Draw pictures of this butterfly and tell something about it that you find interesting. |
| 20 | The famous novel *Gone With the Wind* was written in Georgia. Who wrote it and why is the story so well known? |

**Challenge:** Write a question about the state that isn't addressed above. Then, suggest a website for finding the answer to your question.

**Question 1:** _____

**URL 1:** _____

Name _____    Date _____

# Georgia State Map

**Directions:** Use the key located below to complete the map of the state. Begin by locating the capital city and at least three other major cities. Then, locate and draw two major rivers and/or mountains in the state. Shade in the Okefenokee Swamp. Draw at least two major interstate highways that travel through the state. Finally, label any other states and/or bodies of water that surround the state.

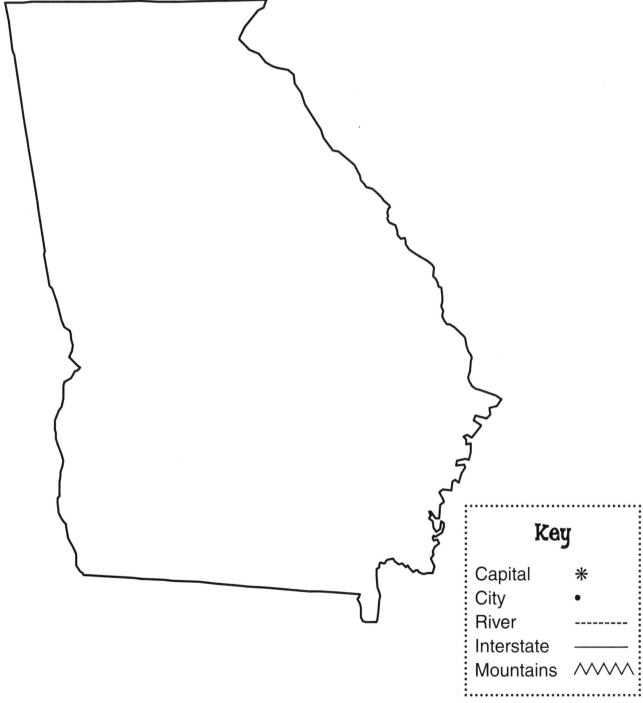

**Key**

| | |
|---|---|
| Capital | ✳ |
| City | • |
| River | - - - - - - - |
| Interstate | —————— |
| Mountains | ∧∧∧∧∧ |

Name _____ Date _____

# Georgia Trivia

In Atlanta, Georgia, it is illegal to tie a giraffe to a telephone pole or street lamp.

Georgia has 75 laws on how to build rice paddies, even though the state has only one rice farm left. Rice was the state's number one crop before the Civil War. But right after the war, a hurricane destroyed all the paddies and ponds. It was too expensive to replace them without slaves, so the Rice State began growing peaches, peanuts, and other crops.

**Directions:** Unscramble the jumbled words to find some critters. Put the numbered letters in order to find out where they live.

1. MANIECAR GIARLLATO

2. HOERGP RITETSOO

3. NAGPSNIP LRUTTE

4. SAEKN

5. KACBL ABRE

6. VIRRE TOERT

7. ROCCAON

8. TABOCB

9. RAEGT LUEB NORHE

10. LBDETE GEIFRKISNH

11. RATGE WEITH TERGE

Name _____ Date _____

# Kentucky Symbols

**http://www.netstate.com/states/**

**Directions:** Use the Internet to locate the symbols of the state to complete the chart below. Then, draw and color the flag, seal, bird, and flower. If you wish, you may instead print the four symbols from a website and paste them on the page.

| State Capital | |
|---|---|
| State Motto | |
| State Nickname | |
| State Flower | |
| State Bird | |
| State Tree | |
| State Song | |

| State Flag | State Seal |
|---|---|
| State Bird | State Flower |

Name _____ Date _____

# Discover Kentucky

**Directions:** Research the Internet to find the answers to these questions. Record your answers below in the space provided, on your own paper, or in a word processing document. You should also include any other interesting places you visited, facts you learned, or opinions you developed.

Begin at the authors' website and then click on the correct state. From there, you can choose the corresponding links to answer the questions.

## http://www.neeleypress.com/usa

| | Questions |
|---|---|
| 1 | The United States' gold is kept in the United States Bullion Depository at Fort Knox, Kentucky. How big is a gold bar? How often is the gold moved? |
| 2 | The new Kentucky State Capitol was built in Frankfort in 1905 after the plans were too big to fit at the old site. Take a look around the statue room and describe it. |
| 3 | The Boy Scouts of America Scouting Museum is located on which university campus? |
| 4 | The Kentucky Derby is the oldest continuously held horse race in the country. It is held at Churchill Downs in Louisville on the first Saturday in May. Retell a horse story from this race's long history. |
| 5 | Mammoth Cave is the world's longest cave in the world. How long is it? When did humans first use the cave? |
| 6 | Before franchising his chicken business at age 65, Colonel Sanders was a streetcar conductor, a railroad fireman, and even a justice of the peace. Where did he open his first Kentucky Fried Chicken®? |
| 7 | Abraham Lincoln was born on February 12, 1809. In what kind of house did his family live? |
| 8 | Mr. Lincoln's great adversary, Jefferson Davis, was born in 1808 in Christian County, Kentucky, and later moved to Mississippi. What did he do during the Civil War? |
| 9 | Cumberland Falls displays a Moonbow on clear nights under a full moon. What is the nickname for these falls? |

# Discover Kentucky *(cont.)*

| | Questions |
|---|---|
| 10 | In 1773, Daniel Boone failed in his first attempt to settle Kentucky, but in 1775 he succeeded in establishing Boonesborough. How many children did he and his wife, Rebecca, have? |
| 11 | Newport is the home of the World Peace Bell, the largest swinging bell in the world. Where was the bell cast? Why was the bell cast? |
| 12 | President Rutherford B. Hayes came to dedicate High Bridge in 1877. Why? Is the bridge still being used? |
| 13 | Alben W. Barkley was 71 years old when he assumed the office of United States Vice President. Under what president did he serve? |
| 14 | Take the virtual tour of the Cathedral Basilica of the Assumption in Covington. It has 82 stained-glass windows. Did you find the beautiful windows? |
| 15 | Frederick Vinson was the thirteenth Chief Justice of the United States Supreme Court. Where was Justice Vinson born? |
| 16 | In 1848, men from Melleray Abbey in France founded Gethsemani in the rolling hills of Kentucky. What do these monks manufacture now? |
| 17 | Muhammad Ali is the three-time world heavy weight champion. What was his name before he changed it to Muhammad Ali? |
| 18 | Enter the Louisville Slugger Museum. Since 1884, Louisville Slugger bats have been in the hands of the greatest players in baseball's history. Look around and read the stories in the "Then and Now" section. Which is your favorite? |
| 19 | Sir Barton was the first Triple Crown winner. What is the Triple Crown? |
| 20 | Barton P. Ambrose was a corporal in the 47th Mounted Infantry Regiment of the Kentucky Volunteers, U. S. Army. Corporal Ambrose returned to farming and requested a pension from the army. How much was he paid per month? |

**Challenge:** Write a question about the state that isn't addressed above. Then, suggest a website for finding the answer to your question.

**Question 1:** _____

**URL 1:** _____

Name _____   Date _____

# Kentucky State Map

**Directions:** Use the key located below to complete the map of the state. Begin by locating the capital city and at least three other major cities. Then, locate and draw two major rivers and/or mountains in the state. What is the highest point in Kentucky? Draw the mountain on the map. Draw at least two major interstate highways that travel through the state. Finally, label any other states and/or bodies of water that surround the state.

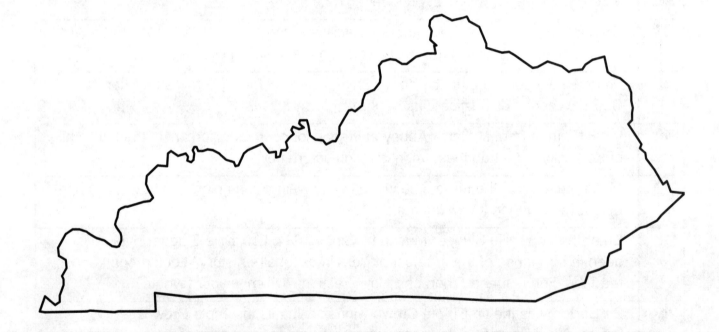

## Key

| Capital | * |
| Capital | * |
| City | • |
| River | ----------- |
| Interstate | ———— |
| Mountains | ΛΛΛΛΛΛ |

Name _____ Date _____

# Kentucky Trivia

Supposedly by law, every citizen of Kentucky is required to take a bath once a year.

In Kentucky, it is against the law to throw eggs at a public speaker.

Kentucky is the state where both Abraham Lincoln, President of the Union, and Jefferson Davis, President of the Confederacy, were born. They were born less than one hundred miles and one year apart.

Two Louisville sisters wrote the "Happy Birthday to You" song in 1893.

More than 100 native Kentuckians have been elected governors of other states.

Mary S. Wilson, a teacher, held the first observance of Mother's Day in Henderson in 1887. It was made a national holiday in 1916.

**Directions:** Use this key to reveal the phrase below.

| | | | | | |
|---|---|---|---|---|---|
| 12–A | 23–B | 34–C | 45–D | 56–E | 67–F |
| 68–G | 69–H | 90–I | 21–J | 32–K | 43–L |
| 54–M | 65–N | 76–O | 87–P | 98–Q | 09–R |
| 13–S | 24–T | 35–U | 46–V | 57–W | 68–X |
| 80–Y | 42–Z | | | | |

_____     \_\_\_\_\_     _____

35-65-90-24-56-45     57-56     13-24-12-65-45

_____     \_\_\_\_\_     _____

45-90-46-90-45-56-45     57-56     67-12-43-43

Name _____  Date _____

# Louisiana Symbols

## http://www.netstate.com/states/

**Directions:** Use the Internet to locate the symbols of the state to complete the chart below. Then, draw and color the flag, seal, bird, and flower. If you wish, you may instead print the four symbols from a website and paste them on the page.

| | |
|---|---|
| **State Capital** | |
| **State Motto** | |
| **State Nickname** | |
| **State Flower** | |
| **State Bird** | |
| **State Tree** | |
| **State Song** | |

| State Flag | State Seal |
|---|---|
| | |
| **State Bird** | **State Flower** |
| | |

Name _____ Date _____

# Discover Louisiana

**Directions:** Research the Internet to find the answers to these questions. Record your answers below in the space provided, on your own paper, or in a word processing document. You should also include any other interesting places you visited, facts you learned, or opinions you developed.

Begin at the authors' website and then click on the correct state. From there, you can choose the corresponding links to answer the questions.

## http://www.neeleypress.com/usa

| | Questions |
|---|---|
| 1 | Who is the present governor of Louisiana? What kind of farming did he do after he returned from the Korean War? |
| 2 | How much did the United States pay for the Louisiana territory? What year was it purchased? |
| 3 | What states were made from the Louisiana Purchase? |
| 4 | What are wetlands? What are some beneficial uses of the wetlands? |
| 5 | What is Mardi Gras? Design and produce a brochure advertising Mardi Gras. |
| 6 | What flags have flown over Louisiana? |
| 7 | What is a Cajun? Where do they live? Where did they originate? Write a few paragraphs about Cajuns. |
| 8 | Read the poem, "Evangeline," and the story behind it. Paraphrase the poem. |
| 9 | Louisiana is home to many different kinds of wildlife. Take the animal trivia quiz and see how well you know your animals. |

# Discover Louisiana *(cont.)*

| | Questions |
|---|---|
| 10 | The capital of Louisiana is Baton Rouge. What does that name mean? |
| 11 | The state capitol in Baton Rouge has 48 steps in the staircase to the entrance. What is the significance of this number? What else makes the capitol unique? |
| 12 | What type of people lived in the area of the Poverty Point State Park in about 1500 B.C.? Were they indicative of most people of that era? Why or why not? Add Poverty Point to your map. |
| 13 | Pick one famous person from Louisiana and write a short essay about him or her. |
| 14 | What is the highest point in Louisiana? What else is famous about this hilltop? |
| 15 | What is the Snow White of the Louisiana Swamp? |
| 16 | Where did Louisiana get its name? |
| 17 | Visit the historic city of New Orleans. What did you like best? |
| 18 | What are the "cities of the dead" in New Orleans? Why were they necessary? |
| 19 | Most states are made up of counties. What is the governing division in Louisiana? Why was this chosen? |
| 20 | For what is Rayne, Louisiana, famous? Why did it become famous? What makes the fame continue? |

**Challenge:** Write a question about the state that isn't addressed above. Then, suggest a website for finding the answer to your question.

**Question 1:** _____

**URL 1:** _____

Name _____ Date _____

# Louisiana State Map

**Directions:** Use the key located below to complete the map of the state. Begin by locating the capital city and at least three other major cities. Then, locate and draw two major rivers and/or mountains in the state. Draw at least two major interstate highways that travel through the state. Finally, label any other states and/or bodies of water that surround the state.

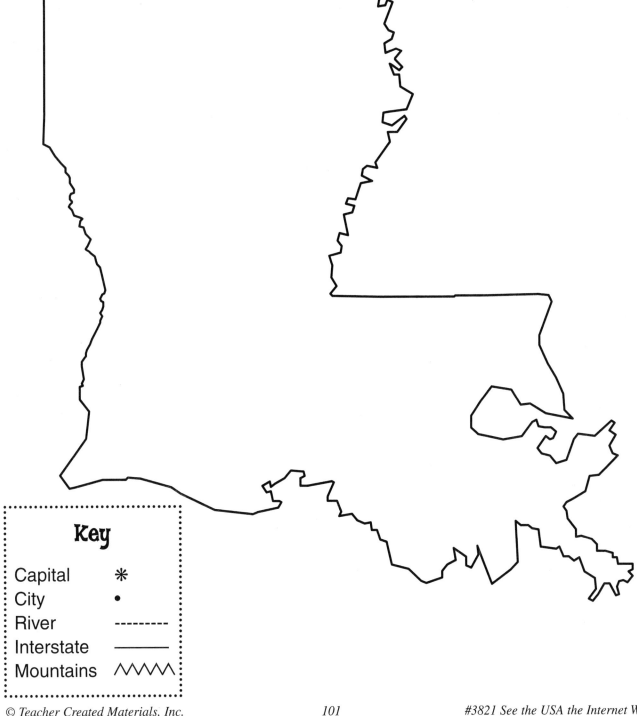

**Key**

| Capital | ✳ |
|---|---|
| City | • |
| River | ------- |
| Interstate | ——— |
| Mountains | ∧∧∧∧ |

Name _____  Date _____

# Louisiana Trivia

The alligator can grow up to 19 feet in length, and is generally found in the swamplands of Louisiana and the Gulf States.

Each two-ounce bottle of Tabasco® Sauce contains at least 720 drops of sauce. The fiery pepper sauce is produced by the McIlhenny family. The McIlhenny Company was founded in 1868 at Avery Island, Louisiana.

The state of Louisiana has two official state songs: "Give Me Louisiana" and "You Are My Sunshine."

In New Orleans, it is against the law to tie an alligator to a fire hydrant.

**Directions:** Unscramble each of the clue words. Copy the letters in the numbered cells to other cells with the same number.

1. NOISALUAI PACSEUHR

2. MADRI SAGR

3. JUACN

4. LEANENGIEV

5. BAOTN GOERU

6. GOLRITLAA

7. EWN SELRONA

8. TAF DEAUTSY

Name _____ Date _____

# Mississippi Symbols

## http://www.netstate.com/states/

**Directions:** Use the Internet to locate the symbols of the state to complete the chart below. Then, draw and color the flag, seal, bird, and flower. If you wish, you may instead print the four symbols from a website and paste them on the page.

| | |
|---|---|
| **State Capital** | |
| **State Motto** | |
| **State Nickname** | |
| **State Flower** | |
| **State Bird** | |
| **State Tree** | |
| **State Song** | |

| **State Flag** | **State Seal** |
|---|---|
| | |
| **State Bird** | **State Flower** |
| | |

Name _____     Date _____

# Discover Mississippi

**Directions:** Research the Internet to find the answers to these questions. Record your answers below in the space provided, on your own paper, or in a word processing document. You should also include any other interesting places you visited, facts you learned, or opinions you developed.

Begin at the authors' website and then click on the correct state. From there, you can choose the corresponding links to answer the questions.

### http://www.neeleypress.com/usa

| | Questions |
|---|---|
| 1 | What is the story of the Friendship Cemetery in Columbus, Mississippi? |
| 2 | The "Teddy Bear" was created because of an incident that happened in Mississippi. What was the incident? |
| 3 | When did Mississippi become a territory? A state? |
| 4 | Find the pledge to the Mississippi state flag and record it. |
| 5 | How many flags have flown over Mississippi? |
| 6 | What is the state beverage of Mississippi? |
| 7 | What Native American groups lived in Mississippi? |
| 8 | One of Mississippi's nicknames is the Bayou State. What is a bayou? |

# Discover Mississippi *(cont.)*

| | Questions |
|---|---|
| 10 | What famous singer was born in Tupelo, Mississippi? |
| 11 | Where did Mississippi get its name? |
| 12 | Visit the capitol building.  From where did the funding come to build the present capitol? |
| 13 | Who is the present governor of Mississippi? |
| 14 | What are the state's most valuable mineral resources?  Agricultural products? |
| 15 | Vicksburg was one of the most decisive battles of the Civil War.  Visit Vicksburg National Military Park, look at the photo album, and take a tour.  Why was it so important? |
| 16 | Natchez is the oldest settlement on the Mississippi River.  Visit some of the historic homes there.  What is the word for these pre-civil war homes? |
| 17 | When, where, and by whom was the first human to human lung transplant? |
| 18 | What did this same doctor and his team do the following year? |
| 19 | The Mississippi Sandhill Crane is critically endangered.  Why? |
| 20 | What four carnivorous plants live in the Mississippi Sandhill Crane National Wildlife Refuge? |

**Challenge:** Write a question about the state that isn't addressed above. Then, suggest a website for finding the answer to your question.

**Question 1:** _____

**URL 1:** _____

Name _____ Date _____

# Mississippi State Map

**Directions:** Use the key located below to complete the map of the state. Begin by locating the capital city and at least three other major cities. Then, locate and draw two major rivers and/or mountains in the state. Locate the Vicksburg National Military Park. Draw at least two major interstate highways that travel through the state. Finally, label any other states and/or bodies of water that surround the state.

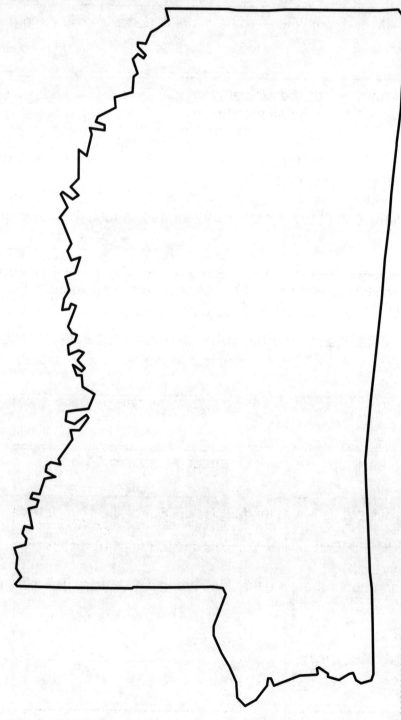

### Key

| | |
|---|---|
| Capital | ✳ |
| City | • |
| River | ‑‑‑‑‑‑‑‑‑ |
| Interstate | ——— |
| Mountains | ᐱᐱᐱᐱᐱ |

Name _____     Date _____

# Mississippi Trivia

The Mississippi State Penitentiary is the largest prison in America.

Mississippi has more churches per capita than any other state in the United States.

Coca Cola® was first bottled in Mississippi.

The first football player on a Wheaties® box was Walter Payton of Columbia, Mississippi.

Mississippi was the first state to ratify the 18th amendment, Prohibition, and has yet to ratify the 21st amendment, which repealed prohibition.

Luka native H.T. Merrell made the world's first transoceanic flight in 1928. He flew to England in a plane loaded with ping-pong balls.

The United States' only cactus plantation is near Edwards, Mississippi.

The Mississippi River is the major river of the United States and is 2,330 miles long from northern Minnesota to the Gulf of Mexico.

Mississippi is the world's largest commercial breeder, producer, and seller of cotton planting seed.

**Directions:** Make a children's alphabet book using things you have learned about Mississippi. Two example pages are given below.

**A** is for Mississippi's animals like the white-tailed deer.

Deer are seen in Mississippi all through the year.

**B** is for Bayou— There are quite a few.

Bringing "crawdads," fishing, and camping to you.

Name _____  Date _____

# North Carolina Symbols

**http://www.netstate.com/states/**

**Directions:** Use the Internet to locate the symbols of the state to complete the chart below. Then, draw and color the flag, seal, bird, and flower. If you wish, you may instead print the four symbols from a website and paste them on the page.

| | |
|---|---|
| **State Capital** | |
| **State Motto** | |
| **State Nickname** | |
| **State Flower** | |
| **State Bird** | |
| **State Tree** | |
| **State Song** | |

| **State Flag** | **State Seal** |
|---|---|
| | |
| **State Bird** | **State Flower** |
| | |

Name _____ Date _____

# Discover North Carolina

**Directions:** Research the Internet to find the answers to these questions. Record your answers below in the space provided, on your own paper, or in a word processing document. You should also include any other interesting places you visited, facts you learned, or opinions you developed.

Begin at the authors' website and then click on the correct state. From there, you can choose the corresponding links to answer the questions.

### http://www.neeleypress.com/usa

| | Questions |
|---|---|
| 1 | What is the tallest mountain peak in North Carolina? How tall is it? In what mountain range is it located? |
| 2 | Write a brochure or flyer describing the Woolly Worm Festival. |
| 3 | Where was the first successful powered flight? |
| 4 | Read (or listen to) the ABCs in the NCMA with art from the North Carolina Museum of Art. Don't forget to click on the question marks to learn about each work. Which is your favorite letter? |
| 5 | North Carolina can be divided into three distinct geographical regions. What are they and where are they located? |
| 6 | What are some of the crops in North Carolina? |
| 7 | During the 30 years before the Civil War, some 50,000 people left North Carolina and moved to Ohio or Indiana in protest. What were they protesting? |
| 8 | Years ago, in order to be prepared to listen to Cherokee stories, what did you have to have done to you? |
| 9 | Who are the Lumbee? |

# Discover North Carolina *(cont.)*

| | Questions |
|---|---|
| 10 | What mountain range is in North Carolina? |
| 11 | What two presidents were born in North Carolina? |
| 12 | Where would you go to see the ship, the USS *North Carolina*? In what war did the USS *North Carolina* see battle? |
| 13 | Visit the mascot of the USS *North Carolina*. What is Charlie? Is there more than one Charlie? Explain. |
| 14 | Choose one famous North Carolinian and write a short essay about his or her life and accomplishments. |
| 15 | Who is the current governor of North Carolina? What is the page program? |
| 16 | Name four national forests in North Carolina. Take a tour of some beautiful forest waterfalls. Describe your favorite one. |
| 17 | What is a shrew? Visit the Western North Carolina Nature Center to find out all about them. |
| 18 | What is the capital of North Carolina? Take a virtual tour of the capitol building. There is a statue of George Washington in the rotunda. How is he dressed? Why do you think the sculptor dressed him this way? |
| 19 | Jump back on the tour bus now and go to New Bern. Tour Tryon Palace. Who first lived there? What was his job? |
| 20 | The last stop on the tour today is the North Carolina Museum of History. Enjoy your tour of the collections and the exhibits. Before you leave, go to the "teasers" and see how many of the answers you can find. |

**Challenge:** Write a question about the state that isn't addressed above. Then, suggest a website for finding the answer to your question.

**Question 1:** _____

**URL 1:** _____

Name _____   Date _____

# North Carolina State Map

**Directions:** Use the key located below to complete the map of the state. Begin by locating the capital city and at least three other major cities. Then, locate and draw two major rivers and/or mountains in the state. Draw at least two major interstate highways that travel through the state. Finally, label any other states and/or bodies of water that surround the state.

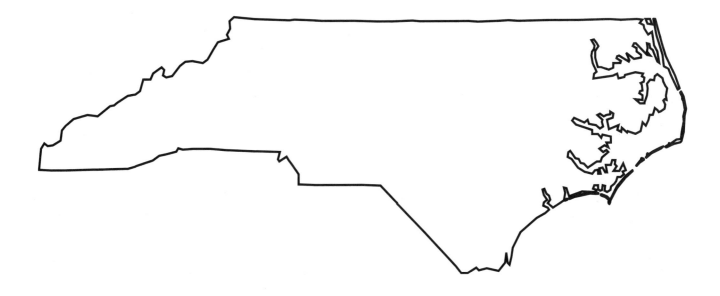

## Key

| Capital | ✳ |
|---|---|
| City | • |
| River | - - - - - - - - - |
| Interstate | ———— |
| Mountains | ∧∧∧∧∧ |

Name _____ Date _____

# North Carolina Trivia

High Point is known as the Furniture Capital of the World.

Beaufort is home of Blackbeard, the pirate.

Pepsi® was invented in New Bern.

In 1803, North Carolina (not California) was the site of the first United States gold rush. The state supplied all the domestic gold coined for currency by the United States Mint in Philadelphia until 1828.

Thomas Jefferson's father was one of the surveyors who laid out the Virginia–North Carolina border.

President Woodrow Wilson, known as "Tommy Wilson" to his classmates at Davidson College in North Carolina, was fined 20 cents in 1873 for "improper conduct in the hall."

It is illegal in North Carolina to use elephants to plow cotton fields.

In Berber, fights between cats and dogs are prohibited.

In Forest City, you must stop and call City Hall before entering town in an automobile. This is so the townspeople will have time to go out and hold their horses until you get through town.

**Directions:** Circle the North Carolina symbols that you find in the puzzle. When you finish, some of the letters that are left will show you a North Carolina slogan.

```
F  I  R  M  S  S  T  I  N  F  E  L  I  D  G
G  H  I  I  Y  W  Q  V  Z  V  F  N  O  K  G
G  R  G  L  R  D  E  D  X  G  E  G  I  F  Q
F  R  A  K  V  F  C  E  A  L  W  K  X  P  T
Y  F  A  Y  W  X  Q  S  T  O  U  C  F  W  Z
L  A  Y  N  S  J  W  R  O  P  A  K  K  L  J
W  C  B  M  I  Q  U  D  Y  R  O  H  V  M  I
C  Q  R  B  F  T  U  R  D  Q  E  T  E  X  M
U  G  F  J  X  H  E  I  T  G  E  A  A  Z  T
E  N  V  O  F  X  N  I  R  O  B  X  M  T  T
G  G  B  J  O  A  R  V  I  R  Y  W  M  O  O
G  I  T  V  L  I  N  Y  D  S  E  M  Y  W  Z
T  F  C  F  J  Q  E  E  J  F  N  L  X  U  K
C  Q  S  O  A  A  N  P  U  J  O  S  H  D  H
G  A  W  F  G  W  D  Q  Y  K  H  X  E  V  L
```

## Word Bank

| | | | | |
|---|---|---|---|---|
| box turtle | cardinal | dogwood | granite | gray squirrel |
| honey bee | milk | pine | sweet potato | |

**North Carolina Slogan:** _____

Name _____  Date _____

# South Carolina Symbols

**http://www.netstate.com/states/**

**Directions:** Use the Internet to locate the symbols of the state to complete the chart below. Then, draw and color the flag, seal, bird, and flower. If you wish, you may instead print the four symbols from a website and paste them on the page.

| | |
|---|---|
| **State Capital** | |
| **State Motto** | |
| **State Nickname** | |
| **State Flower** | |
| **State Bird** | |
| **State Tree** | |
| **State Song** | |

| **State Flag** | **State Seal** |
|---|---|
| | |
| **State Bird** | **State Flower** |
| | |

Name _____ Date _____

# Discover South Carolina

**Directions:** Research the Internet to find the answers to these questions. Record your answers below in the space provided, on your own paper, or in a word processing document. You should also include any other interesting places you visited, facts you learned, or opinions you developed.

Begin at the authors' website and then click on the correct state. From there, you can choose the corresponding links to answer the questions.

**http://www.neeleypress.com/usa**

| | Questions |
|---|---|
| 1 | What were the largest two groups of Native Americans found by the Spanish and French explorers when they arrived in what is now South Carolina? |
| 2 | Choose one South Carolina mammal, one South Carolina bird, and one reptile or amphibian. Write down some interesting facts about them or draw a picture. |
| 3 | What is the capital of South Carolina? Why were the streets built so widely? |
| 4 | What happened in 1865 that suspended work on the new State House? |
| 5 | Take a tour of the State House. What are the bronze stars on the outside of the State House? |
| 6 | Who is the current governor of South Carolina? |
| 7 | What United States president was born in South Carolina? |
| 8 | Where did South Carolina get its name? |
| 9 | What is Gullah? |

# Discover South Carolina *(cont.)*

| | Questions |
|---|---|
| 10 | At the beginning of the Revolution, a battle at Sullivan's Island, South Carolina, saved Charleston from British invasion. What part did the state tree of South Carolina play in this victory? |
| 11 | Who was Francis Marion? Explore the National Forest that bears his name. |
| 12 | Where is Ft. Sumter and what was its significance in the Civil War? Explore more about Ft. Sumter. |
| 13 | Hop back on the tour bus. Visit some other great spots in South Carolina. Describe where you visit. |
| 14 | More wonderful places await you. Choose from one of these great destinations and tell about what you find. |
| 15 | Send an e-postcard to your teacher, a friend, or the authors of this book from one of your favorite spots in South Carolina. |
| 16 | Rich in history and influenced by many cultures, Beaufort is a "must see" in the South Carolina Low Country. In the early 1700s, what two crops were introduced that led to great prosperity for this region? |
| 17 | A cruel pirate named Stede Bonnet was hanged in the port city of Charles Town, named for a British king. Today Charles Town is Charleston, one of South Carolina's most beautiful cities. Read the story of Stede Bonnet. Why do you think he became a pirate? |
| 18 | What are the Appalachians, and how were they formed? |
| 19 | What is the highest mountain in South Carolina? Where is it located? |
| 20 | What were the first dinosaur fossils found in South Carolina? When were they found? |

**Challenge:** Write a question about the state that isn't addressed above. Then, suggest a website for finding the answer to your question.

**Question 1:** _____

**URL 1:** _____

Name _____ Date _____

# South Carolina State Map

**Directions:** Use the key located below to complete the map of the state. Begin by locating the capital city and at least three other major cities. Then, locate and draw two major rivers and/or mountains in the state. Draw at least two major interstate highways that travel through the state. Finally, label any other states and/or bodies of water that surround the state.

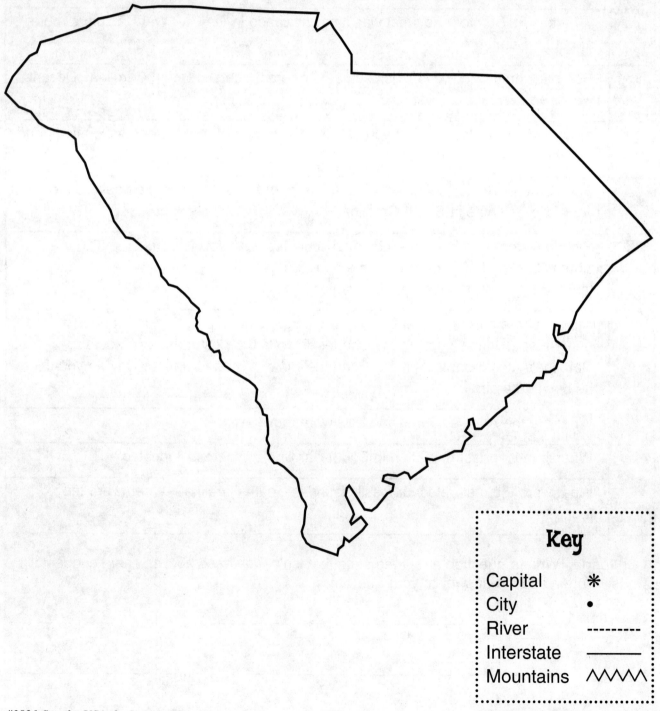

**Key**

| | |
|---|---|
| Capital | ✳ |
| City | • |
| River | --------- |
| Interstate | ——— |
| Mountains | ∧∧∧∧ |

Name _____ Date _____

# South Carolina Trivia

Michael Jackson owns the rights to the South Carolina state anthem.

The first tea farm in the United States was created in 1890 near Summerville, South Carolina.

The walls of the American fort on Sullivan Island, in Charleston Harbor, were made of spongy Palmetto logs. This was helpful in protecting the fort because the British cannonballs bounced off the logs.

Before being known as the Palmetto State, South Carolina was known as, and had emblazoned on their license plates, the Iodine State.

The Isle of Palms was originally named Hunting Island and then Long Island. It's thought to be at least 25,000 years old, and was first inhabited by the indigenous Seewee Indians.

The first boll weevil found in South Carolina is on display at the Pendleton District Agricultural Museum.

It is a state law that horses may not be kept in bathtubs.

Horses are to wear pants at all times in Fountain Inn.

In Spartanburg, eating watermelons in the Magnolia Street cemetery is forbidden.

**Directions:** Unscramble each of the words. Copy the letters in the numbered cells to other cells with the same number.

1. RERISV GERBID      8 28    9 16

2. TF METRUS      11  20  12

3. HALREOTCNS BHARRO      1 22 10  27    19    30

4. MISLGBRLA DILNANG      25    24 5   15

5. MIOSSNM FULFB      2    18   13

6. LEESEINVCOSISL      23    26  3

7. FT REGWAN      21  6 7  17

8. HEONY LIHL      29 14    4

1 2 3 4 5   6 7 8   9 10 11 12 13 14 15   16 17

18 19 20 21 22   23 24 25 26 27 28 29 30

Name _____   Date _____

# Tennessee Symbols

### http://www.netstate.com/states/

**Directions:** Use the Internet to locate the symbols of the state to complete the chart below. Then, draw and color the flag, seal, bird, and flower. If you wish, you may instead print the four symbols from a website and paste them on the page.

| | |
|---|---|
| **State Capital** | |
| **State Motto** | |
| **State Nickname** | |
| **State Flower** | |
| **State Bird** | |
| **State Tree** | |
| **State Song** | |

| State Flag | State Seal |
|---|---|
| | |
| **State Bird** | **State Flower** |
| | |

Name _____ Date _____

# Discover Tennessee

**Directions:** Research the Internet to find the answers to these questions. Record your answers below in the space provided, on your own paper, or in a word processing document. You should also include any other interesting places you visited, facts you learned, or opinions you developed.

Begin at the authors' website and then click on the correct state. From there, you can choose the corresponding links to answer the questions.

## http://www.neeleypress.com/usa

| | Questions |
|---|---|
| 1 | Ruby Falls is America's highest underground waterfall. Where is it located? How was it discovered? |
| 2 | Early in the United States' history, the State of Franklin was started after the citizens of North Carolina became unhappy. For whom was the state named? What happened to this mystery state? |
| 3 | Graceland is Elvis Presley's mansion in Memphis, Tennessee. People travel from all over the world to visit Graceland. You can tour it, too. What are some of the amazing things that you see in the mansion? |
| 4 | Sequoyah, Sogwali, and George Guess are names for one Native American. What was his tribe? What significant contribution did he make to them? |
| 5 | Construction on the Tennessee capitol started in 1845. Who was the architect for the building? Where is he buried? Who else is buried near the capitol? |
| 6 | Gatlinburg is known as the gateway to the Great Smoky Mountains. What was its first name? What family first settled this area? |
| 7 | The Tennessee Valley Authority was started to find solutions to power production, navigation, flood control, and erosion control. Which president signed the TVA Act in 1933? Why did he want the TVA? |
| 8 | Davy Crockett was not "born on a mountaintop in Tennessee." Those were simply words used by Disney for a television show. Where was he actually born? What year was he born? |
| 9 | Oak Ridge National Laboratories was first called Clinton Laboratories when it opened in 1943. What was its original, well-defined mission? |

# Discover Tennessee *(cont.)*

| | Questions |
|---|---|
| 10 | R. T. Raccoon works for the Tennessee Department of Environment and Conservation. Go on R.T.'s adventure. Where did you go? |
| 11 | Reelfoot Lake is called the Turtle Capital of the World. What other wildlife can you find at Reelfoot Lake? |
| 12 | Who convinced President Roosevelt that an atomic bomb was feasible? Where was the bomb built? |
| 13 | Alex Haley was raised in this Tennessee town. Haley wrote *Roots*, an ancestral history of an African family. His boyhood home is an historic site devoted to African Americans. What is the name of the town? |
| 14 | Mr. and Mrs. Willis P. Davis began asking, "Why can't we have a national park in the Smokies?" after they returned from a trip to see the western national parks. How many years did it take before the park was opened? |
| 15 | The National Civil Rights Museum in Memphis is at the Lorraine Motel. Who was assassinated on this spot on April 4, 1968? |
| 16 | Indian Chief Craighead discovered a cavern opening to the Lost Sea which is the largest underground lake in the United States. For what was the cave used during the Civil War? |
| 17 | Andrew Jackson was called Old Hickory, Hero of the Common Man, Hero of the Battle of New Orleans, Self-Made Man, King Andrew, General, and Mr. President. What was the name of his home in Tennessee? |
| 18 | Nashville has the only full-size replica of the ancient Parthenon in Athens. The columns in the building differ in diameter from the ones beside them and all are spaced differently. How tall is the Athena statue in Nashville? |
| 19 | The Country Music Hall of Fame is located in Nashville. What are some of the events that occurred in the years 1953 to 1959? |
| 20 | Tennessee is known as "The Volunteer State." What is the origin of this name? |

**Challenge:** Write a question about the state that isn't addressed above. Then, suggest a website for finding the answer to your question.

**Question 1:** _____

**URL 1:** _____

Name _____ Date _____

# Tennessee State Map

**Directions:** Use the key located below to complete the map of the state. Begin by locating the capital city and at least three other major cities. Where is the largest Tennessee city on the Mississippi located? Where is the Country Music Hall of Fame? Then, locate and draw two major rivers and/or mountains in the state. Draw at least two major interstate highways that travel through the state. Finally, label any other states and/or bodies of water that surround the state.

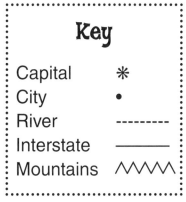

**Key**

| | |
|---|---|
| Capital | ✳ |
| City | • |
| River | - - - - - - |
| Interstate | ——— |
| Mountains | ∧∧∧∧∧ |

Name _____     Date _____

# Tennessee Trivia

Thomas Edison developed a device to electrocute cockroaches while living in Tennessee.

The largest city on the Mississippi River is Memphis, Tennessee.

Tennessee was the last state to secede from the Union during the Civil War and the first state to be readmitted after the war.

Seventy-seven thousand people lived in Tennessee when it became a state in 1796.

The name "Tennessee" originated from the old Yuchi word, *tana-see*, and means the meeting place.

**Directions:** Use these Tennessee terms to complete this word fill-in. The words may be upside down.

**3–letter**
oak

**4–letter**
ruby

**5–letter**
yuchi
civil
April
Elvis

**6–letter**
atomic

**7–letter**
hickory
raccoon

**8–letter**
reelfoot
Franklin
Sequoyah

**9–letter**
Parthenon
Roosevelt

Name _____     Date _____

# Virginia Symbols

## http://www.netstate.com/states/

**Directions:** Use the Internet to locate the symbols of the state to complete the chart below. Then, draw and color the flag, seal, bird, and flower. If you wish, you may instead print the four symbols from a website and paste them on the page.

| | |
|---|---|
| **State Capital** | |
| **State Motto** | |
| **State Nickname** | |
| **State Flower** | |
| **State Bird** | |
| **State Tree** | |
| **State Song** | |

| | |
|---|---|
| **State Flag** | **State Seal** |
| **State Bird** | **State Flower** |

Name _____     Date _____

# Discover Virginia

**Directions:** Research the Internet to find the answers to these questions. Record your answers below in the space provided, on your own paper, or in a word processing document. You should also include any other interesting places you visited, facts you learned, or opinions you developed.

Begin at the authors' website and then click on the correct state. From there, you can choose the corresponding links to answer the questions.

## http://www.neeleypress.com/usa

| | Questions |
|---|---|
| 1 | Who is the governor of Virginia? |
| 2 | Where did Virginia's General Assembly, the earliest elective legislature in America, meet for the first eleven years? |
| 3 | Which eight presidents were from Virginia? |
| 4 | Design and make your own game, using the questions and answers found at "Did You Know . . . ." |
| 5 | Write the salute to the Virginia Flag. |
| 6 | Who designed the capitol building in Richmond? |
| 7 | Take a virtual tour (requires *QuickTime*™) or look at pictures of the grounds, buildings, and statues around the capitol. |
| 8 | How did Virginia get its name? |
| 9 | Is a *common shoveler* an unimportant ditch digger?  What is a *common shoveler*? |

# Discover Virginia *(cont.)*

| | Questions |
|---|---|
| **10** | Which United States presidents are buried in Arlington National Cemetery? |
| **11** | Who was the first person buried in Arlington National Cemetery? |
| **12** | What is the Flowerdew Hundred? |
| **13** | What was George Washington's farm called?  What crops did he grow there?  How did he improve the soil? |
| **14** | What buildings can you see in Capitol Square in Richmond? |
| **15** | What is Monticello?  Describe a typical day in Thomas Jefferson's life. |
| **16** | What was the earliest English settlement in America?  For whom was it named? |
| **17** | Was this first English settlement successful?  Why or why not? |
| **18** | What eight tribes of Native Americans are recognized by the Commonwealth of Virginia? |
| **19** | Where did Cornwallis surrender to Washington?  What was the significance of this surrender? |
| **20** | Who is Lawrence Douglass Wilder?  Why is he important in Virginia's history? |

**Challenge:** Write a question about the state that isn't addressed above. Then, suggest a website for finding the answer to your question.

**Question 1:** _____

**URL 1:** _____

Name _____   Date _____

# Virginia State Map

**Directions:** Use the key located below to complete the map of the state. Begin by locating the capital city and at least three other major cities. Then, locate and draw two major rivers and/or mountains in the state. Draw at least two major interstate highways that travel through the state. Finally, label any other states and/or bodies of water that surround the state.

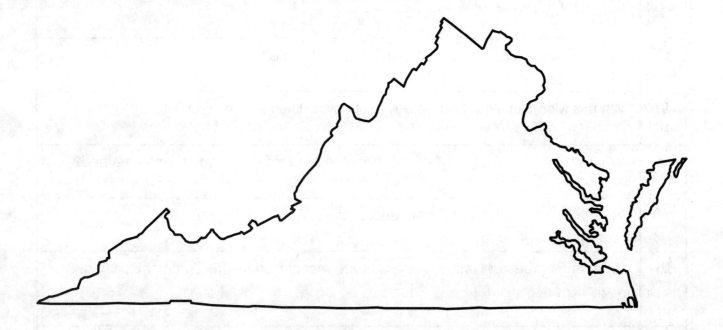

## Key

| | |
|---|---|
| Capital | ✳ |
| City | • |
| River | - - - - - - |
| Interstate | ——— |
| Mountains | ∧∧∧∧ |

Name _____   Date _____

# Virginia Trivia

Virginia extends 95 miles farther west than West Virginia.

Bullets that met in midair have been found in Civil War battlefields in Virginia.

Pocahontas and her husband, John Rolfe, had one son named Thomas who was born and educated in England, but settled in Virginia.

In colonial America, tobacco was acceptable legal tender in several southern colonies, and in Virginia, taxes were paid in tobacco.

Civil War General Thomas Jonathan "Stonewall" Jackson has two separate burial sites. His left arm, which was amputated after the battle of Chancellorsville, was buried on a nearby farm. A week later, Jackson died and was buried in Lexington, Virginia.

The Pentagon building in Arlington, Virginia, has nearly 68,000 miles of telephone lines.

Richmond is Virginia's third capital city. Lawmakers first met in a warehouse.

Urging his fellow Virginians to take up weapons in self-defense in 1775, Patrick Henry spoke these inspiring words: "I know not what course others may take; but as for me, give me liberty or give me death."

In Richmond, it is illegal to flip a coin in a restaurant to see who pays for the coffee.

In Lebanon, Virginia, it is illegal to kick your wife out of bed.

In Norfolk, you may not legally spit on a seagull.

In Waynesboro, it is illegal for a woman to drive a car up Main Street unless her husband is walking in front of the car waving a red flag.

A Virginia law requires all bathtubs to be kept out in the yards, not inside the houses.

**Directions:** Match each description to the city name by writing the letter on the line provided.

| | | |
|---|---|---|
| _____ | Colonial Williamsburg | a. George Washington's home |
| _____ | Jamestown | b. Thomas Jefferson's home |
| _____ | Yorktown | c. Virginia's capital |
| _____ | Mount Vernon | d. Virginia's capital 200 years ago |
| _____ | Richmond | e. first permanent settlement |
| _____ | Chesapeake Bay | f. part of Virginia's eastern border |
| _____ | Monticello | g. British surrendered to America |

Name _____   Date _____

# West Virginia Symbols

## http://www.netstate.com/states/

**Directions:** Use the Internet to locate the symbols of the state to complete the chart below. Then, draw and color the flag, seal, bird, and flower. If you wish, you may instead print the four symbols from a website and paste them on the page.

| | |
|---|---|
| **State Capital** | |
| **State Motto** | |
| **State Nickname** | |
| **State Flower** | |
| **State Bird** | |
| **State Tree** | |
| **State Song** | |

| | |
|---|---|
| **State Flag** | **State Seal** |
| **State Bird** | **State Flower** |

Name _____   Date _____

# Discover West Virginia

**Directions:** Research the Internet to find the answers to these questions. Record your answers below in the space provided, on your own paper, or in a word processing document. You should also include any other interesting places you visited, facts you learned, or opinions you developed.

Begin at the authors' website and then click on the correct state. From there, you can choose the corresponding links to answer the questions.

## http://www.neeleypress.com/usa

| | Questions |
|---|---|
| 1 | Over the years, the West Virginia State Capitol has moved between Charleston and Wheeling several times. Why is it referred to as the floating capitol? |
| 2 | Purloo (or pilau) is a classic dish in Charleston, West Virginia. What are the ingredients in purloo? |
| 3 | Green Bank, West Virginia, is the home to the National Radio Astronomy Observatory. What is a radio telescope? |
| 4 | The Seneca Rocks are a magnificent formation rising nearly 900 feet above the North Fork River in the Monongahela National Forest. What is the legend of Seneca Rocks? |
| 5 | West Virginia's largest and most beautiful caverns are the Seneca Caverns. The Seneca tribe used the caverns for ceremonies and as refuge. |
| 6 | Thomas Jonathon Jackson was orphaned at age seven, graduated from West Point, and became a Confederate hero. What was his famous nickname? |
| 7 | The New River Gorge Bridge near Fayetteville is the longest steel arch bridge (1,700 feet) in the world. How did people cross the New River Gorge before the bridge was built? |
| 8 | Chuck Yeager of West Virginia was a young Air Force test pilot. They say he was the man who "punched a hole in the sky." What was his accomplishment? |
| 9 | The first celebrations of Mother's Day were in Greece. In the United States, West Virginia was first to recognize the holiday. What year was it? |

# Discover West Virginia *(cont.)*

| | Questions |
|---|---|
| 10 | James Rumsey was a skilled cabinet-maker, blacksmith, and millwright as well as a scientist. Which president hired him to build a house? What invention did Rumsey show the president? Did the president like what he saw? |
| 11 | The Adena people created earthen burial mounds during the time period of 1000 B.C. and A.D. 1. One of the nation's oldest and largest Native American burial grounds is located in Moundsville. What is another name for this historic mound? |
| 12 | Fifteen percent of the nation's total coal production comes from West Virginia. When did extensive coal mining begin in West Virginia? |
| 13 | Long before the first European settlers arrived, who used the warm spring waters at Berkeley Springs for health remedies? What was the original name? |
| 14 | Harpers Ferry area has served in a pivotal role in several events that impacted the nation's history. How did the town get its name? |
| 15 | Paul Stark found "gold" in the hills of West Virginia. What did he find? |
| 16 | The Wheeling Suspension Bridge was at one time the longest suspension bridge in the world. It was opened August 1, 1850, fell in 1854, but was rebuilt. What caused it to fall? |
| 17 | Cass Scenic Railroad is the same line built in 1901 to haul lumber to the mill in Cass. What kind of locomotive is used on the Cass Railroad? |
| 18 | Coal House in White Sulphur Springs was occupied on June 1, 1961. How many tons of coal were used to build the house? |
| 19 | Native Americans and pioneers used the brine from wells in the Kanawha Valley for many years. What early industry was developed from this resource? |
| 20 | In Elkins, West Virginia, you can compete in the Mountain State Forest Festival's Lumberjack Contest. What events are in the competition? |

**Challenge:** Write a question about the state that isn't addressed above. Then, suggest a website for finding the answer to your question.

**Question 1:** _____

**URL 1:** _____

Name _____  Date _____

# West Virginia State Map

**Directions:** Use the key located below to complete the map of the state. Begin by locating the capital city and at least three other major cities. What mountain range runs through the eastern part of the state? What river borders the northwest side of the state? What river is on the northeast border? Draw at least two major interstate highways that travel through the state. Finally, label any other states and/or bodies of water that surround the state.

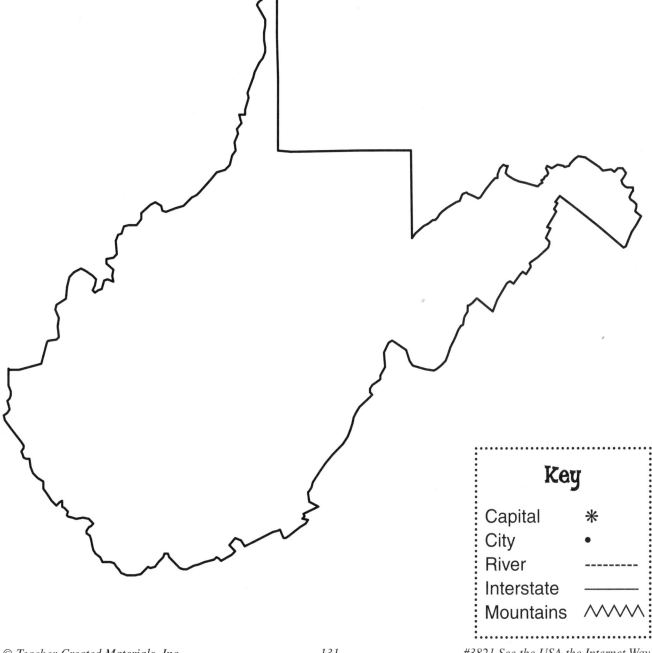

**Key**

| | |
|---|---|
| Capital | ✳ |
| City | • |
| River | -------- |
| Interstate | ———— |
| Mountains | ∧∧∧∧∧ |

Name _____     Date _____

# West Virginia Trivia

Virginia extends 95 miles farther west than West Virginia.

West Virginia is the only state in the Union to have acquired its sovereignty by proclamation of the President of the United States.

West Virginia is considered the southern most northern state and the northern most southern state.

Stone that was quarried near Hinton was contributed by West Virginia for the Washington Monument.

**Directions:** Use this key to reveal the phrase below.

| | | | | | | | |
|---|---|---|---|---|---|---|---|
| 12–A | 23–B | 34–C | 45–D | 56–E | 67–F | 68–G | 69–H |
| 90–I | 21–J | 32–K | 43–L | 54–M | 65–N | 76–O | 87–P |
| 98–Q | 09–R | 13–S | 24–T | 35–U | 46–V | 57–W | 68–X |
| 80–Y | 42–Z | | | | | | |

_____          _____
54-76-65-24-12-65-90                 13-56-54-87-56-09

_____
43-90-23-56-09-90

**which means**

_____          _____
54-76-35-65-24-12-90-65-56-56-09-13            12-09-56

_____          _____
12-43-57-12-80-13            67-09-56-56

Name _____    Date _____

# Illinois Symbols

## http://www.netstate.com/states/

**Directions:** Use the Internet to locate the symbols of the state to complete the chart below. Then, draw and color the flag, seal, bird, and flower. If you wish, you may instead print the four symbols from a website and paste them on the page.

| | |
|---|---|
| **State Capital** | |
| **State Motto** | |
| **State Nickname** | |
| **State Flower** | |
| **State Bird** | |
| **State Tree** | |
| **State Song** | |

| **State Flag** | **State Seal** |
|---|---|
| | |
| **State Bird** | **State Flower** |
| | |

Name _____   Date _____

# Discover Illinois

**Directions:** Research the Internet to find the answers to these questions. Record your answers below in the space provided, on your own paper, or in a word processing document. You should also include any other interesting places you visited, facts you learned, or opinions you developed.

Begin at the authors' website and then click on the correct state. From there, you can choose the corresponding links to answer the questions.

## http://www.neeleypress.com/usa

| | Questions |
|---|---|
| 1 | Take a virtual tour of the Illinois State Capitol. Can you find the rotunda? Describe the ceiling of the rotunda. |
| 2 | The famous architect, Frank Lloyd Wright, designed several homes in Oak Park, Illinois. Take a tour of the neighborhood and describe what you see. |
| 3 | In 1885, Major William Le Baron Jenney created the first skyscraper using the first load-carrying structural frame. What was different about his building's frame? |
| 4 | Two famous old professional baseball parks are located in Chicago. Can you name them? |
| 5 | The Sears Tower in Chicago is the tallest building on the North American continent. The Skydeck is 1,353 feet above the ground. What four states can you see on a clear day from the Skydeck? |
| 6 | The Chicago Water Tower survived the Great Chicago Fire. What year was the water tower built? |
| 7 | In southern Illinois, the ancient city of Cahokia can be found. This is the most sophisticated prehistoric native civilization north of Mexico. What can you see there? |
| 8 | In 1942, Enrico Fermi and a small band of scientists and engineers demonstrated the first nuclear fission reactor at the University of Chicago. Fermi later helped in the development of what kind of bomb in the Manhattan Project? |
| 9 | Though the McDonald brothers opened their first hamburger stand in California, Ray Kroc opened the first McDonald's® in 1995 in what Illinois city? |

# Discover Illinois *(cont.)*

| | Questions |
|---|---|
| 10 | The 40th president of the United States was born in Tampico, Illinois. What is his name? What is his birth date? |
| 11 | Springfield is the home of the National Historic Site of the home of President and Mrs. Abraham Lincoln. How many of their sons were born here? |
| 12 | Legend says that Mrs. O'Leary's cow kicked over a lantern and started the great Chicago fire. When was the great fire? |
| 13 | In 1836, John Deere moved from Vermont to Grand Detour, Illinois, where he started making farming equipment. What did he invent first? |
| 14 | William Sullivan reinvented the wheel when he made this change to the ferris wheel in 1897. What change did he make? |
| 15 | Frank H. Hall invented a machine to help people who are blind to read. What did he invent? What year did he invent it? |
| 16 | Forty feet under the streets and businesses of Chicago lie 62 miles of tunnels that were used from 1899 until 1959. For what were they used? |
| 17 | The world's largest, most complete, and best-preserved Tyrannosaurus-rex is at the Field Museum in Chicago, Illinois. What is her name? |
| 18 | The World's Largest Catsup Bottle stands proudly next to Route 159, just south of downtown Collinsville, Illinois. What is the structure's real function? |
| 19 | Walter Elias Disney was born in Chicago. What was his birth date? |
| 20 | Wild Bill Hickok was a gunfighter of legendary status. Though truly a gunfighter and gambler, he joined a famous Wild West show for a while. Whose show did he join? |

**Challenge:** Write a question about the state that isn't addressed above. Then, suggest a website for finding the answer to your question.

**Question 1:** _____

**URL 1:** _____

Name _____  Date _____

# Illinois State Map

**Directions:** Use the key located below to complete the map of the state. Begin by locating the capital city and at least three other major cities. Then, locate and draw two major rivers and/or mountains in the state. What large river borders the southwest side of Illinois? What lake touches the northwest part of Illinois? Label both bodies of water on the map. Draw at least two major interstate highways that travel through the state. Finally, label any other states and/or bodies of water that surround the state.

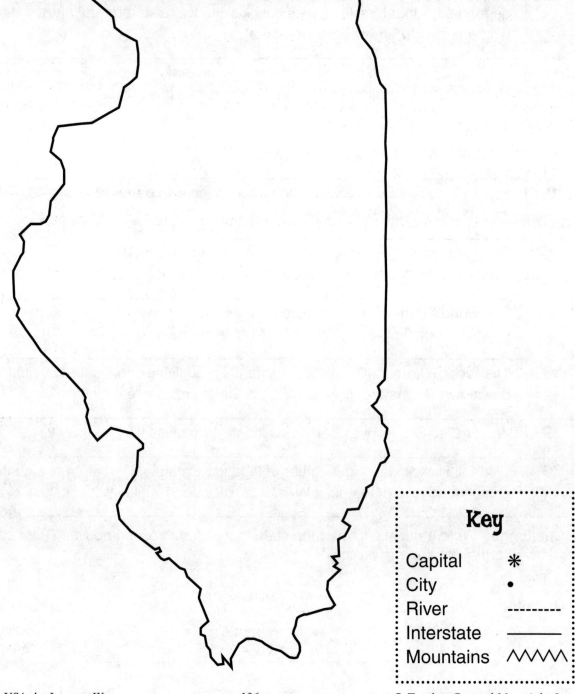

**Key**

| | |
|---|---|
| Capital | ✳ |
| City | • |
| River | ---------- |
| Interstate | —————— |
| Mountains | ∧∧∧∧∧∧ |

Name _____  Date _____

# Illinois Trivia

The first round silo for farm grain storage was constructed on a farm in Spring Grove.

The Illinois state dance is square dancing.

In Mount Pulaski, Illinois, it is illegal for boys to hurl snowballs at trees. Girls are allowed to do that, however.

The Chicago River is dyed green on Saint Patrick's Day.

Chicago, Illinois, was nicknamed the "Windy City" because during the Columbian Exhibition of 1893 the citizens did so much bragging. Chicago has actually been rated as only the 16th breeziest city in America.

Metropolis, the home of Superman, really exists in southern Illinois.

**Directions:** Find the six professional sports teams of Illinois in the word search.

```
B   I   L   K   J   M   F   D   I   K   N   D
U   L   K   L   I   N   K   B   E   S   R   M
L   Q   A   L   W   X   L   M   N   W   O   I
L   K   J   C   U   B   S   Z   K   F   E   T
S   E   R   K   K   T   U   V   B   I   J   N
M   C   V   F   E   H   C   K   E   R   A   M
Z   L   V   R   S   R   A   E   B   E   O   P
R   N   I   W   H   G   D   W   K   L   S   A
L   P   Q   O   W   I   E   R   K   T   I   K
N   B   V   M   W   H   I   T   E   S   O   X
```

## Word Bank

Bears                 Blackhawks                 Bulls
Cubs                  White Sox                  Fire

Name _____   Date _____

# Indiana Symbols

## http://www.netstate.com/states/

**Directions:** Use the Internet to locate the symbols of the state to complete the chart below. Then, draw and color the flag, seal, bird, and flower. If you wish, you may instead print the four symbols from a website and paste them on the page.

| | |
|---|---|
| **State Capital** | |
| **State Motto** | |
| **State Nickname** | |
| **State Flower** | |
| **State Bird** | |
| **State Tree** | |
| **State Song** | |

| **State Flag** | **State Seal** |
|---|---|
| | |
| **State Bird** | **State Flower** |
| | |

Name _____ Date _____

# Discover Indiana

**Directions:** Research the Internet to find the answers to these questions. Record your answers below in the space provided, on your own paper, or in a word processing document. You should also include any other interesting places you visited, facts you learned, or opinions you developed.

Begin at the authors' website and then click on the correct state. From there, you can choose the corresponding links to answer the questions.

### http://www.neeleypress.com/usa

| | Questions |
|---|---|
| 1 | What is unique about the animals you will find at Black Pine Animal Park? |
| 2 | Another place to see animals is the Fort Wayne Children's Zoo. This is one of the top four zoos in the nation for kids. Visit the Central Zoo, the African Veldt, take an Australian Adventure, and wander through the Indonesian Rain Forest. Which was your favorite part and why? |
| 3 | Vice President Dan Quayle, who served under President George Bush, was born in Indianapolis. What other vice presidents were from Indiana and under which presidents did they serve? |
| 4 | Where is the geographic center of Indiana? |
| 5 | Explore the exhibits and the grounds at Angel Mounds State Historic Site. Who built this city and when did they live there? Why do you think they built their houses off the ground on stilts? |
| 6 | Indiana's first State House in Indianapolis was modeled after what famous structure? |
| 7 | Indiana is called the "Hoosier State" and its people are known as "Hoosiers." No one knows for sure where this nickname originated. Read the theories and either choose one or make up a story of your own about why people from Indiana are called Hoosiers. |
| 8 | What is the most important economic activity in Indiana? What are some of the goods produced? |
| 9 | Let's visit Wyandotte Cave, one of the largest caverns in the United States. What use do archeologists think the Native Americans found for the cave? |

# Discover Indiana *(cont.)*

| | Questions |
|---|---|
| 10 | Where is the Calumet region of Indiana and for what is it famous? |
| 11 | When the first Europeans arrived in what is now Indiana, they found only a few hundred Native Americans. To what tribe did most of these people belong, and who had the greatest effect on the development of Indiana? Who was the main leader of this tribe? |
| 12 | What was the first road to cross the state from east to west? Why was this road needed? Tell about its history. |
| 13 | Who is the present governor of Indiana? |
| 14 | Who was the first territorial governor of Indiana? |
| 15 | This governor later ran for president of the United States. His campaign slogan was "Tippecanoe and Tyler, too." To what did that refer? |
| 16 | How long did Tyler serve as president? What happened? |
| 17 | Another president who hailed from Indiana (though not born there) was the grandson of the first territorial governor of Indiana. Who was he? Did he share his grandfather's reputation for fighting Native Americans? Explain. |
| 18 | Vincennes was the first territorial capital. What was the first state capital? How long was it the capital? |
| 19 | When did Indianapolis become the capital? Describe the different State Houses. |
| 20 | What famous sporting event is held in Indianapolis? When is it held? When was the first one and how has the track changed? |

**Challenge:** Write a question about the state that isn't addressed above. Then, suggest a website for finding the answer to your question.

**Question 1:** _____

**URL 1:** _____

Name _____ Date _____

# Indiana State Map

**Directions:** Use the key located below to complete the map of the state. Begin by locating the capital city and at least three other major cities. Then, locate and draw two major rivers and/or mountains in the state. Draw at least two major interstate highways that travel through the state. Finally, label any other states and/or bodies of water that surround the state.

**Key**

| | |
|---|---|
| Capital | ✳ |
| City | • |
| River | - - - - - - - |
| Interstate | ——— |
| Mountains | ∧∧∧∧∧ |

Name _____  Date _____

# Indiana Trivia

There was only one battle in Indiana during the Civil War—the Battle of Coyton.

The marsupial Virginia opossum is found in Indiana.

Born in Fort Wayne, Indiana, Shelly Long played the ditzy barmaid at the "Cheers" bar.

Jim Davis, the creator of the comic strip cat Garfield, lives near Muncie, Indiana.

State Law:  Pedestrians crossing the highway at night are prohibited from wearing tail lights.

In Elkhart, it is illegal for barbers to threaten to cut off kids' ears.

Within four hours of eating garlic, a person may not enter a movie house, theater, or ride a public streetcar in Gary.

**Directions:**  Each letter is represented by a number in the puzzle.  Three letters have been done for you.  **Hint:**  Look for a pattern (plus a number, then minus a number).

| A | B | C | D | E | F | G | H | I | J | K | L | M | N | O | P | Q | R | S | T | U | V | W | X | Y | Z |
|---|---|---|---|---|---|---|---|---|---|---|---|---|---|---|---|---|---|---|---|---|---|---|---|---|---|
| 2 |   |   |   |   |   |   |   | 10 |   |   |   |   |   |   |   |   |   |   | 23 |   |   |   |   |   |   |

I   1854,   T       A       A               T
10 17      23 11 6   2 25 6 21 2 8 6   15 6 17 8 23 11

        T                   T               I           I       I A   A
16 9   23 11 6   20 4 11 16 16 15   23 6 21 14   10 17   10 17 7 10 2 17 2

        A               T   T       A                   A
24 2 20   13 22 20 23   23 24 16   2 17 7   16 17 6   11 2 15 9

                T,               I               A           A T
14 16 17 23 11 20   19 16 20 20 10 5 15 26   5 6 4 2 22 20 6   2 23

T       T I       I T       A       I       A       T
23 11 6   23 10 14 6   10 23   24 2 20   10 15 15 6 8 2 15   23 16

T A       A       A T       I       T       I   T
23 2 12 6   2   5 2 23 11   10 17   23 11 6   24 10 17 23 6 21.

Name _____ Date _____

# Iowa Symbols

## http://www.netstate.com/states/

**Directions:** Use the Internet to locate the symbols of the state to complete the chart below. Then, draw and color the flag, seal, bird, and flower. If you wish, you may instead print the four symbols from a website and paste them on the page.

| | |
|---|---|
| **State Capital** | |
| **State Motto** | |
| **State Nickname** | |
| **State Flower** | |
| **State Bird** | |
| **State Tree** | |
| **State Song** | |

| State Flag | State Seal |
|---|---|
| | |
| **State Bird** | **State Flower** |
| | |

Name _____  Date _____

# Discover Iowa

**Directions:** Research the Internet to find the answers to these questions. Record your answers below in the space provided, on your own paper, or in a word processing document. You should also include any other interesting places you visited, facts you learned, or opinions you developed.

Begin at the authors' website and then click on the correct state. From there, you can choose the corresponding links to answer the questions.

## http://www.neeleypress.com/usa

| | Questions |
|---|---|
| 1 | The dome of the Iowa State Capitol is covered with 23-karat gold. Take a tour through this beautiful 19th century building. What other interesting sights do you see? |
| 2 | In the 1840s, Fort Atkinson was built in Iowa. This army post had a very specific purpose, but was then abandoned in 1849. Why was the fort built? |
| 3 | Snake Alley is a crooked street in Burlington, Iowa. Why was the street built with all the twists and turns? |
| 4 | Where can you find the world's largest strawberry? |
| 5 | Scranton is home to Iowa's oldest water tower still in service. In 1907, the water tower actually caught on fire. Describe how the fire happened. |
| 6 | Imes Bridge was built in 1871 and moved in 1887. What kind of bridge is the Imes Bridge? |
| 7 | Elk Horn is the largest Danish settlement in the United States. Visit the Danish Immigration Museum and describe what you see. |
| 8 | Kalona is the largest Amish Mennonite settlement west of the Mississippi River. What year did the Amish arrive in Kalona? |
| 9 | Fenlon Place Elevator in Dubuque is the world's steepest and shortest railway. Why did Mr. Graves want this inclined railway built? |

# Discover Iowa *(cont.)*

| | Questions |
|---|---|
| **10** | In 1901, John Stuart, his son Robert, and his partner George Douglas started the Quaker Oats Company in what Iowa town? |
| **11** | Cornell College is the only school in the nation to have its entire campus listed on the National Register of Historic Places. What year was the college founded? |
| **12** | The Sergeant Floyd Monument in Sioux City honors the only man to die during which 1804 expedition? |
| **13** | George Washington Carver received two college degrees from what Iowa university? What years did he earn his degrees? |
| **14** | Herbert Hoover, the son of a Quaker blacksmith, became the 31st president of the United States. He was the first president born west of what? |
| **15** | Where is the Herbert Hoover Presidential Library located? |
| **16** | Where is the hometown of baseball great Bob Feller? On what team did he play? What position did he play? |
| **17** | Born Marion Robert Morrison in Winterset, Iowa, this famous movie cowboy was the son of a pharmacist. Who was he? |
| **18** | The Kate Shelley Bridge is the highest double track railroad bridge in the world. Read the story of young Kate Shelley and describe her act of heroism to save a passenger train. |
| **19** | Watch the corn grow in Iowa! Describe what you see. |
| **20** | One town in Iowa is located on an island surrounded by lakes. What is its name? How big is it? |

**Challenge:** Write a question about the state that isn't addressed above. Then, suggest a website for finding the answer to your question.

**Question 1:** _____

**URL 1:** _____

Name _____ Date _____

# Iowa State Map

**Directions:** Use the key located below to complete the map of the state. Begin by locating the capital city and at least three other major cities. Then, locate and draw two major rivers and/or mountains in the state. What large river borders the eastern side of the state? Find Storm Lake. Label both bodies of water on the map. Draw at least two major interstate highways that travel through the state. Finally, label any other states and/or bodies of water that surround the state.

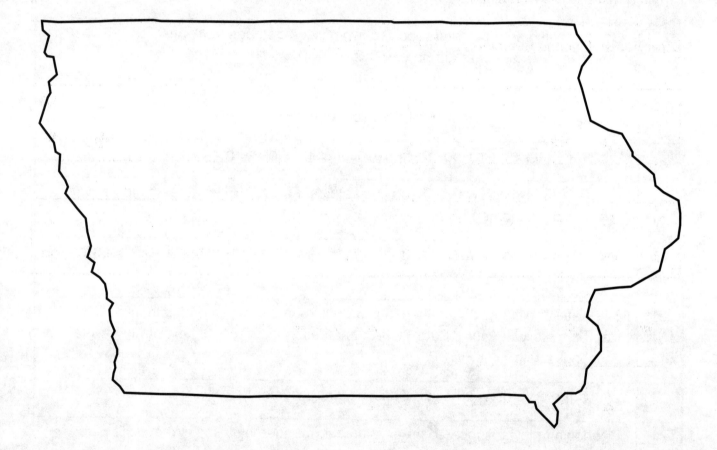

### Key

| | |
|---|---|
| Capital | ✳ |
| City | • |
| River | - - - - - - - |
| Interstate | ———— |
| Mountains | ∧∧∧∧∧ |

Name _____  Date _____

# Iowa Trivia

Iowa is the only state whose east and west borders are 100% formed by water—the Missouri and Mississippi rivers.

Iowa is the only state name that starts with two vowels.

The musical, "The Music Man," was set in a small town in Iowa.

**Directions:** Decode the message below using this key.

| A | B | C | D | E | F | G | H | I | J | K | L | M |
|---|---|---|---|---|---|---|---|---|---|---|---|---|
| ○ | ◻ | ♥ | ✳ | ▲ | ❄ | ✧ | ➙ | ☆ | ✪ | ⇨ | ♣ | ▼ |

| N | O | P | Q | R | S | T | U | V | W | X | Y | Z |
|---|---|---|---|---|---|---|---|---|---|---|---|---|
| 🐿 | ☛ | ✂ | ✈ | ❖ | ◖ | ◼ | ✏ | ✍ | ✚ | ☆ | ◉ | ✿ |

Name _____ Date _____

# Michigan Symbols

## http://www.netstate.com/states/

**Directions:** Use the Internet to locate the symbols of the state to complete the chart below. Then, draw and color the flag, seal, bird, and flower. If you wish, you may instead print the four symbols from a website and paste them on the page.

| | |
|---|---|
| **State Capital** | |
| **State Motto** | |
| **State Nickname** | |
| **State Flower** | |
| **State Bird** | |
| **State Tree** | |
| **State Song** | |

| State Flag | State Seal |
|---|---|
| | |
| **State Bird** | **State Flower** |
| | |

Name _____ Date _____

# Discover Michigan

**Directions:** Research the Internet to find the answers to these questions. Record your answers below in the space provided, on your own paper, or in a word processing document. You should also include any other interesting places you visited, facts you learned, or opinions you developed.

Begin at the authors' website and then click on the correct state. From there, you can choose the corresponding links to answer the questions.

### http://www.neeleypress.com/usa

| | Questions |
|---|---|
| **1** | What does the name Michigan mean? |
| **2** | Take a tour of the historical Michigan State Capitol. How many capitol buildings has the state had? What year was the latest building dedicated? |
| **3** | St. Mary's River is the only water connection between Lake Superior and the other Great Lakes. Watch the animation of how the locks work, and describe them in a paragraph. |
| **4** | The University of Michigan Health System is one of the oldest transplant centers in the nation. What organs are successfully transplanted at UMHC? |
| **5** | The first car to be driven on the streets of Detroit was built by Charles Bradley King. What was the vehicle called? |
| **6** | Sault Ste. Marie was established in 1668. It is the third oldest remaining settlement in the United States. Why did people initially gather there? |
| **7** | Henry Ford's first car was called a Quadricycle. In 1903, he founded what company? |
| **8** | Legends surround Michigan's state stone, the Petoskey. Read the legend. What does the word Petoskey mean? |
| **9** | What does the Mackinac Bridge connect? How long is it? What kind of bridge is it? |

# Discover Michigan *(cont.)*

| | Questions |
|---|---|
| 10 | The walk from St. Ignace to the island, around to the town, and back is how many miles? For how long of a duration is the ice bridge safe to cross? |
| 11 | When you walk onto Mackinac Island, you will notice a very special and quaint characteristic. What is it? |
| 12 | Gerald R. Ford grew up in Grand Rapids and became the 38th president of the United States. President Ford was sworn into office after who resigned? |
| 13 | Battle Creek, Michigan, is the Cereal Capital of the World where the Kellogg brothers began producing and selling cereal. What was the name of their company in 1906? |
| 14 | Michigan's state reptile is a *chrysemys picta*. What is it? |
| 15 | Vernors® ginger ale was the first soda pop made in the United States. Pharmacist James Vernor created the beverage when he returned from serving in the Civil War. What is the main ingredient in the soda? |
| 16 | The Ambassador Bridge spans the Detroit River and serves as an important link between the United States and Canada. Check out the current traffic on the bridge. How long would it take you to cross right now? |
| 17 | Who was Michigan's first state geologist? What year did he call the nation's attention to the huge copper deposits? |
| 18 | The Detroit-Windsor tunnel is the first international sub-aqueous border crossing. Take a look at the history of the tunnel. What is a sub-aqueous tunnel? |
| 19 | The world's first international submarine railway tunnel was opened between Port Huron, Michigan and Sarnia, Ontario, Canada in 1891. How many feet underwater is the tunnel? |
| 20 | Grand Rapids is home to the 24-foot Leonardo da Vinci horse called *Il Gavallo*. It is the largest equestrian bronze sculpture in the western hemisphere. Do you like it? |

**Challenge:** Write a question about the state that isn't addressed above. Then, suggest a website for finding the answer to your question.

**Question 1:** _____

**URL 1:** _____

Name _____ Date _____

# Michigan State Map

**Directions:** Use the key located below to complete the map of the state. Begin by locating the capital city and at least three other major cities. Then, locate and draw two major rivers and/or mountains in the state. How many Great Lakes touch Michigan? Draw at least two major interstate highways that travel through the state. Finally, label any other states and/or bodies of water that surround the state. Do you see the mitten shape in the southern part of Michigan?

**Key**

| | |
|---|---|
| Capital | ✳ |
| City | • |
| River | --------- |
| Interstate | —— |
| Mountains | ∧∧∧∧∧ |

Name _____  Date _____

# Michigan Trivia

Although Michigan is often called the "Wolverine State," there are no longer any wolverines in Michigan.

Michigan has the longest freshwater shoreline in the world.

Michigan has more shoreline than any other state except Alaska.

Michigan has 116 lighthouses and navigational lights.

Standing anywhere in the state, a person is within 85 miles of one of the Great Lakes.

**Directions:** Can you name all of the Great Lakes?

Lake H_____

Lake O_____

Lake M_____

Lake E_____

Lake S_____

Name _____  Date _____

# Minnesota Symbols

**http://www.netstate.com/states/**

**Directions:** Use the Internet to locate the symbols of the state to complete the chart below. Then, draw and color the flag, seal, bird, and flower. If you wish, you may instead print the four symbols from a website and paste them on the page.

| State Capital | |
|---|---|
| State Motto | |
| State Nickname | |
| State Flower | |
| State Bird | |
| State Tree | |
| State Song | |

| State Flag | State Seal |
|---|---|
| State Bird | State Flower |

Name _____ Date _____

# Discover Minnesota

**Directions:** Research the Internet to find the answers to these questions. Record your answers below in the space provided, on your own paper, or in a word processing document. You should also include any other interesting places you visited, facts you learned, or opinions you developed.

Begin at the authors' website and then click on the correct state. From there, you can choose the corresponding links to answer the questions.

**http://www.neeleypress.com/usa**

| | Questions |
|---|---|
| 1 | The official state mushroom of Minnesota is the morel. |
| 2 | Charles Lindberg was a famous American aviator. What important flight did he make in 1927? |
| 3 | The Great Lakes Aquarium opened in July 2000. It is the first aquarium dedicated to what kind of fish? |
| 4 | The Mall of America is the largest, fully enclosed retail and family entertainment complex in America. How many Yankee stadiums would fit inside the Mall? |
| 5 | A single storm in 1905 damaged 20 ships on Minnesota's rocky coastline. Split Rock Lighthouse was built to warn ships of the danger. Beside what body of water does the lighthouse stand? |
| 6 | Minnesotan Richard Drew needed a solution to a problem in the Roaring Twenties. His invention, masking tape, was the answer. What was the problem? |
| 7 | The St. Lawrence Seaway opened in 1959 allowing ocean going ships to reach Duluth. What year was construction started on the first canal in this location? |
| 8 | Minneapolis has 62 bridges that connect buildings and stores to protect people from the harsh winter weather. Altogether, how many miles can you walk using the skyway system without going outside? |
| 9 | Minnesota Governor Jesse Ventura had a very different job before politics. What did he do for 11 years? |

# Discover Minnesota *(cont.)*

| | Questions |
|---|---|
| 10 | The Mayo Clinic is a teaching and working medical facility in Rochester. Who are the two doctors who started the clinic? |
| 11 | Ralph W. Samuelson invented the first practical water skis and tested them on Lake Pepin. What was the year the water skis were tested? What did he try to use first? |
| 12 | Olivia is known as the Corn Capital of Minnesota. Describe the "sculpture" that sits on top of the city's gazebo. |
| 13 | Between Duluth and Minnesota Point, the first aerial ferry carried cars, people, and horses over the shipping canal. How did it work? It was later modified into another type of bridge. How did this bridge work? |
| 14 | In-line skates were actually invented before "standard" roller skates. Scott and Brennan Olson found one of these old skates and modified it with hard rubber wheels to make today's skates. What is the well-known name of these skates? |
| 15 | TONKA® trucks were developed in Minnetonka, Minnesota. What year was the first truck made? The toys were made in the basement of what type of building? |
| 16 | The Control Data 6600, the first supercomputer, was used by the military to simulate nuclear explosions and break Soviet codes. Who was the founder of Control Data Corporation? |
| 17 | Author Laura Ingalls Wilder moved to many towns during her life. Just as in her books, at one point, she lived on the banks of Plum Creek near Walnut Grove. Read about her life and describe some interesting parts. |
| 18 | Greyhound Lines, Inc. opened the first bus line (with one bus) between the towns of Hibbing and Alice in 1914. What was the company's first name? |
| 19 | Alexander Anderson discovered the processes to puff wheat and rice. He was raised in what Minnesota town? |
| 20 | The Kensington Rune stone carvings allegedly tell of a journey of a band of Vikings in 1362. Where was the stone found in 1898? |

**Challenge:** Write a question about the state that isn't addressed above. Then, suggest a website for finding the answer to your question.

**Question 1:** _____

**URL 1:** _____

Name _____     Date _____

# Minnesota State Map

**Directions:** Use the key located below to complete the map of the state. Begin by locating the capital city and at least three other major cities. What cities are called the Twin Cities? Then, locate and draw two major rivers and/or mountains in the state. Draw at least two major interstate highways that travel through the state. Finally, label any other states and/or bodies of water that surround the state.

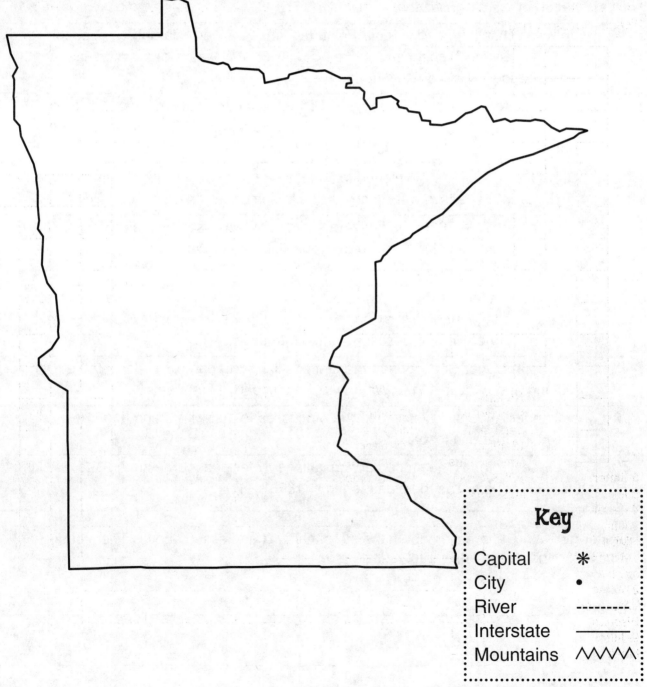

**Key**

| Capital | ✳ |
|---|---|
| City | • |
| River | --------- |
| Interstate | ——— |
| Mountains | ∧∧∧∧∧ |

Name _____  Date _____

# Minnesota Trivia

Reportedly, it is illegal to tease a skunk in Minnesota.

In Minnesota, you will find TYME Machines (TYME is an acronym for Take Your Money Everywhere) instead of ATMs (automatic teller machines).

Minnesota has 90,000 miles of shoreline, which is more than California, Florida, and Hawaii combined.

**Directions:** The following items were invented in Minnesota. Complete the word fill-in with these words. (The light gray squares represent spaces between words.)

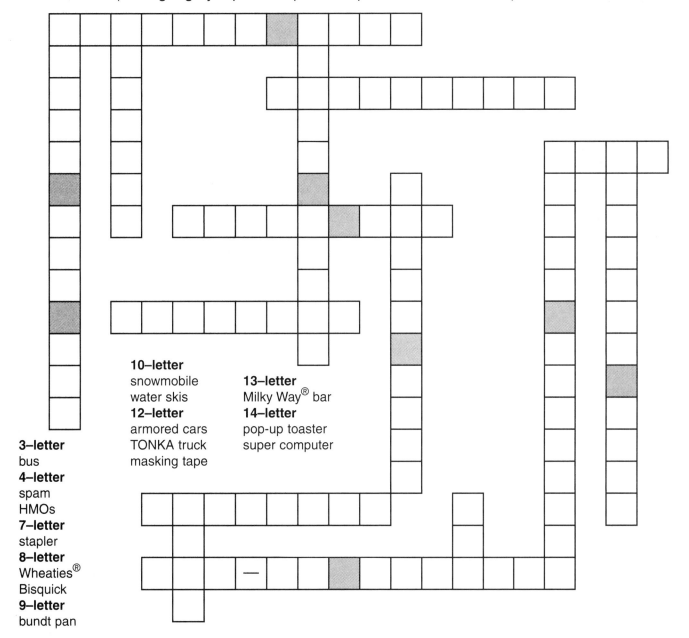

**10–letter**
snowmobile
water skis
**12–letter**
armored cars
TONKA truck
masking tape

**13–letter**
Milky Way® bar
**14–letter**
pop-up toaster
super computer

**3–letter**
bus
**4–letter**
spam
HMOs
**7–letter**
stapler
**8–letter**
Wheaties®
Bisquick
**9–letter**
bundt pan

Name _____  Date _____

# Missouri Symbols

## http://www.netstate.com/states/

**Directions:** Use the Internet to locate the symbols of the state to complete the chart below. Then, draw and color the flag, seal, bird, and flower. If you wish, you may instead print the four symbols from a website and paste them on the page.

| | |
|---|---|
| **State Capital** | |
| **State Motto** | |
| **State Nickname** | |
| **State Flower** | |
| **State Bird** | |
| **State Tree** | |
| **State Song** | |

| **State Flag** | **State Seal** |
|---|---|
| | |
| **State Bird** | **State Flower** |
| | |

Name _____ Date _____

# Discover Missouri

**Directions:** Research the Internet to find the answers to these questions. Record your answers below in the space provided, on your own paper, or in a word processing document. You should also include any other interesting places you visited, facts you learned, or opinions you developed.

Begin at the authors' website and then click on the correct state. From there, you can choose the corresponding links to answer the questions.

## http://www.neeleypress.com/usa

| | Questions |
|---|---|
| 1 | George Washington Carver developed 300 peanut-based products after attending Iowa State University. Where was he born? |
| 2 | Jefferson City was named after which president? Take a tour of the Missouri State Capitol. |
| 3 | Hannibal, Missouri is the boyhood home of Samuel Langhorne Clemens. What is the pen name of this famous writer? |
| 4 | The first successful parachute jump to be made from a moving airplane was made by Captain Berry of St. Louis, in 1912. Where did he make the jump? |
| 5 | At the St. Louis World's Fair in 1904, Richard Blechyden served tea with ice and invented what popular drink? |
| 6 | The 1904 World's Fair celebrated the centennial of the Louisiana Purchase. Take a tour through the Palaces at the Fair and describe what you see. |
| 7 | Mozarkite was adopted as the official state rock on July 21, 1967, by the 74th General Assembly. What is mozarkite? |
| 8 | The crinoid became the state's official fossil on June 16, 1989. Who worked through the legislative process to promote it as a state symbol? |
| 9 | Gateway Arch is located in the middle of what park? The arch was designed by architect Eero Saarinen to celebrate the spirit of the western pioneers. |

# Discover Missouri *(cont.)*

| | Questions |
|---|---|
| 10 | The tallest man in documented medical history was Robert Pershing Wadlow from St. Louis. How tall was he? How much did he weigh? |
| 11 | One of the most powerful earthquakes to strike the United States occurred in 1811, centered in New Madrid, Missouri. Why is this considered an odd place for an earthquake to occur? |
| 12 | Upon the death of President Roosevelt, this thirty-third President was sworn into office. Who was this man? Where was he born? |
| 13 | Saint Genevieve is Missouri's oldest community. What architectural style are the buildings in this town? |
| 14 | As an early historian of the city wrote, "Laclede founded, and Auguste Chouteau built, St. Louis." Who was Auguste Chouteau? |
| 15 | "Madonna of the Trail" monument in Lexington tells the story of the brave women who helped conquer the west. This is one of 12 monuments placed in every state crossed by the National Old Trails Road. Describe the sculpture. |
| 16 | Jesse James was born near Centerville, Missouri, in 1847. The James Gang was famous for robbing what? |
| 17 | The beginning of the Pony Express route started at St. Joseph, Missouri. How old were the riders? What kind of horses did they ride? |
| 18 | Lawrence Peter "Yogi" Berra was born on May 12, 1925, in St. Louis. Where did Yogi get his nickname? |
| 19 | Missouri has 5,380 registered and mapped caves underneath its surface. What is a "show" cave? |
| 20 | Two weeks before the stock market crash of 1929, C. L. Grigg introduced the Bib-Label Lithiated Lemon-Lime Soda. In 1936, he changed the name and people started buying it. What did he call it? |

**Challenge:** Write a question about the state that isn't addressed above. Then, suggest a website for finding the answer to your question.

**Question 1:** _____

**URL 1:** _____

Name _____   Date _____

# Missouri State Map

**Directions:** Use the key located below to complete the map of the state. Begin by locating the capital city and at least three other major cities. What city is in both Missouri and Kansas? Then, locate and draw two major rivers and/or mountains in the state. Draw at least two major interstate highways that travel through the state. Finally, label any other states and/or bodies of water that surround the state.

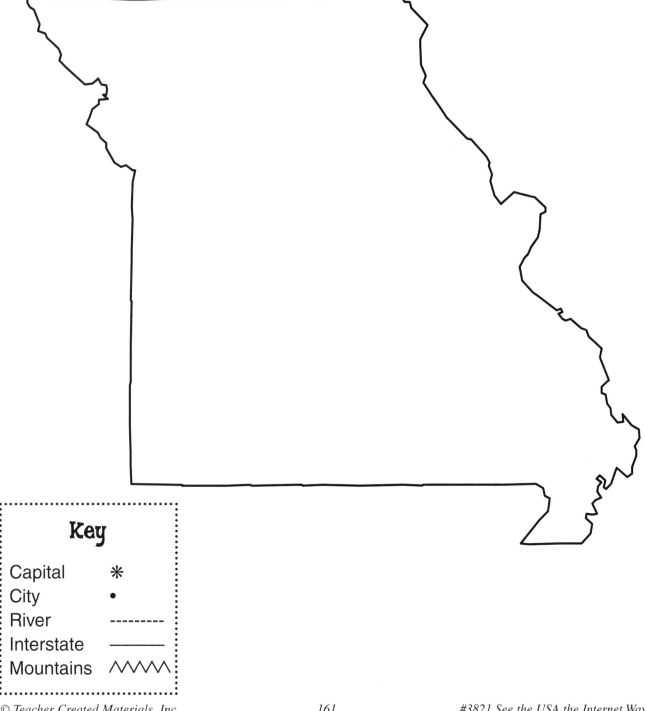

### Key

| Capital | ✳ |
|---|---|
| City | • |
| River | -------- |
| Interstate | ——— |
| Mountains | /\/\/\/\ |

Name _____     Date _____

# Missouri Trivia

In 1865, Missouri became the first slave state to free its slaves.

During Abraham Lincoln's campaign for the presidency, a dyed-in-the-wool Democrat named Valentine Tapley from Pike County, Missouri, swore that he would never shave again if Lincoln were elected. Tapley kept his word and his chin whiskers went unshorn from November 1860 until he died in 1910, attaining a length of twelve feet six inches.

Missouri ties with Tennessee as the neighborliest state in the union, bordered by eight states.

When Mark Twain was born on November 30, 1835, Halley's comet was visible in the sky over Florida, Missouri. Aware that he was born when Halley's comet was visible, Mark Twain predicted in 1909 that he would die when it returned. He was right. When Mark Twain died on April 21, 1910, Halley's comet was once again visible in the sky.

**Directions:** Unscramble these cities in Missouri.

1. SAKSAN TYIC      _____

2. NITSA USOIL      _____

3. DSPLERIINFG      _____

4. EEEEICNDNPND     _____

5. BACIOLUM         _____

6. TASIN POJHES     _____

7. SATIN SHRALEC    _____

Name _____    Date _____

# Ohio Symbols

### http://www.netstate.com/states/

**Directions:** Use the Internet to locate the symbols of the state to complete the chart below. Then, draw and color the flag, seal, bird, and flower. If you wish, you may instead print the four symbols from a website and paste them on the page.

| | |
|---|---|
| **State Capital** | |
| **State Motto** | |
| **State Nickname** | |
| **State Flower** | |
| **State Bird** | |
| **State Tree** | |
| **State Song** | |

| **State Flag** | **State Seal** |
|---|---|
| | |
| **State Bird** | **State Flower** |
| | |

Name _____     Date _____

# Discover Ohio

**Directions:** Research the Internet to find the answers to these questions. Record your answers below in the space provided, on your own paper, or in a word processing document. You should also include any other interesting places you visited, facts you learned, or opinions you developed.

Begin at the authors' website and then click on the correct state. From there, you can choose the corresponding links to answer the questions.

## http://www.neeleypress.com/usa

| | Questions |
|---|---|
| 1 | Thomas A. Edison said, "Genius is 1% inspiration and 99% perspiration." What inventions did Mr. Edison develop with his genius? |
| 2 | On a tour of the Ohio State Capitol, you will see several statues. Describe three of the statues. |
| 3 | Ermal Fraze invented the pop-top can in Kettering. Have you ever collected pop tabs for charity? Describe how your pop tabs can help others. |
| 4 | The Cincinnati Reds were the first professional baseball team. What teams played in the first game? What date did they play? What is the Reds' full name? |
| 5 | The Y Bridge, built in 1814, allowed you to cross the bridge and still be on the same side of the river. How does that work? |
| 6 | Ohio Senator John Glenn has made two trips into space, setting records both times. What were his missions? How old was he on each one? |
| 7 | Rock 'n Roll is here to stay! Visit Cleveland's Rock and Roll Hall of Fame and describe your favorite part. |
| 8 | What day was the National Football League started? Where? |
| 9 | Neil Armstrong became the first man to walk on the moon. When did he become an astronaut? |

# Discover Ohio *(cont.)*

| | Questions |
|---|---|
| **10** | The Wright Brothers are acknowledged as inventors of the first airplane. How far did they fly on the first flight? How long did the flight last? |
| **11** | Seven United States presidents were born in Ohio. One of them, the 18th president, may be better known for what he did prior to becoming president. Give some background information about this man's experience during the Civil War. |
| **12** | The 19th and the 20th presidents were also born in Ohio. What are their names? List two important facts about them. |
| **13** | Who was the president between the 25th and 27th presidents (two Ohio-born presidents)? What is special about him and his family? |
| **14** | Warren G. Harding, the 29th president, was also born in Ohio. What are at least three interesting events that occurred during his years in office? |
| **15** | Harry M. Stevens created the first hot dining dog. What was his business? |
| **16** | Oberlin College was founded in 1833. When were women and minorities allowed to attend this college? |
| **17** | Paul Laurence Dunbar of Dayton is known as the poet laureate of African Americans. When was he born? Who were his parents? |
| **18** | Natural rubber was not useful to industry in the early 1800s. Charles Goodyear accidentally discovered how to make the rubber more useable. How did he make the discovery? |
| **19** | In 1938, Roy J. Plunkett accidentally invented Teflon®. How did he make the discovery? |
| **20** | DeHart Hubbard was the first African American to earn an Olympic Gold Medal. What year did he earn the award? What was his event? |

**Challenge:** Write a question about the state that isn't addressed above. Then, suggest a website for finding the answer to your question.

**Question 1:** _____

**URL 1:** _____

Name _____ Date _____

# Ohio State Map

**Directions:** Use the key located below to complete the map of the state. Begin by locating the capital city and at least three other major cities. Then, locate and draw two major rivers and/or mountains in the state. What river runs along Ohio's south and east borders? Draw at least two major interstate highways that travel through the state. Finally, label any other states and/or bodies of water that surround the state.

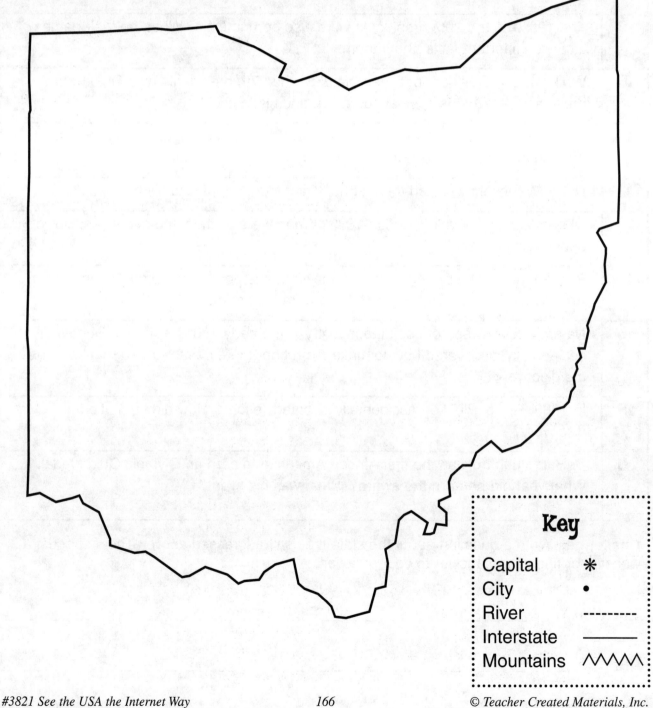

**Key**

| | |
|---|---|
| Capital | ✳ |
| City | • |
| River | - - - - - - |
| Interstate | ——— |
| Mountains | ∧∧∧∧∧ |

Name _____ Date _____

# Ohio Trivia

"Hang On Sloopy" is the official rock song of the state of Ohio.

Ohio's state flag is a pennant design. It is the only state flag of that design in the United States.

Akron was the first city to use police cars, and Cincinnati had the first professional city fire department and ambulance service.

The first full time automobile service station was opened in 1899 in Ohio.

Cleveland became the world's first city to be lighted electrically in 1879. (I wonder if Thomas Edison had anything to do with that!)

**Directions:** Match each description with the correct person by writing the letter on the line provided.

| | | |
|---|---|---|
| _____ Neil Alden Armstrong | A. | astronaut, first man on the moon |
| _____ Annie Oakley | B. | Hopalong Cassidy |
| _____ Arsenio Hall | C. | voice of Bart Simpson |
| _____ Benjamin Harrison | D. | United States Army officer |
| _____ Bill Boyd | E. | inventor |
| _____ Cy Young | F. | 20th U. S. president |
| _____ George Armstrong Custer | G. | talk show host |
| _____ Jack Nicklaus | H. | astronaut, first man to orbit Earth |
| _____ James Abram Garfield | I. | 18th U. S. president |
| _____ Jesse Owens | J. | author |
| _____ John Herschel Glenn | K. | 29th U. S. president |
| _____ Judith Resnik | L. | 19th U. S. president |
| _____ Kenisaw Mountain Landis | M. | 23rd U. S. president |
| _____ Nancy Cartwright | N. | first baseball commissioner |
| _____ Orville Wright | O. | 25th U. S. president |
| _____ Rutherford B. Hayes | P. | golfer |
| _____ Steven Spielberg | Q. | markswoman |
| _____ Tecumseh | R. | Olympic gold medal winner |
| _____ Ted Turner | S. | shuttle astronaut |
| _____ Thomas Alva Edison | T. | Union Army general |
| _____ Ulysses Simpson Grant | U. | movie director |
| _____ Warren Gamaliel Harding | V. | 27th U. S. president |
| _____ William Howard Taft | W. | Shawnee chief |
| _____ William McKinley | X. | broadcasting magnet |
| _____ William Tecumseh Sherman | Y. | inventor, pilot |
| _____ Zane Grey | Z. | baseball player |

Name _____  Date _____

# Wisconsin Symbols

**http://www.netstate.com/states/**

**Directions:** Use the Internet to locate the symbols of the state to complete the chart below. Then, draw and color the flag, seal, bird, and flower. If you wish, you may instead print the four symbols from a website and paste them on the page.

| | |
|---|---|
| **State Capital** | |
| **State Motto** | |
| **State Nickname** | |
| **State Flower** | |
| **State Bird** | |
| **State Tree** | |
| **State Song** | |

| State Flag | State Seal |
|---|---|
| | |

| State Bird | State Flower |
|---|---|
| | |

Name _____ Date _____

# Discover Wisconsin

**Directions:** Research the Internet to find the answers to these questions. Record your answers below in the space provided, on your own paper, or in a word processing document. You should also include any other interesting places you visited, facts you learned, or opinions you developed.

Begin at the authors' website and then click on the correct state. From there, you can choose the corresponding links to answer the questions.

## http://www.neeleypress.com/usa

| | Questions |
|---|---|
| 1 | Who is the governor of Wisconsin? |
| 2 | Create a postcard to send a friend or your teacher from Wisconsin. |
| 3 | What groups of Native Americans lived in Wisconsin? |
| 4 | What are two events that make Cassville, Wisconsin, special? |
| 5 | Who was the first European to reach Wisconsin? |
| 6 | Where was the first capital of the territory of Wisconsin? |
| 7 | Which two of the Great Lakes border Wisconsin? |
| 8 | Wisconsin leads the nation in production of what agricultural product? |
| 9 | When did Madison become the capital? |

# Discover Wisconsin *(cont.)*

| | Questions |
|---|---|
| 10 | Who donated most of the black angels in the Angel Museum? |
| 11 | Send a postcard from the Circus World Museum in Baraboo, Wisconsin. |
| 12 | Who was the first schoolteacher in Madison, and what was her salary? |
| 13 | What percentage of the nation's cheese is produced in Wisconsin? |
| 14 | What NFL Football team is based in Wisconsin? |
| 15 | Where did the state get its name? What does it mean? |
| 16 | What is the Racine Zoo's claim to fame? How many animals started the zoo? |
| 17 | Who was Joseph McCarthy? What does the word McCarthyism mean? |
| 18 | Solve the Mammoth Mystery at this website. |
| 19 | When and where was the Republican Party born? What did Margarethe Meyer Schurz start? Who designed and built the first steam-powered automobile? Do you think his name had anything to do with what we call automobiles? Is it Arthur P. Warner's fault if I get a speeding ticket? |
| 20 | Find a good place to go snowshoeing for a vacation. Where is it? |

**Challenge:** Write a question about the state that isn't addressed above. Then, suggest a website for finding the answer to your question.

**Question 1:** _____

**URL 1:** _____

Name _____    Date _____

# Wisconsin State Map

**Directions:** Use the key located below to complete the map of the state. Begin by locating the capital city and at least three other major cities. Then, locate and draw two major rivers and/or mountains in the state. Draw at least two major interstate highways that travel through the state. Finally, label any other states and/or bodies of water that surround the state.

**Key**

| | |
|---|---|
| Capital | ✳ |
| City | • |
| River | - - - - - - - |
| Interstate | ——— |
| Mountains | /\/\/\/\ |

Name _____ Date _____

# Wisconsin Trivia

The first kindergarten was in Watertown, Wisconsin.

The nation's largest water-theme park, Noah's Ark, is in the Wisconsin Dells.

Green Bay is known as the Toilet Paper Capital of the World.

Mount Horeb is known as the Troll Capital of the World.

Milwaukee is home of Harley Davidson® motorcycles.

**Directions:** Draw lines to match the symbols.

| | |
|---|---|
| 1. animal, domestic | a. trilobite |
| 2. animal, forest | b. sugar maple |
| 3. animal, wildlife | c. "On, Wisconsin" |
| 4. beverage | d. milk |
| 5. bird | e. badger |
| 6. dog | f. honeybee |
| 7. fish | g. robin |
| 8. flower | h. dairy cow |
| 9. fossil | i. American water spaniel |
| 10. insect | j. red granite |
| 11. mineral | k. galena |
| 12. rock | l. white-tailed deer |
| 13. song | m. muskellunge |
| 14. tree | n. wood violet |

Name _____   Date _____

# Kansas Symbols

## http://www.netstate.com/states/

**Directions:** Use the Internet to locate the symbols of the state to complete the chart below. Then, draw and color the flag, seal, bird, and flower. If you wish, you may instead print the four symbols from a website and paste them on the page.

| | |
|---|---|
| **State Capital** | |
| **State Motto** | |
| **State Nickname** | |
| **State Flower** | |
| **State Bird** | |
| **State Tree** | |
| **State Song** | |

| **State Flag** | **State Seal** |
|---|---|
| | |
| **State Bird** | **State Flower** |
| | |

Name _____    Date _____

# Discover Kansas

**Directions:** Research the Internet to find the answers to these questions. Record your answers below in the space provided, on your own paper, or in a word processing document. You should also include any other interesting places you visited, facts you learned, or opinions you developed.

Begin at the authors' website and then click on the correct state. From there, you can choose the corresponding links to answer the questions.

## http://www.neeleypress.com/usa

| | Questions |
|---|---|
| 1 | The Kansas State Capitol is a few feet taller than the United States Capitol. How many years did it take to build the state capitol? |
| 2 | Where is the world's largest ball of twine? How much does it weigh? When was it started? |
| 3 | In 1951, Kansas experienced its worst flood in history. What happened to the Rock Island Railroad Bridge during that flood? How long did the flood last? |
| 4 | Susan Madora Salter was the first woman mayor in the United States. What was her nickname? Mrs. Salter was active in the founding of what union? |
| 5 | Who was Amelia Earhart? Learn more about her by playing this game. |
| 6 | The first African-American woman to win an Academy Award was Hattie McDaniel. She won the award for what movie? |
| 7 | Almon Stowger of El Dorado invented automatic switching for telephones in 1889. What was his profession? What did his wife do? |
| 8 | In 1909, William Purvis and Charles Wilson quit their regular jobs to invent the predecessor of the helicopter. What kind of wings did it have? |
| 9 | Omar Knedlik owned a Dairy Queen® in Coffeyville. He invented the first frozen carbonated drink machine in 1961. How did he come up with the idea? |

# Discover Kansas *(cont.)*

| | Questions |
|---|---|
| 10 | The 34th President of the United States was born in Texas, but was raised in Abilene, Kansas.  He was the commanding general in World War II.  Who was this president?  How many terms did he serve as president? |
| 11 | Fort Riley was the cradle of the United States Cavalry for 83 years.  The fort was established along what two important trails during the 1850s? |
| 12 | Cedar Crest was built in 1928 by Topeka newspaper publisher Frank P. MacLennan on a wooded hilltop in Topeka.  How did this private home become the governor's mansion? |
| 13 | Civil War veteran Samuel Perry Dinsmoor used 113 tons of concrete to build the Garden of Eden in Lucas.  What did he use to make his cabin? |
| 14 | Hutchinson is built above some of the richest salt deposits in the world.  Read the history of salt.  For what has salt been used throughout history? |
| 15 | John Brown followed his five sons to Kansas in 1855 and stayed at his half-sister's home.  He was a steadfast abolitionist.  What does this mean? |
| 16 | Where is the geographic (geodetic) center of the contiguous 48 United States?  This is the beginning point of reference for land surveying in North America. |
| 17 | The graham cracker was named after whom?  He was a Presbyterian minister who strongly believed in eating whole wheat flour products. |
| 18 | The rocks at Rock City are huge sandstone concretions.  How do geologists believe that these huge rocks got to Kansas? |
| 19 | Russell Springs located in Logan County is known as the Cow Chip Capital of Kansas.  What year was it established?  What is the old courthouse used for now? |
| 20 | Kansas has named many of their cities as capitals of bizarre things and places.  What is the Sunflower Capital? |

**Challenge:** Write a question about the state that isn't addressed above. Then, suggest a website for finding the answer to your question.

**Question 1:** _____

**URL 1:** _____

Name _____   Date _____

# Kansas State Map

**Directions:** Use the key located below to complete the map of the state. Begin by locating the capital city and at least three other major cities. Then, locate and draw two major rivers and/or mountains in the state. Draw at least two major interstate highways that travel through the state. Finally, label any other states and/or bodies of water that surround the state.

## Key

| | |
|---|---|
| Capital | ✳ |
| City | • |
| River | ---------- |
| Interstate | ——— |
| Mountains | ∧∧∧∧∧ |

Name _____ Date _____

# Kansas Trivia

**Directions:** Many Kansas towns have been named the capitals for almost everything under the sun (and the sun as well). How many of these capitals can you figure out? The words in italics are hints to the answers.

1. **Abilene** — _____ Capital (*a bus or a dog*)

2. **Cassoday** — Prairie_____ Capital (*like a hen or a rooster*)

3. **Chetopa** — _____ Capital (*swimming kitty*)

4. **Cloud County** — _____ Capital (*think colorful, pretty glass*)

5. **Dodge City** — _____ Capital (*Roy Rogers or John Wayne, for instance*)

6. **Downs** — _____ Capital (*Once upon a time . . . .*)

7. **Geary County** — _____ Capital (*grab your pole and bait*)

8. **Goodland** — _____ Capital (*get a tan from this bloom*)

9. **Johnson County** — _____ Capital (*not a redbird but a . . . .*)

10. **Kechi** — _____ Capital (*really old things*)

11. **Kirwin** — _____ Capital (*gander*)

12. **LaCrosse** — _____ Capital (*a very prickly wire fence*)

13. **Lenexa** — _____ Capital (*Popeye's favorite food*)

14. **McPherson** — _____ Capital (*as in bulbs and switches*)

15. **Phillips County** — _____ Capital (*mom and baby moo*)

16. **Russell Springs** — _____ Capital (*this could be very stinky from baby moo*)

17. **Thayer** — _____ Capital (*Seed spitting contest anyone?*)

18. **Wichita** — _____ Capital (*breathe in and you've got it*)

Name _____  Date _____

# Nebraska Symbols

**http://www.netstate.com/states/**

**Directions:** Use the Internet to locate the symbols of the state to complete the chart below. Then, draw and color the flag, seal, bird, and flower. If you wish, you may instead print the four symbols from a website and paste them on the page.

| | |
|---|---|
| **State Capital** | |
| **State Motto** | |
| **State Nickname** | |
| **State Flower** | |
| **State Bird** | |
| **State Tree** | |
| **State Song** | |

| State Flag | State Seal |
|---|---|
| | |

| State Bird | State Flower |
|---|---|
| | |

Name _____ Date _____

# Discover Nebraska

**Directions:** Research the Internet to find the answers to these questions. Record your answers below in the space provided, on your own paper, or in a word processing document. You should also include any other interesting places you visited, facts you learned, or opinions you developed.

Begin at the authors' website and then click on the correct state. From there, you can choose the corresponding links to answer the questions.

## http://www.neeleypress.com/usa

| | Questions |
|---|---|
| 1 | Which expedition established Fort Atkinson in 1819? Where was it built? |
| 2 | Union Pacific Railroad originated in Omaha as the first railway in 1862. How many miles of track ran through Nebraska at that time? |
| 3 | There is only one roller skating museum in the world. Where is it? |
| 4 | When was the Nebraska territory established? Which president signed the act creating Nebraska? What was the capital city's first name? |
| 5 | Nebraska's capitol building is different from most state capitols. What is different about it compared to others that you have seen? Take a tour of this beautiful building. |
| 6 | Who invented the microwave oven? When did that happen? What was discovered about the microwave first, before discovering that microwaves could cook food? |
| 7 | The powdered soft drink Kool-Aid® was invented in Hastings, Nebraska, in 1927. Who was the inventor? What were his interests before this invention? |
| 8 | J. Sterling Morton founded Arbor Day in 1872. What did Mr. Morton encourage people to do? |
| 9 | The Naval Ammunition Depot located in Hastings provided 40% of WWII's ammunition. Why was this location selected? |

# Discover Nebraska *(cont.)*

| | Questions |
|---|---|
| 10 | The Lied Jungle is the world's largest indoor rain forest. Where is the Lied Jungle located? |
| 11 | An aquifer is an underground lake or water supply. The largest in the United States is the Ogalala aquifer. What states does this aquifer touch? |
| 12 | What is unique about Nebraska's legislature? When did they vote out half of their legislature? |
| 13 | Father Edward Flanagan founded Boys Town in 1917 to help children in trouble. Now, thanks to Girls and Boys Town, what have some of the graduates accomplished? |
| 14 | Toadstool Park has large sandstone formations left by ancient volcanoes. Describe this geological marvel. |
| 15 | Nebraska adopted the woolly mammoth as its state fossil on the state's 100th birthday. How many skeletons of woolly mammoths are believed to be in Nebraska? |
| 16 | Weeping Water is the world's largest natural limestone deposit. How many years ago was it formed? |
| 17 | The North Platte's Red Cross Canteen served a very specific purpose in the two world wars. What did these dedicated women do for the United State's servicemen? |
| 18 | Take a look at downtown Lincoln, Nebraska. What is the current weather in Lincoln? |
| 19 | Dr. Harold Edgerton was the inventor of the strobe light. Where did he work in the summers after high school? Where did he go to college? |
| 20 | The Stuhr Museum was designed by architect, Edward Durrell Stone. What is the focus of this museum? |

**Challenge:** Write a question about the state that isn't addressed above. Then, suggest a website for finding the answer to your question.

**Question 1:** _____

**URL 1:** _____

Name _____  Date _____

# Nebraska State Map

**Directions:** Use the key located below to complete the map of the state. Begin by locating the capital city and at least three other major cities. Then, locate and draw two major rivers and/or mountains in the state. Draw at least two major interstate highways that travel through the state. Shade the region in which most people live. Finally, label any other states and/or bodies of water that surround the state.

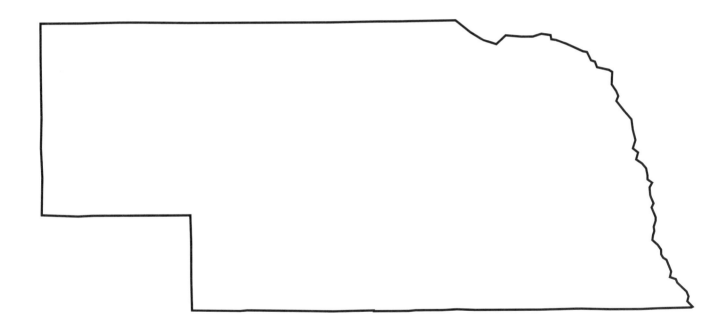

## Key

| | |
|---|---|
| Capital | ✳ |
| City | • |
| River | -------- |
| Interstate | ——— |
| Mountains | ∧∧∧∧ |

Name _____   Date _____

# Nebraska Trivia

In Blue Hill, Nebraska, no female wearing a "hat that would scare a timid person" can be seen eating onions in public.

The largest porch swing in the world is located in Hebron, Nebraska, and it can sit 25 adults.

Nature's totem, the awe-inspiring, 325-foot spire of Chimney Rock in Nebraska, informed Pony Express riders and frontiersmen they had crossed the American plains and that mountains lay ahead.

Nebraska was the first state to complete its segment of the nation's mainline interstate system, a 455-mile stretch of four-lane highway.

The 9-1-1 system of emergency communications, now used nationwide, was developed and first used in Lincoln, Nebraska.

The world's largest hand-planted forest is Halsey National Forrest near Thedford, Nebraska.

In 1950, Omaha became the home of the College World Series.

Kearney, Nebraska, is located exactly halfway between Boston and San Francisco.

**Directions:** Unscramble the following words. Once you write the words on the lines, the letters in the boxes will spell the nickname of the state.

1. YCHENMI  ☐ _____

2. AOHMA  ☐ _____

3. KOCR  ☐ _____

4. ANEKSBAR  ☐ _____

5. LEYSAH  ☐ _____

6. BELBELUNIEVA  ☐ _____

7. ESTTA  ☐ _____

8. YKEAENR  ☐ _____

9. SEPREXS  ☐ _____

10. DRE  ☐ _____

11. REEISS  ☐ _____

State Nickname: _____

182

Name _____  Date _____

# North Dakota Symbols

### http://www.netstate.com/states/

**Directions:** Use the Internet to locate the symbols of the state to complete the chart below. Then, draw and color the flag, seal, bird, and flower. If you wish, you may instead print the four symbols from a website and paste them on the page.

| | |
|---|---|
| **State Capital** | |
| **State Motto** | |
| **State Nickname** | |
| **State Flower** | |
| **State Bird** | |
| **State Tree** | |
| **State Song** | |

| State Flag | State Seal |
|---|---|
| | |

| State Bird | State Flower |
|---|---|
| | |

Name _____     Date _____

# Discover North Dakota

**Directions:** Research the Internet to find the answers to these questions. Record your answers below in the space provided, on your own paper, or in a word processing document. You should also include any other interesting places you visited, facts you learned, or opinions you developed.

Begin at the authors' website and then click on the correct state. From there, you can choose the corresponding links to answer the questions.

## http://www.neeleypress.com/usa

| | Questions |
|---|---|
| 1 | What three Native American tribes contributed to the success of the Lewis & Clark expedition in North Dakota? |
| 2 | Where do the people of these three tribes live today? |
| 3 | What is the origin of North Dakota's name? |
| 4 | From what are the Nokota horses supposedly descended? |
| 5 | When was North Dakota admitted to the United States? |
| 6 | The 26th president, though not born in North Dakota, spent several years there as a young man. He said that had he not spent time in North Dakota, he would never have been president. Who was he? |
| 7 | Who is the current governor of North Dakota? |
| 8 | Jump in the time machine and watch the seasons change at the capitol complex. Which do you like best? |
| 9 | When was the present capitol building built? What happened to the first capitol building? |

# Discover North Dakota *(cont.)*

| | Questions |
|---|---|
| 10 | Four new members joined the Lewis and Clark expedition in North Dakota. Who were they? |
| 11 | Sacagawea did many things to help the Lewis and Clark expedition. Tell about some of them. What are some of the other spellings of her name? |
| 12 | What are some of the kinds of wildlife you can see in North Dakota? |
| 13 | In what types of houses did the Mandan, Hidatsa, and Arikara live? |
| 14 | How did Devil's Lake get its name? Devil's Lake has at least three claims to fame. What are they? It is the largest what, is the _____ capital of the world, and it has its very own what? |
| 15 | North Dakota grows more _____ than any other state. |
| 16 | What are some of the other crops grown in North Dakota? |
| 17 | What was the highest temperature ever recorded in North Dakota? What was the lowest? |
| 18 | What percentage of North Dakota is used for farming? |
| 19 | Investigate some of the threatened and endangered species in North Dakota. Write a few paragraphs about one of them. |
| 20 | What is the largest city in North Dakota? What river is it on? How often does this area flood? Why so often? |

**Challenge:** Write a question about the state that isn't addressed above. Then, suggest a website for finding the answer to your question.

**Question 1:** _____

**URL 1:** _____

Name _____ Date _____

# North Dakota State Map

**Directions:** Use the key located below to complete the map of the state. Begin by locating the capital city and at least three other major cities. Then, locate and draw two major rivers and/or mountains in the state. Draw at least two major interstate highways that travel through the state. Finally, label any other states and/or bodies of water that surround the state.

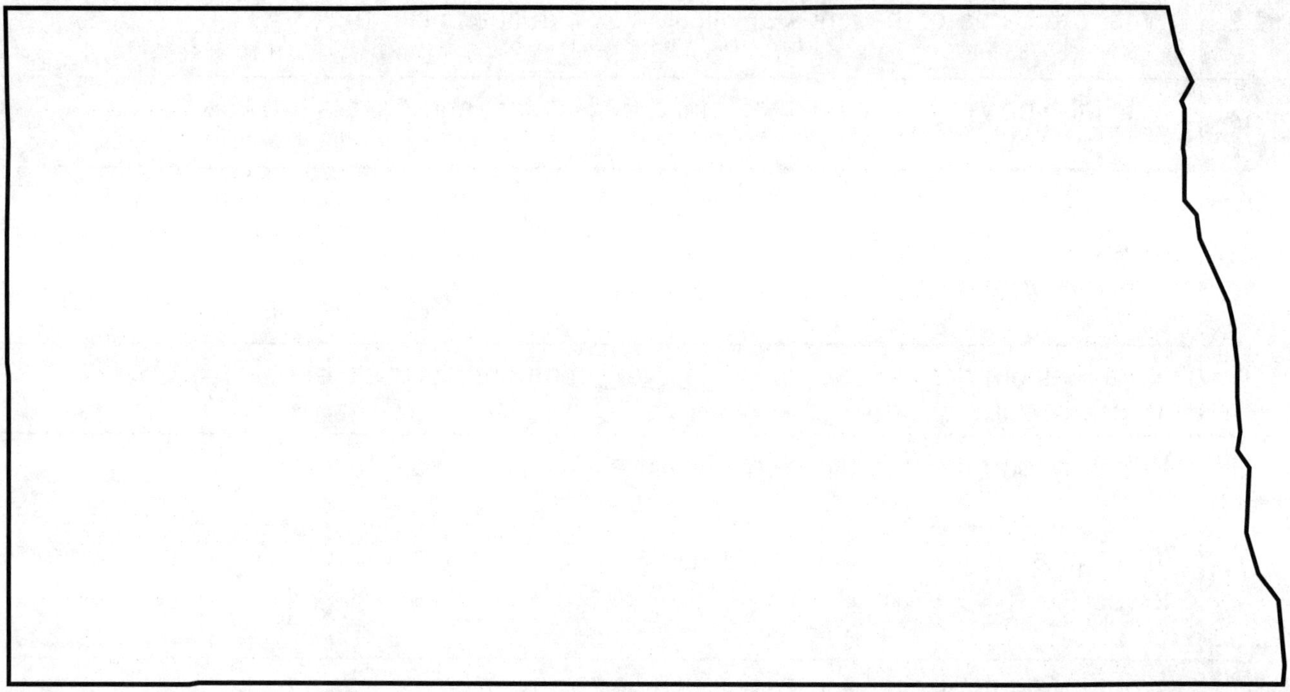

## Key

Capital   ✳

City   •

River   - - - - - - -

Interstate   ———

Mountains   ∧∧∧∧

Name _____ Date _____

# North Dakota Trivia

> Rugby, North Dakota, is the geographical center of North America.

> North Dakota is the nation's top sunflower grower, producing 50 percent of the United States crop.

> James Zaharee of North Dakota, using a fine pen and a microscope, printed Abraham Lincoln's Gettysburg Address on a human hair less than three inches long. (Imagine finding that in your soup.)

> The tallest artificial structure in the world is the KTHI-TV tower in North Dakota, at a height of 2,063 feet.

> Dakota Gasification Company in Beulah is the nation's only synthetic natural gas producer.

> The Dakota Dinosaur Museum in Dickinson houses twelve full-scale dinosaurs, thousands of rock, mineral, and fossil specimens, and a complete triceratops and edmontosaurus.

> Kenmare is the Goose Capital of North Dakota. Kenmare is the hunting haven of the north with an annual snow goose count being over 400,000 birds.

> Flickertail refers to the Richardson ground squirrels which are abundant in North Dakota. The animal flicks or jerks its tail in a characteristic manner while running or just before entering its burrow.

> The Lewis and Clark expedition encountered their first grizzly (brown) bears in North Dakota.

> In Fargo, one may be jailed for wearing a hat while dancing, or even for wearing a hat to a function where dancing is taking place.

> It is illegal to lie down and fall asleep with your shoes on.

> The average annual temperature in North Dakota is 70 degrees Fahrenheit in summer, and 7 degrees Fahrenheit in the winter.

> In a 1990 national survey, North Dakota 8th grade students ranked first nationally in math tests. In 1992, North Dakota 4th grade students tied for third in reading proficiency.

**Directions:** Finish this North Dakota limerick. These words might help you (or might not): Bismarck, dark, hark, bark, flickertail, wild prairie rose, doze, flows, Meadowlark, Nokota horse, pike, and American Elm.

There once was a ranger from _____
Who sought things North Dakotan in his park.
He smelled a _____ _____ _____,
Saw a _____ pose,
But alas, no Western _____ .

Name _____     Date _____

# South Dakota Symbols

## http://www.netstate.com/states/

**Directions:** Use the Internet to locate the symbols of the state to complete the chart below. Then, draw and color the flag, seal, bird, and flower. If you wish, you may instead print the four symbols from a website and paste them on the page.

| | |
|---|---|
| **State Capital** | |
| **State Motto** | |
| **State Nickname** | |
| **State Flower** | |
| **State Bird** | |
| **State Tree** | |
| **State Song** | |

| **State Flag** | **State Seal** |
|---|---|
| | |
| **State Bird** | **State Flower** |
| | |

Name _____ Date _____

# Discover South Dakota

**Directions:** Research the Internet to find the answers to these questions. Record your answers below in the space provided, on your own paper, or in a word processing document. You should also include any other interesting places you visited, facts you learned, or opinions you developed.

Begin at the authors' website and then click on the correct state. From there, you can choose the corresponding links to answer the questions.

### http://www.neeleypress.com/usa

| | Questions |
|---|---|
| 1 | Who first explored and claimed what is now South Dakota? |
| 2 | In 1804, President Jefferson sent Meriwether Lewis and William Clark and their Corps of Discoverers to explore the part of the Louisiana Purchase that included present day South Dakota. Take an online tour and travel with them up the Missouri River. What were some of the things they saw that they had not seen before and some of the adventures they had? |
| 3 | In 1874, General George Custer entered the Black Hills of South Dakota. What did his men find? |
| 4 | Who was Sitting Bull? For what was he famous? |
| 5 | What are the four land regions in South Dakota? Shade them and label them on your map. |
| 6 | What is the highest point in South Dakota? |
| 7 | Who is Sue from Faith, South Dakota? How long has she been in South Dakota? |
| 8 | Take a tour through Bear Country, USA in the Black Hills. Choose an animal and write a paragraph about it. |
| 9 | Visit the Crazy Horse memorial in the Black Hills. Describe the plans for the memorial. |

# Discover South Dakota *(cont.)*

| | Questions |
|---|---|
| 10 | How long has the work on the Crazy Horse memorial been going on? |
| 11 | When did the carving on Mount Rushmore begin?  How old was the sculptor when he started carving it? |
| 12 | Whose faces are carved into the stone of Mount Rushmore?  Indicate the location of Mount Rushmore on your map. |
| 13 | Where is the world famous Mashed Potato Wrestling Contest held?  Why do they celebrate Potato Day? |
| 14 | The remains of what animals have been found at the Mammoth Site near Hot Springs, South Dakota?  How do scientists think so many happened to be in one place?  Take a tour of the museum to find out. |
| 15 | The capital of South Dakota is Pierre.  Pierre wasn't always the capital.  What other cities shared this honor?  How did Pierre finally become the capital? |
| 16 | Take a tour through the capitol building.  Most of the floors are made of terrazzo tile.  What do the little blue tiles mean? |
| 17 | As you continue your tour, look for the answers to these questions.  What does the word "rotunda" mean?  How many murals of Greek goddesses are there and for what do they stand?  What is scagliola and what are the ingredients?  What is unusual about the grand marble staircase? |
| 18 | Who is the current governor of South Dakota? |
| 19 | Who was Martha J. Burke? |
| 20 | Who was James Butler Hickok?  How did he die? |

**Challenge:** Write a question about the state that isn't addressed above.  Then, suggest a website for finding the answer to your question.

**Question 1:** _____

**URL 1:** _____

Name _____    Date _____

# South Dakota State Map

**Directions:** Use the key located below to complete the map of the state. Begin by locating the capital city and at least three other major cities. Then, locate and draw two major rivers and/or mountains in the state. Draw at least two major interstate highways that travel through the state. Finally, label any other states and/or bodies of water that surround the state.

## Key

| | |
|---|---|
| Capital | ✳ |
| City | • |
| River | -------- |
| Interstate | —— |
| Mountains | /\/\/\/\ |

Name _____ Date _____

# South Dakota Trivia

The fastest temperature change on record is a rise of 49° Fahrenheit in two minutes, from -4° to 45° Fahrenheit. This occurred in Spearfish, South Dakota, on January 1943, between 7:30 and 7:32 A.M.

The geographical center of the United States is located in Butte County, South Dakota, on the state's western border.

A state law: No horses are allowed into Fountain Inn unless they are wearing pants.

**Directions:** Draw lines to match the symbols and signs of South Dakota. Then find them in the puzzle.

| | |
|---|---|
| Black Hills spruce | mineral |
| coyote | capital |
| "Great Faces, Great Places" | bird |
| "Hail, South Dakota" | flower |
| honeybee | dessert |
| kuchen | tree |
| pasque | fossil |
| Pierre | animal |
| Rose Quartz | slogan |
| triceratops | insect |
| walleye | song |
| Chinese ring neck pheasant | fish |

```
E U C N P C F D Y D G R J W J T X A V Z V L Q G E A
C H I N E S E R I N G N E C K E D P H E A S A N T B
U F S T O H H V L S E M Q S D B Z B F T Q E T O A L
R V S H K J C V Z T M W G A E R S L I B Z C K S G U
P M T H O J E U O H P J B M S C O P S R G A E N A J
S O E R Z C H Y K X A E I Q S W A F H J D L N A N N
S R F L I K O U P H V N B S E C L F E H W P O G R A
L U W V C C N S U E E Z E R R E I P T N D T T O U C
L N B L T B E Y N R B Y Y U T K U U P A T A S L B C
I I P T U T Y R A J L D E X Q X O D D T E E M S R U
H K S Z Q L B L A C K H I L L S G O L D Q R E T I W
K F D S T C E E R T I O F V L A A D Y U N G G M A J
C N I U O M E W C G O A N I M A L P A Y L I T P F H
A N G I X F T E O K V P A Q E G W R M H N J Y U P O
L G J T P T S J C V V H S B V L T F P E M S F F E S
B I T X T N X M S O C B M S L Z E S O N H H C D U A
O C H T I J H W Q U D C Z X K M J F M T I H J Q B
```

Name _____    Date _____

# Arizona Symbols

## http://www.netstate.com/states/

**Directions:** Use the Internet to locate the symbols of the state to complete the chart below. Then, draw and color the flag, seal, bird, and flower. If you wish, you may instead print the four symbols from a website and paste them on the page.

| | |
|---|---|
| State Capital | |
| State Motto | |
| State Nickname | |
| State Flower | |
| State Bird | |
| State Tree | |
| State Song | |

| State Flag | State Seal |
|---|---|
| | |
| **State Bird** | **State Flower** |
| | |

Name _____　　Date _____

# Discover Arizona

**Directions:** Research the Internet to find the answers to these questions. Record your answers below in the space provided, on your own paper, or in a word processing document. You should also include any other interesting places you visited, facts you learned, or opinions you developed.

Begin at the authors' website and then click on the correct state. From there, you can choose the corresponding links to answer the questions.

## http://www.neeleypress.com/usa

| | Questions |
|---|---|
| 1 | How did Arizona get its name? |
| 2 | There are four types of deserts in Arizona. What are they? |
| 3 | How was the Grand Canyon formed? |
| 4 | In what mine might you find smithsonite? Take a tour through the *Cave & Minerals* exhibit at the Arizona Sonoran Desert Museum to find out. |
| 5 | How fast can a roadrunner run? Look in the *Walk In Aviary* to discover interesting facts. Then, take a walk down the *Riparian Corridor* to find an animal that can drink up to two gallons of water in a few minutes. |
| 6 | The Navajo Nation is the largest group of Native Americans. How large is their reservation? |
| 7 | The Coyote is important in the legends, myths, and stories of Native Americans. Read some of the Coyote stories and then write one of your own. |
| 8 | Traditionally a bead of turquoise (one of the sacred stones of the Navajo) was fastened to a lock of hair to protect the Navajo from what danger? |
| 9 | The name "Apache" comes from the Yuma word meaning what and the Zuni word meaning what? Why do you think the Apache were given this name? |

# Discover Arizona *(cont.)*

| | Questions |
|---|---|
| 10 | In what kind of homes did the Hopi live?  Describe and draw a picture of one of their homes. |
| 11 | What is a *kiva*? |
| 12 | The Tohono O'odham, or Papago people, lived in houses that resemble what? |
| 13 | What were the three ancient cultures in Arizona? |
| 14 | The Petrified Forest is part of a national park in Arizona.  What is petrified wood?  How does it become petrified? |
| 15 | Explore some of the ghost towns at this website.  What do you think could cause a town to be abandoned?  Are there any ghost towns near where you live? |
| 16 | Most states have official trees, birds, flags, etc. to symbolize the states.  Arizona has an official state liar!  Read some of his journal and respond to it in a paragraph or two. |
| 17 | Who chose the Arizona state mammal, fish, reptile, and amphibian?  Name each official animal. |
| 18 | Who is the governor of Arizona?  Tell a few interesting facts about the governor. |
| 19 | Why is the star in the Arizona flag the color it is?  Does it have a special meaning? |
| 20 | Along with 60% of the different types of wildlife in America, Arizona has 43 species of lizards and 27 species of bats. What is the most widespread of all North American bats? |

**Challenge:** Write a question about the state that isn't addressed above. Then, suggest a website for finding the answer to your question.

**Question 1:** _____

**URL 1:** _____

Name _____     Date _____

# Arizona State Map

**Directions:** Use the key located below to complete the map of the state. Begin by locating the capital city and at least three other major cities. Then, locate and draw two major rivers and/or mountains in the state. Label the Grand Canyon and the Colorado River. Draw at least two major interstate highways that travel through the state. Finally, label any other states, countries, and/or bodies of water that surround the state.

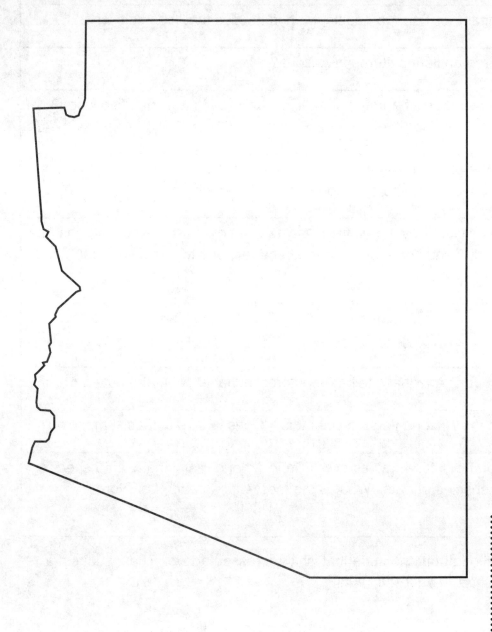

## Key

| | |
|---|---|
| Capital | ✳ |
| City | • |
| River | - - - - - - - - |
| Interstate | ———— |
| Mountains | ∧∧∧∧∧ |

Name _____ Date _____

# Arizona Trivia

One of Geronimo's raids interrupted a baseball game.

At the Four Corners, the states of Utah, New Mexico, Colorado, and Arizona come together. You can stand on the monument and be in four states at the same time! This is the only spot in America where that is possible.

Oraibi, a Hopi village on the Third Mesa, dates from before A.D.1200 and is believed to be the longest continuously inhabited community in the nation.

Arizona is on Mountain Standard Time and never moves the clocks forward or back. Only the Navajo Nation observes daylight savings time.

**Directions:** Unscramble each of the clue words. Copy the letters in the numbered cells to the other cells with the same number.

1. NEOXIPH

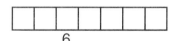

2. LOEVADREP

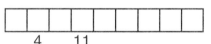

3. RANDG COYNAN

4. PEFTERIDI TORSEF

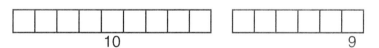

5. TCUCAS WERN

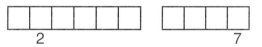

6. LAAJINVE

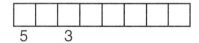

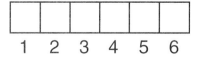

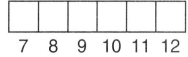

Name _____ Date _____

# New Mexico Symbols

### http://www.netstate.com/states/

**Directions:** Use the Internet to locate the symbols of the state to complete the chart below. Then, draw and color the flag, seal, bird, and flower. If you wish, you may instead print the four symbols from a website and paste them on the page.

| | |
|---|---|
| **State Capital** | |
| **State Motto** | |
| **State Nickname** | |
| **State Flower** | |
| **State Bird** | |
| **State Tree** | |
| **State Song** | |

| State Flag | State Seal |
|---|---|
| | |
| **State Bird** | **State Flower** |
| | |

Name _____ Date _____

# Discover New Mexico

**Directions:** Research the Internet to find the answers to these questions. Record your answers below in the space provided, on your own paper, or in a word processing document. You should also include any other interesting places you visited, facts you learned, or opinions you developed.

Begin at the authors' website and then click on the correct state. From there, you can choose the corresponding links to answer the questions.

## http://www.neeleypress.com/usa

| | Questions |
|---|---|
| 1 | New Mexico has the oldest and the newest state capitols. Describe the newest capitol. |
| 2 | Sid Gutierrez was born in Albuquerque and dreamed of becoming an astronaut. He was the first Hispanic to do what in the space program? |
| 3 | Conrad Hilton was born in 1887 in San Antonio, New Mexico, and attended school at St. Michael's College in Santa Fe, New Mexico, and the New Mexico School of the Mines. He opened his first hotel in Cisco, Texas. What was the name of his second hotel? |
| 4 | Al Unser, Jr. was born in and lives in Albuquerque with his family. He comes from a long line of professional automobile drivers. Who is his father? |
| 5 | The old Spanish Trail was called "The longest, crookedest, most arduous pack mule route in America." What cities did the trail stretch between? What are their names today. |
| 6 | Each October, Albuquerque hosts the world's largest international fiesta. The event is colorful and held outside. What kind of fiesta do they hold? |
| 7 | The world's first atomic bomb was detonated on July 16, 1945, on the White Sands Testing Range. North of the impact point is a small placard marking the area. What is this site known as? |
| 8 | White Sands National Monument is a desert, not of sand, but of gleaming white gypsum crystals. The dunes are located at the north end of what desert? |
| 9 | New Mexico is home of Philmont Scout Ranch located in Cimarron. In what mountains is the ranch located? How many square miles are in the ranch? |

# Discover New Mexico *(cont.)*

| | Questions |
|---|---|
| 10 | Carlsbad Caverns is one of the largest caverns of Permian-age fossil reef.  In the evening, 300,000 bats leave the caverns to look for insects.  What kind of bat lives in Carlsbad Caverns? |
| 11 | Four states all come together in one small spot.  What states touch this spot?  The monument is located on what Native American reservation? |
| 12 | The Palace of Governors in Santa Fe, built in 1610, is one of the oldest public buildings in America.  What was its original use? |
| 13 | Bandelier National Monument has cliff dwellings from what ancient tribe?  These dwellings date back to A.D.1100. |
| 14 | The Anasazi left petraglyphs behind to tell of their lives.  This civilization, which dates from A.D.1100, is the ancestors of what tribe of Native Americans? |
| 15 | In 1950, the little cub that was to become the National Fire Safety symbol was found trapped in a tree in Lincoln National Forest.  What was the little cub named? |
| 16 | The word "Pueblo" is used to describe a group of people and an architectural style.  How long have people lived in the Taos Pueblo? |
| 17 | The father of modern rocketry is scientist Robert Goddard.  Goddard moved to New Mexico to develop supersonic and multi-stage rockets and fin-guided steering.  Many of these inventions are still major parts of today's rockets.  To what town did Goddard move? |
| 18 | After World War II, many scientists moved to New Mexico to participate in scientific research such as nuclear energy research at Sandia National Laboratories.  What is Sandia's motto? |
| 19 | "In the mining industry, it's a fact of life and a philosophy:  everything starts with a hole in the ground."  What are some of the natural resources found in New Mexico? |
| 20 | At Alamogordo, you'll find the International Space Hall of Fame.  In 1976, they received some very special rocks.  What kind of rocks are they?  What else can you see there? |

**Challenge:** Write a question about the state that isn't addressed above.  Then, suggest a website for finding the answer to your question.


**Question 1:** _____


**URL 1:** _____

Name _____     Date _____

# New Mexico State Map

**Directions:** Use the key located below to complete the map of the state. Begin by locating the capital city and at least three other major cities. Then, locate and draw two major rivers and/or mountains in the state. What river borders New Mexico on the south? What two interstate highways cross New Mexico? Where do they meet? Finally, label any other states and/or bodies of water that surround the state.

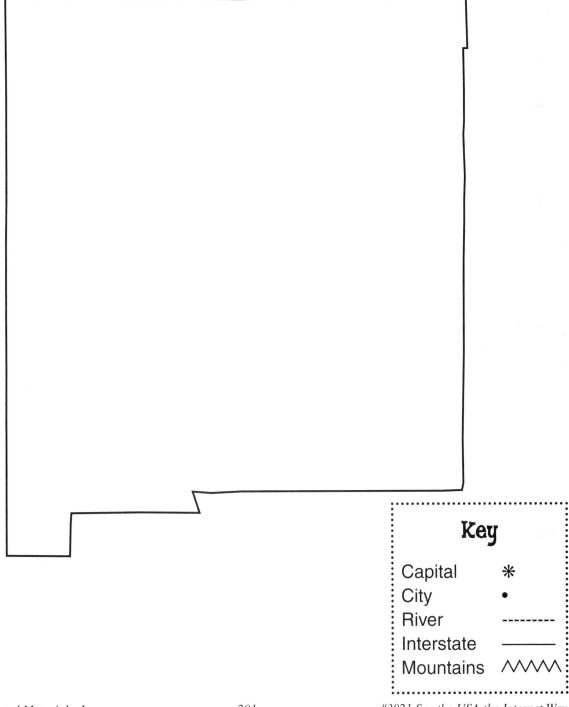

## Key

| | |
|---|---|
| Capital | ✳ |
| City | • |
| River | --------- |
| Interstate | ——— |
| Mountains | ⋀⋀⋀⋀ |

Name _____     Date _____

# New Mexico Trivia

Santa Fe is the highest capital city in the United States at 7,000 feet above sea level.

New Mexico's State Constitution officially states that New Mexico is a bilingual state. One out of three families in New Mexico speak Spanish at home.

New Mexico has far more sheep and cattle than people. There are only about 12 people per square mile.

Native Americans have been living in New Mexico for some twenty thousand years. The Pueblo, Apache, Comanche, Navajo, and Ute peoples were in the New Mexico region when Spanish settlers arrived in the 1600s.

In some isolated villages, such as Truchas, Chimayo', and Coyote in north-central New Mexico, some descendants of Spanish conquistadors still speak a form of 16th century Spanish used nowhere else in the world today.

**Directions:** Find the New Mexico related words in the word search.

```
K S A N B L O R M K W P X R L W
P I A M N O E T A M N A S R V Q
S E T N L R Y T M R W Z A S L P
W R E X G U A D A L U P E I M A
O R H C H R A C H E B I R E T H
S A C R A M E N T O L G D R H R
M D A L I S A D W M A N N R Q S
B E H L R N T A E E C L A A O P
A L N D R E U T C C K Z N C I U
T P U L Y A L I H R R O A A S I
R O O C K Y A L U N A I S F A N
D T O S C U R O S R N E S I S S
C R A M O E O N C T G O O T S C
M I M B R E S U A R E O B A O L
A L C K M O A U N T I Z U N I N
B L C D G H L M O R S T Z T D P
C O M A S R O M L H G D C O C B
```

### Word Bank

| | | | | |
|---|---|---|---|---|
| Black Range | Chusca | Datil | Guadalupe | Hacheta |
| Luna | Mimbres | Oscuro | Rocky | Sacramento |
| San Andreas | San Mateo | Sangre de Cristo | Sierra Cafitan | Sierra del Potrillo |
| Tularosa | Zuni | | | |

Name _____  Date _____

# Oklahoma Symbols

### http://www.netstate.com/states/

**Directions:** Use the Internet to locate the symbols of the state to complete the chart below. Then, draw and color the flag, seal, bird, and flower. If you wish, you may instead print the four symbols from a website and paste them on the page.

| State Capital | |
|---|---|
| State Motto | |
| State Nickname | |
| State Flower | |
| State Bird | |
| State Tree | |
| State Song | |

| State Flag | State Seal |
|---|---|
| State Bird | State Flower |

Name _____ Date _____

# Discover Oklahoma

**Directions:** Research the Internet to find the answers to these questions. Record your answers below in the space provided, on your own paper, or in a word processing document. You should also include any other interesting places you visited, facts you learned, or opinions you developed.

Begin at the authors' website and then click on the correct state. From there, you can choose the corresponding links to answer the questions.

## http://www.neeleypress.com/usa

| | Questions |
|---|---|
| 1 | How did Oklahoma get its name? |
| 2 | Read the story about the land rush of 1889. Write your own illustrated version of the story. |
| 3 | How many counties are in Oklahoma? How many counties have had oil wells drilled? |
| 4 | What is the Trail of Tears? |
| 5 | About how many Native Americans live in Oklahoma? |
| 6 | Why is the eagle considered sacred? |
| 7 | A bald eagle frequently keeps the same nest, enlarging it each year. How large was the largest eagle's nest on record? |
| 8 | One of the state's largest maternity colonies of Mexican free-tail bats is near Woodward, Oklahoma. What is the cave named and how do the bats help the farmers? |
| 9 | What are the four mountain ranges in Oklahoma? Show them on your map. |

# Discover Oklahoma *(cont.)*

| | Questions |
|---|---|
| 10 | Describe a pow-wow. |
| 11 | On April 22, 1889, the population of Guthrie increased. How much did it increase, and why? |
| 12 | Who was Will Rogers? Where was he born? |
| 13 | Who is Oklahoma's current governor? |
| 14 | Oklahoma's written history began with the exploration by what Spaniard? For what was this explorer looking? |
| 15 | What is the highest point in Oklahoma? |
| 16 | What is the Chisholm trail? Why did it come into existence? |
| 17 | Take a trip through the capitol. Oklahoma City's capitol is the only one in the United States to have an oil well on the grounds. The well is called "Petunia #1." Why? |
| 18 | At one time there were how many oil wells pumping from beneath the capitol grounds? |
| 19 | Part of the capitol was not completed because of a shortage of funds during World War I. What part of the capitol was that? On July 25, 2000, 86 years after the original groundbreaking, Governor Frank Keating made an exciting announcement. What did he announce? |
| 20 | On April 19, 1995, a massive bomb inside a rental truck exploded, destroying half of the nine-story Murrah Federal Building in downtown Oklahoma City. The bombing left 168 people dead. Five years later, the Oklahoma City National Memorial was dedicated in honor of those who died, those who survived, and all of us who will remember. Describe the memorial. |

**Challenge:** Write a question about the state that isn't addressed above. Then, suggest a website for finding the answer to your question.

**Question 1:** _____

**URL 1:** _____

Name _____  Date _____

# Oklahoma State Map

**Directions:** Use the key located below to complete the map of the state. Begin by locating the capital city and at least three other major cities. Then, locate and draw two major rivers and/or mountains in the state. Draw at least two major interstate highways that travel through the state. Finally, label any other states and/or bodies of water that surround the state.

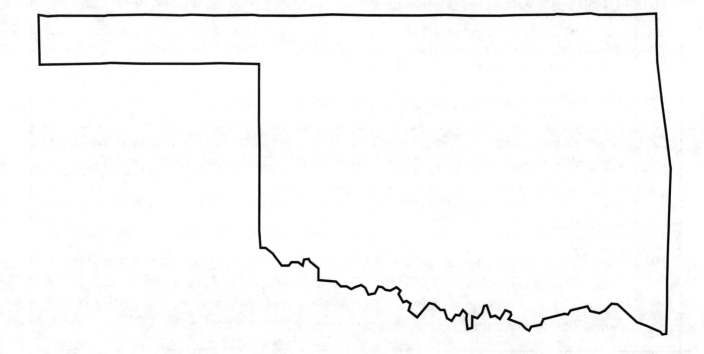

## Key

| | |
|---|---|
| Capital | ✳ |
| City | • |
| River | --------- |
| Interstate | ———— |
| Mountains | ∧∧∧∧∧ |

Name _____   Date _____

# Oklahoma Trivia

During a tornado in Ponca City, Oklahoma, a man and his wife were carried aloft in their house by a tornado. The walls and roof were blown away, but the floor remained intact and eventually glided downward, setting the couple safely back on the ground.

Bore-hole seismometry indicates that the land in Oklahoma moves up and down 25 cm throughout the day, corresponding with the tides. Earth tides are generally about one-third the size of ocean tides.

Per square mile, Oklahoma has the most tornadoes of all the states of the United States.

Sylvan N. Goldman of Humpty Dumpty Stores and Standard Food Markets developed the shopping cart so that people could buy more in a single visit to the grocery store. He unveiled his creation in Oklahoma City on June 4, 1937.

The first parking meter was installed in Oklahoma City, Oklahoma, in 1935.

The town of Beaver claims to be the Cow Chip Throwing Capital of the World. It is here that the World Championship Cow Chip Throw is held each April.

Tahlequah, Oklahoma, is the tribal capital of the Cherokee Nation.

It's a law! Violators can be fined, arrested, or jailed for making ugly faces at a dog.

Whaling is illegal in Oklahoma. (Why is this law funny?)

**Directions:** Find your way from New Mexico to Missouri by following the correct trail across Oklahoma.

New Mexico                                                                Missouri

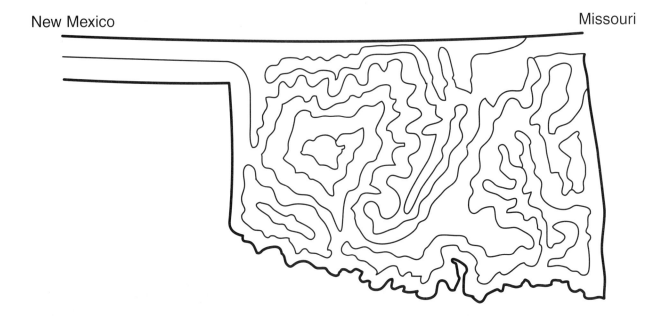

Name _____ Date _____

# Texas Symbols

## http://www.netstate.com/states/

**Directions:** Use the Internet to locate the symbols of the state to complete the chart below. Then, draw and color the flag, seal, bird, and flower. If you wish, you may instead print the four symbols from a website and paste them on the page.

| | |
|---|---|
| **State Capital** | |
| **State Motto** | |
| **State Nickname** | |
| **State Flower** | |
| **State Bird** | |
| **State Tree** | |
| **State Song** | |

| **State Flag** | **State Seal** |
|---|---|
| | |
| **State Bird** | **State Flower** |
| | |

Name _____ Date _____

# Discover Texas

**Directions:** Research the Internet to find the answers to these questions. Record your answers below in the space provided, on your own paper, or in a word processing document. You should also include any other interesting places you visited, facts you learned, or opinions you developed.

Begin at the authors' website and then click on the correct state. From there, you can choose the corresponding links to answer the questions.

**http://www.neeleypress.com/usa**

| | Questions |
|---|---|
| 1 | What is the capital of Texas? |
| 2 | What do you like best about the capitol building? |
| 3 | What do the colors stand for in the Texas flag? |
| 4 | Write the pledge to the Texas flag. |
| 5 | What is the state motto? |
| 6 | Find and record the recipe for the Texas state dish. |
| 7 | What are other common names for the state flower? |
| 8 | Read the legend of the bluebonnet. Summarize it. |
| 9 | Write your own legend about any of the state symbols. |

# Discover Texas *(cont.)*

| | Questions |
|---|---|
| 10 | Read the story of the state tree.  What does Rio Nueces mean in Spanish? |
| 11 | Spend some time with the wildflowers of Texas.  Which is your favorite?  Why? |
| 12 | Listen to some songs about Texas.  Retell your favorite one. |
| 13 | What is the official state song?  Why were some of the words changed in 1959? |
| 14 | Where is the highest point in Texas? |
| 15 | How far is it across Texas east to west? |
| 16 | What is the state bird?  How did it get its name? |
| 17 | What is the state fish?  What is unusual about its name? |
| 18 | What is the state insect? |
| 19 | There are three state mammals.  What are they? |
| 20 | Texas has two national parks.  Visit one and tell about it in a paragraph or two. |

**Challenge:** Write a question about the state that isn't addressed above.  Then, suggest a website for finding the answer to your question.

**Question 1:** _____

**URL 1:** _____

Name _____    Date _____

# Texas State Map

**Directions:** Use the key located below to complete the map of the state. Begin by locating the capital city and at least three other major cities. Then, locate and draw two major rivers and/or mountains in the state. Label the Llano Estacado. Draw at least two major interstate highways that travel through the state. Finally, label any other states and/or bodies of water that surround the state.

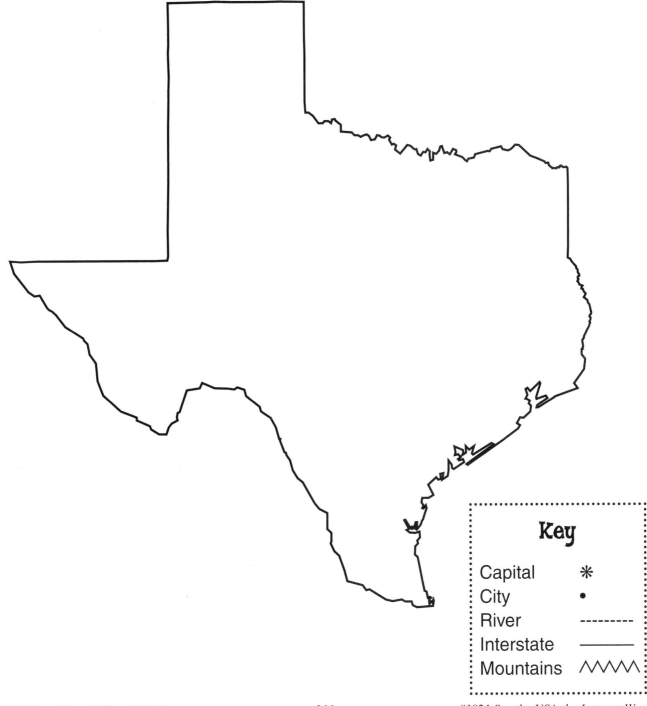

**Key**

| | |
|---|---|
| Capital | ✳ |
| City | • |
| River | --------- |
| Interstate | ———— |
| Mountains | ∧∧∧∧ |

Name _____ Date _____

# Texas Trivia

The tidewater coastline of Texas stretches 624 miles along the Gulf of Mexico and contains more than 600 historic shipwrecks.

Texas has the biggest:  urban bat colony, capitol building, ranch, state fair, and number of counties (254).

Two U. S. presidents were born in Texas, Dwight David Eisenhower, October 14, 1890, in Denison, Texas, and Lyndon Baines Johnson, August 27, 1908, near Johnson City, Texas.

The capitol in Austin, built of Texas pink granite, opened May 16, 1888.  The dome of the capitol stands seven feet higher than that of the nation's capitol in Washington, D.C.

Texas has more churches than any state in the union, with 16,961.

According to Texas law, in some places, running a bakery is considered to be an agricultural business.

Texas law forbids carrying around a fence cutter or a pair of pliers that could cut fence.

Texas was once a country.

In Port Arthur, it is a law that obnoxious odors may not be emitted while in an elevator.

It is illegal in Texas for one to shoot a bison from the second story of a hotel.

**Directions:** Complete this crossword puzzle using facts about Texas.

## Across

4. Texas state bird
6. large Texas city
8. capital city

## Down

1. large Texas mammal
2. neighboring state
3. neighboring state
5. Texas state flower
7. neighboring state

Name _____  Date _____

# California Symbols

## http://www.netstate.com/states/

**Directions:** Use the Internet to locate the symbols of the state to complete the chart below. Then, draw and color the flag, seal, bird, and flower. If you wish, you may instead print the four symbols from a website and paste them on the page.

| | |
|---|---|
| **State Capital** | |
| **State Motto** | |
| **State Nickname** | |
| **State Flower** | |
| **State Bird** | |
| **State Tree** | |
| **State Song** | |

| **State Flag** | **State Seal** |
|---|---|
| | |
| **State Bird** | **State Flower** |
| | |

Name _____ Date _____

# Discover California

**Directions:** Research the Internet to find the answers to these questions. Record your answers below in the space provided, on your own paper, or in a word processing document. You should also include any other interesting places you visited, facts you learned, or opinions you developed.

Begin at the authors' website and then click on the correct state. From there, you can choose the corresponding links to answer the questions.

## http://www.neeleypress.com/usa

| | Questions |
|---|---|
| 1 | Who is California's current governor? Are there any past governors who are well-known around the country? |
| 2 | Take a tour of the historic capitol building. Describe what you see. |
| 3 | Located in Sacramento, the California State Railroad Museum is the largest museum of its kind in North America. What is your favorite exhibit? |
| 4 | California's Mount Whitney is the highest peak in the contiguous 48 states. If you wanted to climb Mount Whitney, what special equipment would you need? |
| 5 | Where is the largest winter population of bald eagles in the continental United States? |
| 6 | How hot can the summer temperatures get in Death Valley? |
| 7 | Visit Sequoia National Park and Muir Woods National Monument. How big is the largest living tree? What is its name? |
| 8 | San Francisco Bay is considered the world's largest landlocked harbor. Take a live look from some of the Bay's famous bridges. Describe what you see. |
| 9 | Where is former President Richard Nixon's library located? Where is the Ronald Reagan Presidential Library and Museum located? |

214

# Discover California *(cont.)*

| | Questions |
|---|---|
| 10 | It is estimated that there are approximately 500,000 detectable seismic tremors in California annually. What was the magnitude of the latest earthquake in California? How is the magnitude of an earthquake measured? |
| 11 | Who are the Sharks? |
| 12 | Visit a real castle in California. Who was the famous person who built this castle? |
| 13 | Read the story of the 160-room house built by Sarah L. Winchester. For how many years was the house under construction? |
| 14 | What prison, located in the middle of San Francisco Bay, was believed to be escape proof? In what way is the old prison used today? |
| 15 | What is the "crookedest" street in the country? |
| 16 | What are the leading agricultural products in California? |
| 17 | What is a condor and why is it special? |
| 18 | During the California Gold Rush, Mr. Strauss noticed that the miners pants couldn't hold up to the hard work in the mines. What did he invent to solve this problem? |
| 19 | In 1975, two men named Steve began building a small computer called an Apple. What are their last names? |
| 20 | Who were the 49ers in the 1800s? |

**Challenge:** Write a question about the state that isn't addressed above. Then, suggest a website for finding the answer to your question.

**Question 1:** _____

**URL 1:** _____

Name _____  Date _____

# California State Map

**Directions:** Use the key located below to complete the map of the state. Begin by locating the capital city and San Francisco, Los Angeles, and San Diego. Then, locate and draw two major rivers and/or mountains in the state. Draw at least two major interstate highways that travel through the state. Finally, label any other states, countries, and/or bodies of water that surround the state.

**Key**

| | |
|---|---|
| Capital | ✳ |
| City | • |
| River | --------- |
| Interstate | ———— |
| Mountains | ∧∧∧∧∧ |

Name _____ Date _____

# California Trivia

The highest and lowest points in the continental United States are within 100 miles of one another in the middle of California. Mount Whitney measures 14,495 feet above sea level and Bad Water in Death Valley is 282 feet below sea level.

Castroville is known as the artichoke capital of the world. In 1947, a young woman named Norma Jean was crowned Castroville's first Artichoke Queen.

Fallbrook County is known as the avocado capital of the world and hosts an annual Avocado Festival. More avocados are grown in the region than in any other county in the nation.

San Francisco Bay is considered the world's largest landlocked harbor.

Sequoia National Park contains the largest living tree. Its trunk is 102 feet in circumference.

California has the largest economy in America.

Totaling nearly three million acres, San Bernardino County is the largest county in the country.

More turkeys are raised in California than in any other state in the United States.

**Directions:** Use the trivia listed above to fill in the blanks below. Be prepared to convert the measurements!

1. The highest point in California is _____ . It is _____ **inches** above sea level.

2. The lowest point in California is _____ . It is _____ **inches** below sea level.

3. Why is Fallbrook County known as the avocado capital of the world? _____

4. The largest county in the country is _____.

5. The largest living tree is in _____ . It measures _____ **inches** in circumference.

6. California raises the most _____ . (That must be very noisy!)

**Bonus Questions:**

1. The young artichoke queen is better known by what name?

2. Why might California have the largest economy in the country?

Name _____ Date _____

# Colorado Symbols

### http://www.netstate.com/states/

**Directions:** Use the Internet to locate the symbols of the state to complete the chart below. Then, draw and color the flag, seal, bird, and flower. If you wish, you may instead print the four symbols from a website and paste them on the page.

| | |
|---|---|
| **State Capital** | |
| **State Motto** | |
| **State Nickname** | |
| **State Flower** | |
| **State Bird** | |
| **State Tree** | |
| **State Song** | |

| | |
|---|---|
| **State Flag** | **State Seal** |
| **State Bird** | **State Flower** |

Name _____     Date _____

# Discover Colorado

**Directions:** Research the Internet to find the answers to these questions. Record your answers below in the space provided, on your own paper, or in a word processing document. You should also include any other interesting places you visited, facts you learned, or opinions you developed.

Begin at the authors' website and then click on the correct state. From there, you can choose the corresponding links to answer the questions.

## http://www.neeleypress.com/usa

| | Questions |
|---|---|
| **1** | Where did Colorado get its name? What does it mean? |
| **2** | Who is the governor of Colorado? |
| **3** | Take a tour of the Colorado State Capitol. What is the altitude where the capitol is located? |
| **4** | There are 40 species of bats in the United States and 18 in the state of Colorado. Name five of the types of Colorado bats. |
| **5** | Read about Buffalo Bill and his Wild West Show. He is buried on Lookout Mountain near what Colorado city? |
| **6** | Tour fifteen of Colorado's ghost towns and mining camps. Why do you think people moved away from these towns? |
| **7** | Take a ride on the Durango & Silverton Narrow Gauge Railroad. What was the train's first use? |
| **8** | The United States Air Force Academy is located in what Colorado city? |
| **9** | Katharine Lee Bates wrote her most famous poem, "America the Beautiful" while looking from this famous mountaintop. What mountain is it? |

# Discover Colorado *(cont.)*

| | Questions |
|---|---|
| 10 | Where can you find the highest suspension bridge in the world? Can you find the special bridge in the bottom of the gorge? |
| 11 | Gold mining is still in operation in Cripple Creek, Colorado. What kind of life do you think the early miners lived? |
| 12 | The trademark for the name Cheeseburger was awarded to Louis Ballast in what city and in what year? |
| 13 | What road is the highest continuously paved highway in the United States? It crosses the Continental Divide at 12,183 feet above sea level and is only open in the summer. |
| 14 | Every day approximately 26,000 vehicles drive under the Continental Divide through this tunnel. What is the name of the tunnel? |
| 15 | Discover the sand dunes in the middle of Colorado! When and how were the dunes probably created? |
| 16 | Read the story of a famous trapper, scout, Native American agent, soldier, and authentic legend of the West who commanded Colorado's first and oldest military post, Fort Garland, in 1858. Who is this man? |
| 17 | What are four professional sports teams in Colorado? |
| 18 | Read about Denver's famous Unsinkable Molly Brown. Summarize her adventures. |
| 19 | Travel back in time on a prehistoric journey. What is your favorite discovery at the museum? |
| 20 | How many kinds of dinosaurs have been found in Colorado? |

**Challenge:** Write a question about the state that isn't addressed above. Then, suggest a website for finding the answer to your question.

**Question 1:** _____

**URL 1:** _____

Name _____ Date _____

# Colorado State Map

**Directions:** Use the key located below to complete the map of the state. Begin by locating the capital city and at least three other major cities. Then, locate and draw two major rivers and/or mountains in the state. What mountain range is located in western Colorado? Draw at least two major interstate highways that travel through the state. Finally, label any other states and/or bodies of water that surround the state.

## Key

| | |
|---|---|
| Capital | ✳ |
| City | • |
| River | - - - - - - - |
| Interstate | —— |
| Mountains | ∧∧∧∧ |

Name _____ Date _____

# Colorado Trivia

The lowest elevation in Colorado is higher that the highest point in Pennsylvania.

The world's largest flat-top mountain is in Grand Mesa.

In Fruita, the town folk celebrate "Mike the Headless Chicken Day." It seems that a farmer named L.A. Olsen cut off Mike's head on September 10, 1945, in anticipation of a chicken dinner. Surprisingly, Mike lived for another four years without a head.

Colfax Avenue in Denver is the longest continuous street in America.

Denver, Colorado, has 300 days of bright sunshine a year! That is more annual hours of sun than San Diego, California, or Miami Beach, Florida.

The world's largest silver nugget, weighing 1,840 pounds, was found in 1894 near Aspen, Colorado.

The United States federal government owns more than one-third of the land in Colorado.

Leadville is the very highest incorporated city in the United States at 10,430 feet in elevation. The town's founding fathers decided that they would rather use the name Leadville, because so many other mining towns had the word silver in their names.

**Directions:** Unscramble the following words from this page and place each word in the spaces. Then, unscramble the letters in the boxes to spell the capital of this state.

1. NESHNUSI    __ __ [ ] __ __ __ __ __

2. LIVADLELE    __ __ __ [ ] __ __ __ __ __

3. VAELEONIT    [ ] __ __ __ __ __ __ __

4. OORPCRTADINE    __ __ __ __ __ __ __ __ __ __ [ ] __

5. HERRAT    [ ] __ __ __ __ __

6. YREV    [ ] __ __ __

Capital: _____

Name _____  Date _____

# Hawaii Symbols

**http://www.netstate.com/states/**

**Directions:** Use the Internet to locate the symbols of the state to complete the chart below. Then, draw and color the flag, seal, bird, and flower. If you wish, you may instead print the four symbols from a website and paste them on the page.

| State Capital | |
|---|---|
| State Motto | |
| State Nickname | |
| State Flower | |
| State Bird | |
| State Tree | |
| State Song | |

| State Flag | State Seal |
|---|---|
| | |
| **State Bird** | **State Flower** |
| | |

Name _____ Date _____

# Discover Hawaii

**Directions:** Research the Internet to find the answers to these questions. Record your answers below in the space provided, on your own paper, or in a word processing document. You should also include any other interesting places you visited, facts you learned, or opinions you developed.

Begin at the authors' website and then click on the correct state. From there, you can choose the corresponding links to answer the questions.

## http://www.neeleypress.com/usa

| | Questions |
|---|---|
| 1 | The state of Hawaii consists of eight main islands: Niihau, Kauai, Oahu, Maui, Molokai, Lanai, Kahoolawe, and Hawaii. Which is the largest island? |
| 2 | What shape are the two legislative chambers in the capitol? Why? |
| 3 | Iolani Palace is the only royal palace in the United States. Which king built the palace? What was the name of his kingdom? |
| 4 | Who was overthrown and was the last royalty in Hawaii? What year was she overthrown? |
| 5 | There are only 12 letters in the Hawaiian alphabet. What are they? |
| 6 | Hawaii has its own time zone, Hawaiian Standard Time. There is no daylight savings time. At 8:00 A.M. in your town, what time is it in Hawaii? |
| 7 | The wind blows east to west in Hawaii. The average daytime temperature in July is 82 degrees Fahrenheit. The average daytime temperature in January is 72 degrees Fahrenheit. What is the current weather in Hawaii? |
| 8 | The world's largest wind generator is on the island of Oahu. The windmill has two blades 400 feet long on the top of a tower twenty stories high. What is the advantage of using wind energy? |
| 9 | Visit Maui's sleeping volcano, Haleakala Crater. How long and wide is the crater? How deep is it? What is the elevation at the crater's rim? |

# Discover Hawaii *(cont.)*

| | Questions |
|---|---|
| 10 | The Hawaiian Islands were formed by a line of volcanoes in the Hawaiian archipelago. What island is the youngest? |
| 11 | Loihi is the newest volcano in the archipelago. When did it first erupt? |
| 12 | Kilauea volcano is possibly the world's most active volcano. What is Kilauea currently doing? |
| 13 | On what island will you find the Hawaii Volcanoes National Park? |
| 14 | What is the southernmost point of the United States? How many miles is it from the middle of the United States? |
| 15 | Diamond Head Crater is Hawaii's most famous landmark. What United States Army fort was built in the crater to defend the harbor? |
| 16 | Hawaii's state fish has quite a name. Can you spell it? Better yet, can you pronounce it? |
| 17 | What does *ukulele* mean in Hawaiian? What is a ukulele? (**Hint:** Scroll down to "Dancing and Music.") |
| 18 | What does *mahalo* mean? What does *Wikiwiki* mean? |
| 19 | Go surfing. How high are the waves on the north shore of Oahu? |
| 20 | On December 7, 1941, the United States was drawn into World War II when Japan dropped bombs on Pearl Harbor. Watch the attack and read the stories. Record your feelings about the event. |

**Challenge:** Write a question about the state that isn't addressed above. Then, suggest a website for finding the answer to your question.

**Question 1:** _____

**URL 1:** _____

Name _____  Date _____

# Hawaii State Map

**Directions:** Use the key located below to complete the map of the state. Begin by locating the capital city and at least three other major cities. Label the islands of Hawaii. Then, locate and draw two major rivers and/or mountains in the state. Where is the Kilauea Volcano? Mark it on the map. Draw at least two major interstate highways that travel through the state. Finally, label any other states and/or bodies of water that surround the state.

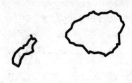

**Key**

| | |
|---|---|
| Capital | ✳ |
| City | • |
| River | --------- |
| Interstate | ———— |
| Mountains | ∧∧∧∧ |

Name _____ Date _____

# Hawaii Trivia

Hawaii is the most isolated population center on the face of the earth. Hawaii is 2,390 miles from California; 3,850 miles from Japan; 4,900 miles from China; and 5,280 miles from the Philippines.

There are no racial or ethnic majorities in Hawaii. Everyone is a minority. Caucasians (Haoles) constitute about 34%; Japanese American about 32%; Filipino American about 16%; and Chinese American about 5%. It is very difficult to determine racial identification as most of the population has some mixture of ethnicities.

Hawaii is the only state that grows coffee. They also grow sugarcane, pineapples, and macadamia nuts.

From east to west, Hawaii is the widest state in the United States.

The Hawaiian Islands are the projecting tops of the biggest mountain range in the world. Under-sea volcanoes that erupted thousands of years ago formed the islands of Hawaii.

Hawaiian's dance the hula wearing grass skirts at a luau.

**Directions:** Find the Hawaiian islands in the word search below!

| A | K | P | O | A | H | U | M | N | L |
|---|---|---|---|---|---|---|---|---|---|
| M | E | A | I | L | E | A | H | R | N |
| N | K | H | H | U | M | U | M | A | I |
| A | A | P | M | O | L | O | K | A | I |
| A | U | W | E | L | O | M | W | U | A |
| L | A | P | L | M | J | L | L | O | A |
| N | I | I | H | A | U | J | A | K | M |
| B | H | I | J | U | K | L | N | W | M |
| R | P | N | I | I | A | W | A | H | E |
| J | H | M | L | K | O | E | I | U | P |

## Word Bank

| Niihau | Kauai | Oahu |
|--------|-------|------|
| Maui | Molokai | Lanai |
| Kahoolawe | Hawaii | |

Name _____ Date _____

# Idaho Symbols

## http://www.netstate.com/states/

**Directions:** Use the Internet to locate the symbols of the state to complete the chart below. Then, draw and color the flag, seal, bird, and flower. If you wish, you may instead print the four symbols from a website and paste them on the page.

| | |
|---|---|
| **State Capital** | |
| **State Motto** | |
| **State Nickname** | |
| **State Flower** | |
| **State Bird** | |
| **State Tree** | |
| **State Song** | |

| **State Flag** | **State Seal** |
|---|---|
| | |
| **State Bird** | **State Flower** |
| | |

Name _____ Date _____

# Discover Idaho

**Directions:** Research the Internet to find the answers to these questions. Record your answers below in the space provided, on your own paper, or in a word processing document. You should also include any other interesting places you visited, facts you learned, or opinions you developed.

Begin at the authors' website and then click on the correct state. From there, you can choose the corresponding links to answer the questions.

### http://www.neeleypress.com/usa

| | Questions |
|---|---|
| 1 | Idaho is actually just an invented word. What state was originally suggested to be called Idaho? |
| 2 | The Snake River Birds of Prey National Conservation Area located in Idaho is home to the United States' largest population of birds of prey with 2,500 nesting birds. Describe the area. |
| 3 | Idaho grows about 27 billion potatoes annually. What makes the soil in Idaho so great for growing potatoes? |
| 4 | Island Park has the longest main street in America. How long is it? How wide is the city at its narrowest point? |
| 5 | Arco, Idaho, with a population of 1,000 became the first United States town powered by nuclear energy. What was the name of the reactor? What year did this happen? When did they quit using the reactor? |
| 6 | Take a tour of Ernest Hemingway's home in Ketchum, Idaho. What did the designer of the website type on Hemingway's typewriter? |
| 7 | Idaho's capitol building was started in 1905. On the top of the dome stands a sculpture. What is it? What metals are used in the sculpture? |
| 8 | The Cataldo Mission is the oldest building in the state. Which Native American tribe invited the Jesuit priests to come build a mission for their people? |
| 9 | Grangeville, Idaho, is the gateway to five wilderness areas and four national forests totaling 5½ million acres. What national forests can you visit near Grangeville? |

# Discover Idaho *(cont.)*

| | Questions |
|---|---|
| 10 | What was the purpose of the Lewis and Clark Expedition? Take a trip down the Lewis and Clark Trail. Read the history of this famous trail. |
| 11 | What was Idaho's first industry? |
| 12 | Bruneau Dunes State Park contains North America's tallest single structured sand dune. It stands 470 feet high. What makes this dune different than others in America? |
| 13 | The Appaloosa horse has several legends surrounding its arrival to the United States. The stories agree that the Nez Perce native Americans bred the horses to be superior mounts. Read the accounts of the history of the horse. What are the three different opinions on how the horse arrived in the United States? |
| 14 | Three million gallons of water run through the Lava Hot Springs each day from the natural underground springs. What is the temperature of the water? |
| 15 | The Snake River runs through Hells Canyon, the deepest gorge in America. How deep is the canyon? Would you like to whitewater raft on the Snake River? |
| 16 | The Shoshone Native Americans used to catch salmon at the foot of Shoshone Falls. The falls have been referred to by what nickname? |
| 17 | The Port of Lewiston is 465 miles from the Pacific Ocean, yet it is called a seaport. What two rivers come together in Lewiston to make this an accurate description? |
| 18 | What if you had an idea that you knew would change the world, but you were only 14 years old? Who was Philo Taylor Farnsworth? |
| 19 | Which president of the United States established the Caribou National Forest in 1907? |
| 20 | Take a look at Idaho's rich history. The first Oregon Trail wagons crossed Idaho in 1843. What was the population of the state in 1900? |

**Challenge:** Write a question about the state that isn't addressed above. Then, suggest a website for finding the answer to your question.

**Question 1:** _____

**URL 1:** _____

Name _____ Date _____

# Idaho State Map

**Directions:** Use the key located below to complete the map of the state. Begin by locating the capital city and at least three other major cities. Then, locate and draw two major rivers and/or mountains in the state. What well-known river is in the southern part of the state? Draw the river on the map. Draw at least two major interstate highways that travel through the state. Finally, label any other states and/or bodies of water that surround the state. What foreign country borders Idaho? Label the country on the map.

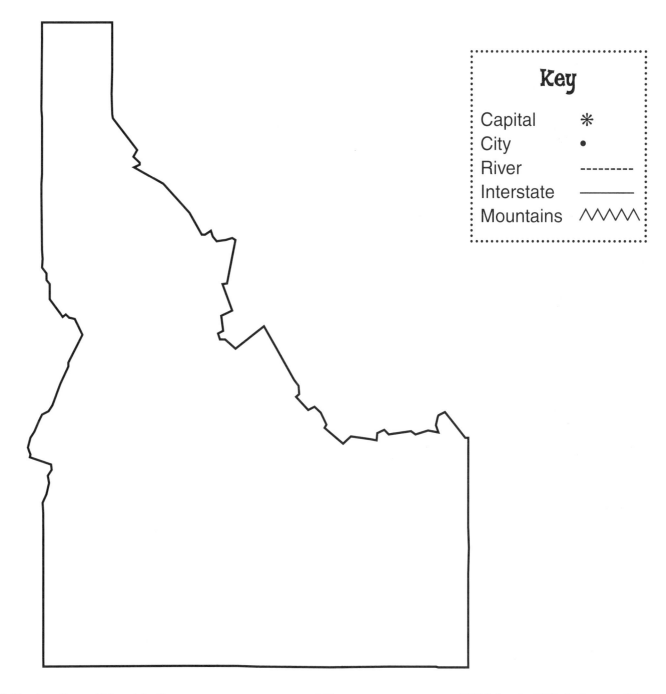

**Key**

| | |
|---|---|
| Capital | ✳ |
| City | • |
| River | - - - - - - - - |
| Interstate | —————— |
| Mountains | /\/\/\/\ |

Name _____  Date _____

# Idaho Trivia

Six states entered the United States during Benjamin Harrison's term as United States president:  North Dakota, South Dakota, Montana, Idaho, Wyoming, and Washington.

In Idaho, a citizen is forbidden by law to give another citizen a box of candy that weighs more than 50 pounds.

In the mid-1920s, the entire town of American Falls was moved when the original American Falls Dam was constructed.

The Idaho Champion Western Red Cedar Tree, the largest tree in the state, is located in Elk River.  It is estimated to be over 3,000 years old.  The tree is more than 18 feet in diameter and stands 177 feet tall.

**Directions:**  Use the names of these Idaho cities to complete this word fill-in.  (The light gray squares represent spaces between words.)

**5–letter**

Boise

Nampa

**6–letter**

Moscow

**8–letter**

Caldwell

Meridian

Lewiston

**9–letter**

Pocatello

Twin Falls

**11–letter**

Coeur d'Alene

Name _____    Date _____

# Montana Symbols

## http://www.netstate.com/states/

**Directions:** Use the Internet to locate the symbols of the state to complete the chart below. Then, draw and color the flag, seal, bird, and flower. If you wish, you may instead print the four symbols from a website and paste them on the page.

| | |
|---|---|
| **State Capital** | |
| **State Motto** | |
| **State Nickname** | |
| **State Flower** | |
| **State Bird** | |
| **State Tree** | |
| **State Song** | |

| **State Flag** | **State Seal** |
|---|---|
| | |
| **State Bird** | **State Flower** |
| | |

Name _____  Date _____

# Discover Montana

**Directions:** Research the Internet to find the answers to these questions. Record your answers below in the space provided, on your own paper, or in a word processing document. You should also include any other interesting places you visited, facts you learned, or opinions you developed.

Begin at the authors' website and then click on the correct state. From there, you can choose the corresponding links to answer the questions.

## http://www.neeleypress.com/usa

| | Questions |
|---|---|
| 1 | Meet Montana's governor. What was the governor's job before being elected to this office? Where was the governor born? |
| 2 | Glacier National Park is in the northwest corner of Montana next to Waterton Lakes National Park. Where does the park get its name? What are two of the nicknames for Glacier National Park? |
| 3 | Montana has incredible wildlife including migratory elk, trumpeter swans, golden eagles, grizzly bears, and more. Which of the animals in Montana's Wildlife Gallery do you like the most? What do you like about the animal? |
| 4 | Can you tell the difference between a golden eagle and a bald eagle? What is a golden eagle's wingspan? Which are the easiest to see? |
| 5 | Jack Horner, a popular paleontologist, has studied the parenting behavior of dinosaurs. Where did he discover Egg Mountain? What did he find there? |
| 6 | Montana is the only state with a triple continental divide allowing water to flow into the Pacific, Atlantic, and Hudson Bay. What is the name of this peak? |
| 7 | What is the plural of moose? What does a moose eat? Can a moose swim? |
| 8 | Montana has the largest grizzly bear population in the lower 48 states. Killing a grizzly bear in the lower 48 is both a state and federal offense. How can you recognize a grizzly? |
| 9 | The first luge run in North America was built at Lolo Hot Springs in 1965. What would it be like to travel 65 miles per hour only three inches above solid ice lying feet first on a tiny sled? |

# Discover Montana *(cont.)*

| | Questions |
|---|---|
| 10 | Virginia City was founded in 1863 and is a remarkably well-preserved old west Victorian gold mining town considered to be the most complete original town of its kind. Where is it located? |
| 11 | George Armstrong Custer and his troops made their last stand on June 26, 1876, at Little Bighorn. Who were the key players in this battle? |
| 12 | Charles M. Russell was a famed western artist known as Charlie Russell. He painted and sculpted many works of art depicting the old West. What did he really want to do when he first came to Montana? |
| 13 | Montana's state gem is the sapphire. Sapphire mining is big business in Philipsburg, Montana. What are some of the colors of sapphires? |
| 14 | Montana's first territorial capital, Bannack, has been preserved as a ghost town state park. Where did people find gold near Bannack? |
| 15 | Take a look at Montana's beautiful countryside. What is the weather today? |
| 16 | Evel Knievel, a daredevil stunt man who attempted to jump the Snake River Canyon, was born in Butte, Montana. What jobs did he have early in life? |
| 17 | Montana has seven Native American reservations. What are they? |
| 18 | Jeanette Rankin was the first woman to serve in the United States Congress. She was elected four years before what significant event? |
| 19 | Pompey's Pillar was a very important landmark for settlers as they traveled westward. How do we know that William Clark saw the pillar during the Lewis and Clark Expedition? |
| 20 | Whitewater rafting, mountain biking, and skiing are some of the outdoor sports that you can do in Montana. Which sport would be the most fun for you? |

**Challenge:** Write a question about the state that isn't addressed above. Then, suggest a website for finding the answer to your question.

**Question 1:** _____

**URL 1:** _____

Name _____     Date _____

# Montana State Map

**Directions:** Use the key located below to complete the map of the state. Begin by locating the capital city and at least three other major cities. Then, locate and draw two major rivers and/or mountains in the state. Mark the location of the Triple Divide Peak and Little Bighorn on the map. Where is Glacier National Park and the road to Yellowstone? Draw at least two major interstate highways that travel through the state. Finally, label any other states and/or bodies of water that surround the state.

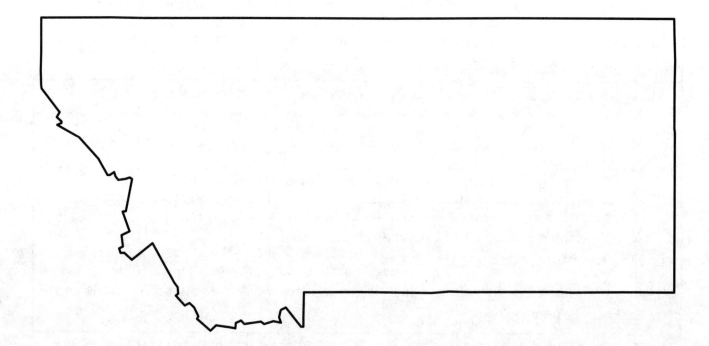

## Key

| Capital | * |
|---|---|
| City | • |
| River | --------- |
| Interstate | ——— |
| Mountains | /\/\/\/\ |

Name _____  Date _____

# Montana Trivia

In 1888, Helena had more millionaires per capita than any other city in the world.

46 out of Montana's 56 counties are considered "frontier counties" with an average population of six or fewer people per square mile.

The notorious outlaw, Henry Plummer, built the first jail constructed in the state.

The Montana Yogo Sapphire is the only North American gem to be included in the Crown Jewels of England.

Combination, Comet, Keystone, Black Pine, and Pony are names of Montana ghost towns.

**Directions:** Help us find Montana's animal friends in the word search below!

```
D  K  I  L  I  D  I  N  O  S  A  U  R  S  O  P  L  M  Q  Z
W  M  O  O  S  E  P  L  E  N  C  B  R  W  O  E  L  M  K  V
K  M  E  E  T  E  R  S  P  E  L  I  C  A  N  S  B  O  U  Z
X  L  W  A  Y  R  E  I  P  K  M  V  T  N  R  P  U  I  E  A
A  M  C  N  D  E  R  W  V  L  N  K  I  S  O  P  F  R  O  U
W  M  V  T  G  O  L  D  E  N  E  A  G  L  E  K  F  W  M  R
U  V  L  E  P  N  W  O  U  K  L  F  A  E  C  B  A  T  L  K
Z  E  T  L  I  M  O  L  B  B  A  L  D  E  A  G  L  E  K  M
O  T  R  O  L  E  E  S  A  B  E  E  T  S  A  S  O  O  P  L
W  K  V  P  O  Y  O  I  Y  R  L  E  K  E  L  D  O  S  A  M
R  Q  T  E  Y  O  P  O  I  E  K  R  A  V  R  G  N  H  G  N
G  R  I  Z  Z  L  Y  B  E  A  R  S  S  A  B  I  S  O  N  E
```

**Word Bank**

| | | | | |
|---|---|---|---|---|
| moose | bald eagle | golden eagle | loons | dinosaurs |
| grizzly bears | elk | swans | pelicans | bison |
| geese | antelope | deer | buffalo | meadowlark |

Name _____ Date _____

# Nevada Symbols

## http://www.netstate.com/states/

**Directions:** Use the Internet to locate the symbols of the state to complete the chart below. Then, draw and color the flag, seal, bird, and flower. If you wish, you may instead print the four symbols from a website and paste them on the page.

| State Capital | |
|---|---|
| State Motto | |
| State Nickname | |
| State Flower | |
| State Bird | |
| State Tree | |
| State Song | |

| State Flag | State Seal |
|---|---|
| | |
| **State Bird** | **State Flower** |
| | |

Name _____     Date _____

# Discover Nevada

**Directions:** Research the Internet to find the answers to these questions. Record your answers below in the space provided, on your own paper, or in a word processing document. You should also include any other interesting places you visited, facts you learned, or opinions you developed.

Begin at the authors' website and then click on the correct state. From there, you can choose the corresponding links to answer the questions.

## http://www.neeleypress.com/usa

| | Questions |
|---|---|
| 1 | The capitol in Carson City was completed in 1871. In 1971, who moved out of the capitol? Where did they go? |
| 2 | Who is the governor? For whom did the governor work before being elected? |
| 3 | Liberace opened the Liberace Museum in 1979. How many pianos did he own? What cars are in the museum? |
| 4 | In Reno, you can see the National Automobile Museum. How many cars are in the museum? |
| 5 | The Black Rock Desert is a prehistoric lake bed. How much precipitation classifies land as a desert? |
| 6 | The Hoover Dam was built to provide water and electricity. What river does the dam control? What lake was formed with the dam? By what other name is Hoover Dam known? |
| 7 | Boulder City was built to house the people who built the dam. What was life like in Boulder City? |
| 8 | Famous tennis player Andre Agassi was born in Las Vegas in 1970. What year did he turn professional? |
| 9 | The wife of the 37th United States President was born in Ely, Nevada. Her mother was from Germany and her father was a miner. She was born on St. Patrick's Day. Who is this First Lady? |
| 10 | The first mechanical slot machine was named the Liberty Bell. The machine was built in 1895 by Charles Fey. What did Mr. Fey do for a living? |

# Discover Nevada *(cont.)*

| | Questions |
|---|---|
| 11 | Bertha the elephant entertained for 37 years at John Ascuaga's Nugget casino. How old was she when she died? |
| 12 | Virginia City was a bustling tent town when gold was discovered at the head of Six-Mile Canyon. The mud from the settlement caused a great deal of trouble. What did they find in the mud? |
| 13 | Virginia City hosts the championship event of a very peculiar type of race. What is the race? Would you want to participate? |
| 14 | Samuel Langhorne Clemens adopted the pen name Josh as a reporter for the Virginia City Territorial Enterprise. What pen name did he later use? |
| 15 | In March 1931, Governor Fred Balzar signed into law the bill legalizing gambling in the state. Las Vegas became a huge city of entertainment. The city is known for its bright lights and entertainers. Can you find Elvis? |
| 16 | In 1999, Nevada produced 75% of the gold in the United States and 10% of all the gold in the world. What was the largest producing mining company that year? Take a look at the bar graph of all the minerals mined in Nevada. |
| 17 | The ghost town of Rhyolyte was once the home to 10,000 people dreaming of becoming rich on gold. Describe the remains of the depot, glass house, bank, and other buildings. |
| 18 | Tonopah, like many other towns, was started after silver was discovered. Jim Butler discovered the vein purely by accident. What does legend tell us about his discovery? |
| 19 | Berlin-Ichthyosaur State Park was first established in 1957 to protect and display North America's most abundant concentration and largest known ichthyosaur fossils. Besides being the state fossil, what is an ichthyosaur? |
| 20 | Area 51 is a secret military base between Alamo and Tonopah. Many stories and legends surround the base including those suggesting extraterrestrial life forms. Do you think the stories are possible? |

**Challenge:** Write a question about the state that isn't addressed above. Then, suggest a website for finding the answer to your question.

**Question 1:** _____

**URL 1:** _____

Name _____  Date _____

# Nevada State Map

**Directions:** Use the key located below to complete the map of the state. Begin by locating the capital city and at least three other major cities. Label Hoover Dam and Lake Mead. Then, locate and draw two major rivers and/or mountains in the state. Draw at least two major interstate highways that travel through the state. Finally, label any other states and/or bodies of water that surround the state.

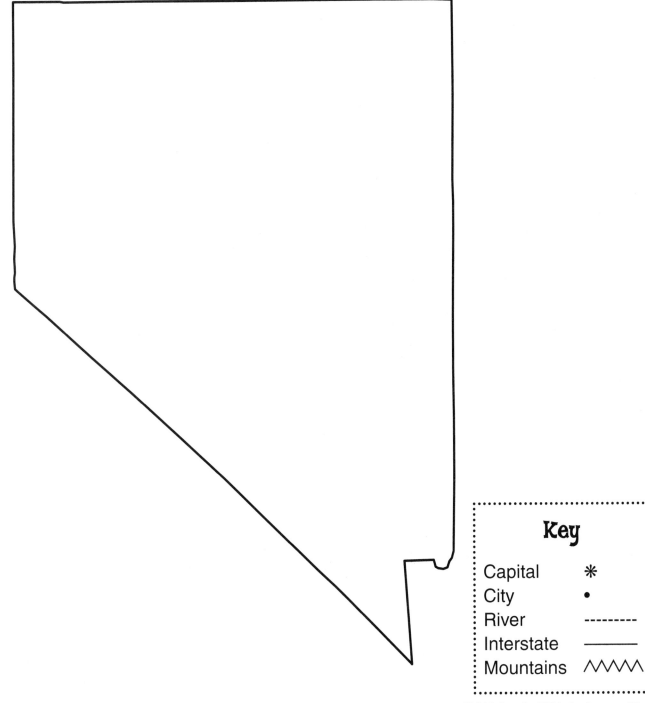

### Key

| | |
|---|---|
| Capital | ✳ |
| City | • |
| River | - - - - - - |
| Interstate | ——— |
| Mountains | ∧∧∧∧ |

Name _____   Date _____

# Nevada Trivia

Construction worker hard hats were first invented specifically for workers on the Hoover Dam in 1933.

Camels were used as pack animals in Nevada as late as 1870.

The name Nevada comes from a Spanish word meaning snow-clad.

The Reno Ice Pavilion is a 16,000-square-foot rink once dismantled and moved to Reno from Atlantic City, New Jersey.

Pershing County features the only round courthouse in the United States.

Nevada has Native American tribes including the Shoshone, Washo, and Paiute.

The state's Highway 50, known as the Loneliest Highway in America, received its name from *Life* magazine in 1986. There are few road stops in the 287-mile stretch between Ely and Fernley.

**Directions:** Place these words in the fill-in. Words can be placed vertically, horizontally, diagonally, and backwards.

silver

gold

copper

aggregate

petroleum

people

Name _____ Date _____

# Utah Symbols

## http://www.netstate.com/states/

**Directions:** Use the Internet to locate the symbols of the state to complete the chart below. Then, draw and color the flag, seal, bird, and flower. If you wish, you may instead print the four symbols from a website and paste them on the page.

| State Capital | |
|---|---|
| State Motto | |
| State Nickname | |
| State Flower | |
| State Bird | |
| State Tree | |
| State Song | |

| State Flag | State Seal |
|---|---|
| | |
| **State Bird** | **State Flower** |
| | |

Name _____    Date _____

# Discover Utah

**Directions:** Research the Internet to find the answers to these questions. Record your answers below in the space provided, on your own paper, or in a word processing document. You should also include any other interesting places you visited, facts you learned, or opinions you developed.

Begin at the authors' website and then click on the correct state. From there, you can choose the corresponding links to answer the questions.

**http://www.neeleypress.com/usa**

| | Questions |
|---|---|
| 1 | Different history books give different meanings for the word *Utah*. Which Native American tribe should know the definition better than anyone else? |
| 2 | *C. parvidens* is the smallest of this kind of animal and it lives in Utah. What do we call these animals? |
| 3 | President Bill Clinton designated a new national monument in 1996. What is the name of this new monument? Where is it located? |
| 4 | The Bingham Canyon copper mine is one of the largest open-pit copper mines in the world. How deep is it? How wide is it? |
| 5 | Nolan Bushnell invented the first home video game, Atari®. Then he invented Pong. What got him interested in electricity and engineering? |
| 6 | Paul Winchell is the voice of Tigger in the Winnie the Pooh films. What did he invent and give the patent for to the University of Utah? |
| 7 | Monument Valley straddles the Utah and Arizona border and is entirely inside an Native American reservation. What tribe calls this area home? |
| 8 | Want to learn more about your family history? The Genealogical Society of Utah is the largest collection of genealogical information. How many records and books do they have? |
| 9 | One of the seven natural wonders of the world is in southern Utah. Rainbow Bridge is the world's largest natural-rock span. What is its height and width? |

# Discover Utah *(cont.)*

| | Questions |
|---|---|
| **10** | Fillmore was Utah's first territorial capital and was named for United States President Millard Fillmore. Where is the state capital now? |
| **11** | Robert Leroy Parker and Harry Longbaugh were famous outlaws in the wild west. What names did they go by? What was the name of their gang? |
| **12** | In 1869, the completion of the world's first transcontinental railroad was celebrated by driving four symbolic spikes. What two railroads met on this site? |
| **13** | The dome-shaped auditorium of the Mormon Tabernacle on Temple Square is so acoustically sensitive that you can hear what? |
| **14** | Swimming in the Great Salt Lake is described as a "once-in-a-lifetime-will-be-quite-enough-thank-you" sort of experience. Can you float in this lake? |
| **15** | Lake Bonneville was a huge ancient lake that covered most of Utah. How big was the lake? What unique lake is a part of the Lake Bonneville area today? |
| **16** | The Wasatch mountain range is named after a Ute name meaning "mountain pass" or "low place in a high mountain." What does the weather look like today on the mountain? |
| **17** | The Heber Valley Railroad has been used in many movies and continues to carry passengers today. What year did it start? What two types of locomotives run on this track? |
| **18** | Capitol Reef National Park protects the Waterpocket Fold, a 90-mile long monocline. What is a monocline? |
| **19** | Debbi Fields was born in 1956 in Utah. What store did she open in 1977? |
| **20** | Philo Farnsworth was born in Indian Creek, Utah, in 1906. As a very young man, he invented the technology for today's television. How old was he? What was his profession? |

**Challenge:** Write a question about the state that isn't addressed above. Then, suggest a website for finding the answer to your question.

**Question 1:** _____

**URL 1:** _____

Name _____ Date _____

# Utah State Map

**Directions:** Use the key located below to complete the map of the state. Begin by locating the capital city and at least three other major cities. Then, locate and draw two major rivers and/or mountains in the state. Draw the Great Salt Lake and color it blue. Where is Monument Valley and Capitol Reef? Draw at least two major interstate highways that travel through the state. Finally, label any other states and/or bodies of water that surround the state.

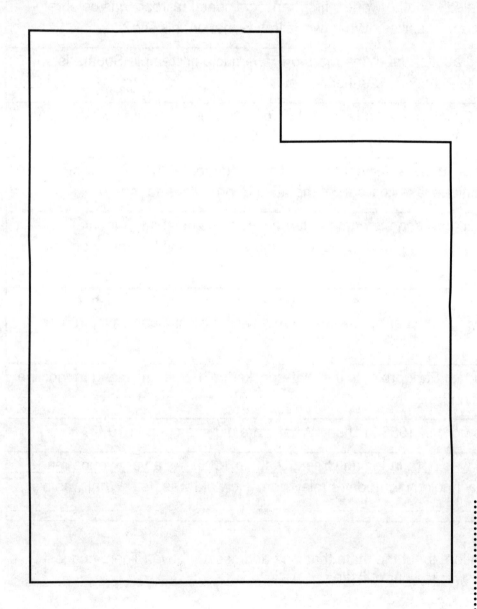

## Key

| Capital | ✳ |
| --- | --- |
| City | • |
| River | - - - - - - - - |
| Interstate | ——— |
| Mountains | ∧∧∧∧ |

Name _____ Date _____

# Utah Trivia

The only teams in the NBA that don't have names ending in the letter "S" are the Utah Jazz, the Miami Heat, and the Orlando Magic.

Salt Lake City was originally named Great Salt Lake City. Great was dropped from the name in 1868.

Utah has the highest literacy rate in the nation.

Mailing an entire building has been illegal in the United States since 1916 when a man mailed a 40,000-ton brick house across Utah to avoid high freight rates.

The controversy surrounding the construction of the Glen Canyon Dam and Lake Powell is often cited as the beginning of the modern-day environmental movement.

The Heber Valley Railroad's magnificent steam engine and ten passenger railroad cars have been filmed in over 31 motion pictures over the past 20 years.

The Uinta mountain range is named after the Ute tribe. The Uinta's are the only east–west axis mountains in North America.

Kanab is known as Utah's Little Hollywood because of the large number of motion pictures that are filmed in the area.

**Directions:** Decipher the words on the lines below using the key.

| A | B | C | D | E | F | G | H | I | J | K | L | M |
|---|---|---|---|---|---|---|---|---|---|---|---|---|
| ◯ | ◻ | ♥ | ✳ | ▲ | ❄ | ✦ | ➜ | ☆ | ✪ | ⇨ | ♣ | ▼ |

| N | O | P | Q | R | S | T | U | V | W | X | Y | Z |
|---|---|---|---|---|---|---|---|---|---|---|---|---|
| ☙ | ☛ | ✂ | ✈ | ❖ | ◗ | ◼ | ✐ | ✑ | ✚ | ☆ | ◉ | ✿ |

Name _____　　　Date _____

# Wyoming Symbols

**http://www.netstate.com/states/**

**Directions:** Use the Internet to locate the symbols of the state to complete the chart below. Then, draw and color the flag, seal, bird, and flower. If you wish, you may instead print the four symbols from a website and paste them on the page.

| | |
|---|---|
| **State Capital** | |
| **State Motto** | |
| **State Nickname** | |
| **State Flower** | |
| **State Bird** | |
| **State Tree** | |
| **State Song** | |

| | |
|---|---|
| **State Flag** | **State Seal** |
| **State Bird** | **State Flower** |

Name _____ Date _____

# Discover Wyoming

**Directions:** Research the Internet to find the answers to these questions. Record your answers below in the space provided, on your own paper, or in a word processing document. You should also include any other interesting places you visited, facts you learned, or opinions you developed.

Begin at the authors' website and then click on the correct state. From there, you can choose the corresponding links to answer the questions.

## http://www.neeleypress.com/usa

| | Questions |
|---|---|
| 1 | Meet the governor of the state of Wyoming. What is the governor's name? Where did the governor go to college? When was the governor born? |
| 2 | Bucking Horse and Rider (BH&R) is a federal and state registered trademark of the State of Wyoming. What is a trademark? |
| 3 | The historic Native Americans in Wyoming were nomadic tribes known as the Plains Indians. What are the names of the tribes that lived in Wyoming? |
| 4 | Mountain Skies Observatory is located in Lyman, Wyoming, at an elevation of 6,900 feet. What astronomical pictures have been taken by the observatory? |
| 5 | Chief Washakie recognized that many people would die if his people took up arms to settle the differences with whites. What did he do for the settlers moving to the West? How was he buried? |
| 6 | Devil's Tower is a 1,267-foot tall formation to which 4,000 people a year travel. Why can it be dangerous to climb the tower? |
| 7 | Fort Laramie was originally located in eastern Wyoming. What were the different uses of this important fort? |
| 8 | Fossil Butte has over 75 fossils on display including a 13-foot crocodile and the oldest known bat. What was Fossil Butte fifty million years ago? |
| 9 | Five mountains make up the Grand Teton National Park. What are the mountains' names? |

# Discover Wyoming *(cont.)*

| | Questions |
|---|---|
| **10** | Architect Robert Reamer designed the Old Faithful Inn to match the beautiful surroundings of Yellowstone. Take a look around at this beautiful inn. What year was the inn completed? |
| **11** | Yellowstone was the first national park in the United States. In 1872, which president set aside this land to preserve it for future generations? |
| **12** | The terraces of Mammoth Hot Springs constantly change as the levels of mineral-laden hot water change. What are the minerals called that form the terraces? |
| **13** | Wind River Canyon is twelve miles long and 2,000 feet deep. What are the names given to the river at the bottom of the canyon? |
| **14** | Jackson Hole, Wyoming, was named after the fur trapper David E. Jackson. What brought Mr. Jackson to this area of the West? |
| **15** | In 1897, the first Frontier Days were held in Cheyenne to attract business and people to the area. What were the first events to be held at Frontier Days? |
| **16** | Nellie Tayloe Ross was the United States' first female governor. How was she first elected to office? |
| **17** | Wyoming's open spaces provide plenty of room for wildlife to roam free. How many of these animals have antlers or horns? |
| **18** | Each geyser has special characteristics and behaviors. How can you tell when Old Faithful is about to erupt? |
| **19** | Geysers, fumaroles, and hot springs are geothermal features of the earth. So, what are geysers, fumaroles, and hot springs? |
| **20** | Yellowstone is an active earthquake region. When did the last earthquake occur? What was its magnitude? |

**Challenge:** Write a question about the state that isn't addressed above. Then, suggest a website for finding the answer to your question.

**Question 1:** _____

**URL 1:** _____

Name _____ Date _____

# Wyoming State Map

**Directions:** Use the key located below to complete the map of the state. Begin by locating the capital city and at least three other major cities. Then, locate and draw two major rivers and/or mountains in the state. Label Yellowstone National Park and Grand Teton National Park on your map. Draw at least two major interstate highways that travel through the state. Finally, label any other states and/or bodies of water that surround the state.

## Key

| | |
|---|---|
| Capital | ✳ |
| City | • |
| River | - - - - - - - - |
| Interstate | ———— |
| Mountains | ∧∧∧∧∧ |

Name _____ Date _____

# Wyoming Trivia

**Directions:** Use the following words to complete the Upper Geyser Basin Thermal Features word fill-in. Words can be forwards, backwards, up, or down.

**multi–word**
Old Faithful
Morning Glory Pool
Upper Geyser Basin
Punch Bowl

**9–letter**
artemisia
riverside
spasmodic

**3–letter**
spa
ear

**4–letter**
cone
lion
pump

**5–letter**
daisy
comet
grand
heart
plume

**6–letter**
grotto
oblong
beauty
turban
castle
canary
rocket

**7–letter**
sawmill
crested
beehive
mastiff

**8–letter**
fountain
splendid

Name _____ Date _____

# Alaska Symbols

## http://www.netstate.com/states/

**Directions:** Use the Internet to locate the symbols of the state to complete the chart below. Then, draw and color the flag, seal, bird, and flower. If you wish, you may instead print the four symbols from a website and paste them on the page.

| State Capital | |
|---|---|
| State Motto | |
| State Nickname | |
| State Flower | |
| State Bird | |
| State Tree | |
| State Song | |

| State Flag | State Seal |
|---|---|
| State Bird | State Flower |

Name _____ Date _____

# Discover Alaska

**Directions:** Research the Internet to find the answers to these questions. Record your answers below in the space provided, on your own paper, or in a word processing document. You should also include any other interesting places you visited, facts you learned, or opinions you developed.

Begin at the authors' website and then click on the correct state. From there, you can choose the corresponding links to answer the questions.

## http://www.neeleypress.com/usa

| | Questions |
|---|---|
| 1 | Alaska was one of the last states admitted to the United States of America. When did this happen and which state was admitted after Alaska? |
| 2 | Eleven distinct cultural groups make up Alaska's native people. What are the eleven groups? |
| 3 | What does *subsistence* mean? Play the subsistence game on the website. Have you ever heard any of these words before? |
| 4 | Did you think that rain forests were only in the tropics? Take a tour of the Alaskan Rain Forest. How big is the Alaskan Rain Forest, and where exactly is it located? |
| 5 | What are some of the wildlife species found in the Alaskan Rain Forest? |
| 6 | Choose an Alaskan animal and describe it. Be sure to include information about its habitat. |
| 7 | What is the capital of Alaska? In land area, how large is the city? |
| 8 | What is the population of Juneau? How does this compare with the population of your city? |
| 9 | Take a virtual tour of Juneau. Describe what you enjoyed most about the tour. |

# Discover Alaska *(cont.)*

| | Questions |
|---|---|
| 10 | What are the *Aurora Borealis*? |
| 11 | Design a brochure to attract tourists to Alaska. |
| 12 | What is the Iditarod?  How did it begin? |
| 13 | How did mushers get that name? |
| 14 | What is the highest point in North America?  Can you find two different names for this mountain? |
| 15 | What is the northernmost point in the United States?  The easternmost?  The westernmost? |
| 16 | What is a glacier?  Read about how glaciers are formed, then write about your favorite Alaskan glacier. |
| 17 | Send an Alaskan e-card to someone you know. |
| 18 | Listen to and read about the Klondike Gold Rush.  Take the quiz on the website. |
| 19 | How many days does it take oil to travel the length of the Trans-Alaska pipeline? Where does it start?  Where does it end? |
| 20 | Describe how an igloo is constructed. |

**Challenge:** Write a question about the state that isn't addressed above. Then, suggest a website for finding the answer to your question.

**Question 1:** _____

**URL 1:** _____

Name _____    Date _____

# Alaska State Map

**Directions:** Use the key located below to complete the map of the state. Begin by locating the capital city and at least three other major cities. Then, locate and draw two major rivers and/or mountains in the state. Label the Alaskan Rain Forest and Mt. McKinley/Denali. Draw at least two major interstate highways that travel through the state. Finally, label any other states, countries, and/or bodies of water that surround the state.

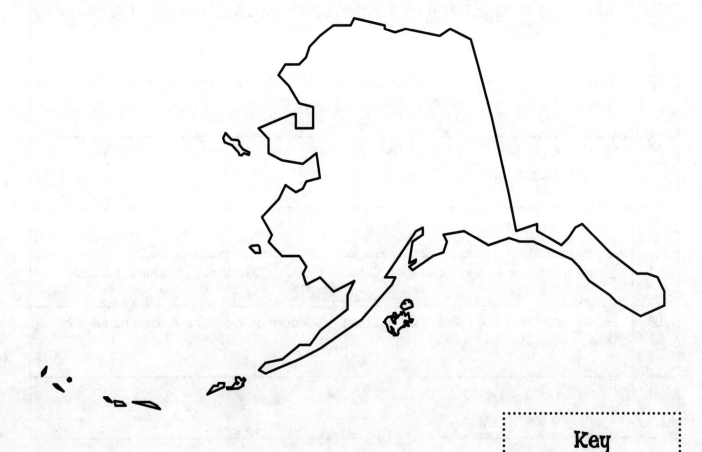

## Key

| | |
|---|---|
| Capital | ✳ |
| City | • |
| River | ------- |
| Interstate | ——— |
| Mountains | ∧∧∧∧ |

Name _____   Date _____

# Alaska Trivia

The United States paid Russia about two cents an acre for Alaska.

Waking a sleeping bear for the purpose of taking a photograph is prohibited.

Rhode Island can fit into Alaska 425 times.

Juneau is the only capital city in the United States that is accessible only by boat or plane.

Alaska is the northernmost, easternmost, and westernmost state in the United States.

**Directions:** Use these clues to complete the crossword puzzle. Use the website as a reference to help you as you work.

## http://home.gci.net/~alaskapage/trivia.htm

**Across**

1. largest lake in Alaska
3. largest glacier in Alaska
5. longest river
6. state bird
7. capital
8. northern lights

**Down**

1. 1,100 mile dog sled race
2. highest mountain
3. state sport
4. state tree

Name _____ Date _____

# Oregon Symbols

**http://www.netstate.com/states/**

**Directions:** Use the Internet to locate the symbols of the state to complete the chart below. Then, draw and color the flag, seal, bird, and flower. If you wish, you may instead print the four symbols from a website and paste them on the page.

| | |
|---|---|
| **State Capital** | |
| **State Motto** | |
| **State Nickname** | |
| **State Flower** | |
| **State Bird** | |
| **State Tree** | |
| **State Song** | |

| **State Flag** | **State Seal** |
|---|---|
| | |
| **State Bird** | **State Flower** |
| | |

Name _____     Date _____

# Discover Oregon

**Directions:** Research the Internet to find the answers to these questions. Record your answers below in the space provided, on your own paper, or in a word processing document. You should also include any other interesting places you visited, facts you learned, or opinions you developed.

Begin at the authors' website and then click on the correct state. From there, you can choose the corresponding links to answer the questions.

## http://www.neeleypress.com/usa

| | Questions |
|---|---|
| 1 | The Oregon Trail was the route used to move westward in the United States. Where did it start? Where did it end? How long was the trip? |
| 2 | What is a f*usitriton oregonensis* ? |
| 3 | What type of architecture is the current capitol? |
| 4 | The flag of Oregon is the only state flag with different pictures on each side. How many stars appear on the front of the flag? What do they mean? |
| 5 | The Columbia River gorge has each of its canyon walls in a different state. What states border in the gorge? |
| 6 | The Columbia River gorge is considered by many to be the best place in the world for what water sport? |
| 7 | Crater Lake is located in a volcanic depression that was formed from an eruption that occurred approximately 7,700 years ago. What was the volcano's name? |
| 8 | Oregon is in the Cascade mountain range that was formed by volcanoes. How many volcanoes have erupted in the last 200 years? |
| 9 | On the top of the Oregon State Capitol building is a statue called the "Oregon Pioneer." How much does the statue weigh? What does it represent? |

# Discover Oregon *(cont.)*

| | Questions |
|---|---|
| **10** | Douglas C. Engelbart invented computer technology that we use every day. What did he invent? |
| **11** | Mount Hood last erupted in 1790. What kind of volcano is Mount Hood? |
| **12** | The Rogue River is 215 miles long and runs through the Cascade Mountains. Where does the river start? |
| **13** | Multnomah Falls is the second tallest waterfall in the United States. What year did Simon Benson build a bridge over the falls? |
| **14** | In 1880, William Cox discovered the Sea Lion Caves. Get on the elevator and take a tour of the cave and listen to the description of the cave. Summarize what you hear. |
| **15** | The H.J. Andrews Experimental Forest is one of the largest long-term ecological research sites. Watch the slide show. How much of the forest has been logged? What university is affiliated with the forest? |
| **16** | Who discovered the caves located in the Oregon Caves National Monument? What was he doing when he made the discovery? |
| **17** | An international museum in Hood City collects a very special kind of horses. What do they collect? |
| **18** | The Tillamook Naval Air Museum is in the world's largest wooden clear-span building. How many football fields could fit into the hangar? |
| **19** | Haystack Rock is 235 feet high. In 1990, the rock received Marine Garden status. What does this status mean? |
| **20** | The Tillamook Rock Lighthouse was built in 1880 and was decommissioned in 1957. How far out to sea is the lighthouse located? What is its nickname? |

**Challenge:** Write a question about the state that isn't addressed above. Then, suggest a website for finding the answer to your question.

**Question 1:** _____

**URL 1:** _____

Name _____ Date _____

# Oregon State Map

**Directions:** Use the key located below to complete the map of the state. Begin by locating the capital city and at least three other major cities. Then, locate and draw two major rivers and/or mountains in the state. What river runs along the northern border? What river is on the east? Draw at least two major interstate highways that travel through the state. Finally, label any other states and/or bodies of water that surround the state.

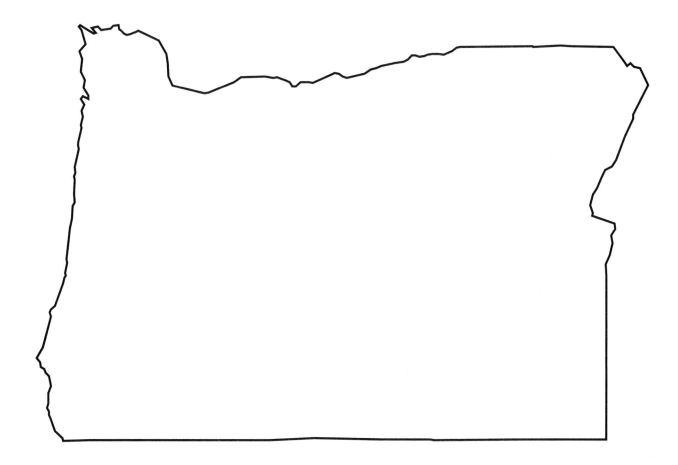

## Key

| | |
|---|---|
| Capital | ✳ |
| City | • |
| River | --------- |
| Interstate | ———— |
| Mountains | ∧∧∧∧ |

Name _____ Date _____

# Oregon Trivia

Eugene was the first city to have one-way streets.

The state of Oregon has one city named Sisters and another called Brothers.

The world's shortest river—the D River in Oregon—is only 121 feet long.

**Directions:** Find your way along the Oregon Trail.

Independence, Missouri

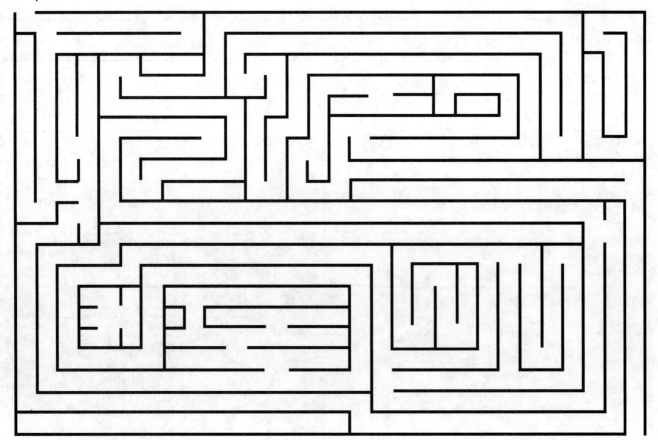

Oregon City, Oregon

Name _____ Date _____

# Washington Symbols

## http://www.netstate.com/states/

**Directions:** Use the Internet to locate the symbols of the state to complete the chart below. Then, draw and color the flag, seal, bird, and flower. If you wish, you may instead print the four symbols from a website and paste them on the page.

| State Capital | |
|---|---|
| State Motto | |
| State Nickname | |
| State Flower | |
| State Bird | |
| State Tree | |
| State Song | |

| State Flag | State Seal |
|---|---|
| State Bird | State Flower |

Name _____ Date _____

# Discover Washington

**Directions:** Research the Internet to find the answers to these questions. Record your answers below in the space provided, on your own paper, or in a word processing document. You should also include any other interesting places you visited, facts you learned, or opinions you developed.

Begin at the authors' website and then click on the correct state. From there, you can choose the corresponding links to answer the questions.

**http://www.neeleypress.com/usa**

| | Questions |
|---|---|
| 1 | Seventh and eighth-grade students from Washington Middle School created this virtual tour of the Washington State Capitol. What famous monument stands in front of the capitol? |
| 2 | The beautiful Washington State Capitol was constructed in 1911. In 2001, a 6.8 earthquake shook the beautiful building. Describe the damage. |
| 3 | Hank Ketcham is the creator and cartoonist of Dennis the Menace. In his biography, Mr. Ketcham says that he got his inspiration from what two men? |
| 4 | Chief Seattle was born on Blake Island in central Puget Sound. He said that all things share the same breath. What do you think he meant? |
| 5 | Mount Rainier is a dormant volcano that is 14,411 feet high. Many people try to climb to the top. Other people wait for its next eruption. When was the last earthquake near Mount Rainier? |
| 6 | Seattle's Space Needle has an observation deck that is 520 feet above the city. How long does it take for the restaurant at the 500-foot level to turn one full revolution? |
| 7 | The eruption of Mount St. Helens had a devastating effect on the terrain. Describe the scene before and after the eruption. |
| 8 | Who is Washington's governor? Where was the governor born? Where did the governor go to college? |
| 9 | Sixty percent of the apples produced in the United States are grown in Washington state. How many apples are grown in a year? |

# Discover Washington *(cont.)*

| | Questions |
|---|---|
| 10 | Washington has more glaciers than the other 47 contiguous states combined. How is a glacier born? |
| 11 | Bill Gates started a computer software company when he was only twenty years old. What company did he start? |
| 12 | The Tacoma Narrows Bridge collapsed in 1940. Watch the video. What caused the bridge to collapse? A new bridge was built in 1950. |
| 13 | The Sea-Tac is the abbreviated name for the Seattle-Tacoma Airport. Take a look at the airport. What is the weather like today? |
| 14 | Rob Angel from Seattle, developed Pictionary®, a game in which partners try to guess phrases based on each other's drawings. How old was he? What was his job? |
| 15 | *Orcinus orca* is the scientific name for Puget Sound's killer whales. Humans impact the population of these beautiful animals. How many orcas were counted in 2000? |
| 16 | Seattle's Museum of Flight provides pictures of most of the airplanes that have been produced. What plane carried Presidents Eisenhower, Kennedy, Johnson, and Nixon? |
| 17 | Where are the San Juan Islands located? What are the names of the islands? |
| 18 | Washington State Ferries move people and their cars from place to place in Puget Sound. What time could you take a ferry from Bainbridge Island to Seattle? |
| 19 | What is the current weather on Mount Rainier? What is the weather in Tacoma? What is the difference in temperature between the mountain's summit and the city? |
| 20 | Visit the Pacific Science Center. Are there aliens out there? Investigate the possibilities. |

**Challenge:** Write a question about the state that isn't addressed above. Then, suggest a website for finding the answer to your question.

**Question 1:** _____

**URL 1:** _____

Name _____    Date _____

# Washington State Map

**Directions:** Use the key located below to complete the map of the state. Begin by locating the capital city and at least three other major cities. Where is the Columbia River? Where is Mount Rainier? Where is Mount St. Helens? What is the inlet on the northwest corner called? Then, locate and draw two major rivers and/or mountains in the state. Draw at least two major interstate highways that travel through the state. Finally, label any other states and/or bodies of water that surround the state.

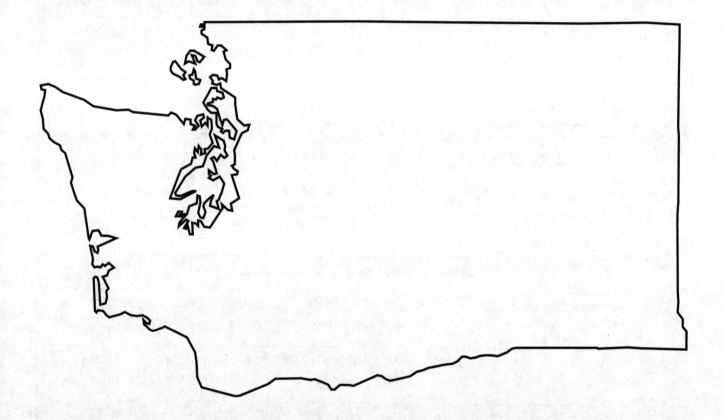

## Key

| | |
|---|---|
| Capital | ✴ |
| City | • |
| River | --------- |
| Interstate | ——— |
| Mountains | ∧∧∧∧∧ |

Name _____ Date _____

# Washington Trivia

The state of Washington is the only state to be named after a United States president.

Cape Flattery on Washington's Olympic Peninsula is the northwesternmost point in the contiguous United States.

Before Washington became a state, the territory was called Columbia. When it was granted statehood, the name was changed to Washington, so people wouldn't confuse it with the District of Columbia.

In 1971–1972, Mount Rainer in Washington accumulated 1,224 inches of snow to set a record in snowfall.

Six states entered the United States during Benjamin Harrison's term as United States president: North Dakota, South Dakota, Montana, Idaho, Wyoming, and Washington.

**Directions:** Find these odd town names from Washington in the word search below.

```
L   K   F   D   S   E   Q   P   K   L   U   W   P
Q   R   L   M   M   U   T   M   U   T   M   U   T
G   H   U   M   P   T   U   L   I   P   S   R   S
W   E   V   B   L   U   U   N   N   F   R   S   P
B   G   C   L   W   K   R   S   D   O   I   L   A
A   R   T   U   M   W   A   T   E   R   L   L   A
T   O   U   M   W   I   T   E   X   K   N   B   C
P   E   Q   L   M   L   N   Q   P   S   D   O   G
E   G   A   L   L   A   W   A   L   L   A   W   N
O   Y   O   P   L   U   L   A   U   R   A   N   C
```

## Word Bank

| | | | |
|---|---|---|---|
| Forks | George | Humptulips | Index |
| Tukwila | Tumtum | Tumwater | Walla Walla |

# State Information Chart

| State | Capital | Admission Date | Admission No. |
|---|---|---|---|
| Alabama | Montgomery | December 14, 1819 | 22 |
| Alaska | Juneau | January 3, 1959 | 49 |
| Arizona | Phoenix | February 14, 1912 | 48 |
| Arkansas | Little Rock | June 15, 1836 | 25 |
| California | Sacramento | September 9, 1850 | 31 |
| Colorado | Denver | August 1, 1876 | 38 |
| Connecticut | Hartford | January 9, 1788 | 5 |
| Delaware | Dover | December 7, 1787 | 1 |
| Florida | Tallahassee | March 3, 1845 | 27 |
| Georgia | Atlanta | January 2, 1788 | 4 |
| Hawaii | Honolulu | August 21, 1959 | 50 |
| Idaho | Boise | July 3, 1890 | 43 |
| Illinois | Springfield | December 3, 1818 | 21 |
| Indiana | Indianapolis | December 11, 1816 | 19 |
| Iowa | Des Moines | December 28, 1846 | 29 |
| Kansas | Topeka | January 29, 1861 | 34 |
| Kentucky | Frankfort | June 1, 1792 | 15 |
| Louisiana | Baton Rouge | April 30, 1812 | 18 |
| Maine | Augusta | March 15, 1820 | 23 |
| Maryland | Annapolis | April 28, 1788 | 7 |
| Massachusetts | Boston | February 6, 1788 | 6 |
| Michigan | Lansing | January 26, 1837 | 26 |
| Minnesota | St. Paul | May 11, 1858 | 32 |
| Mississippi | Jackson | December 10, 1817 | 20 |
| Missouri | Jefferson City | August 10, 1821 | 24 |

# State Information Chart *(cont.)*

| State | Capital | Admission Date | Admission No. |
|---|---|---|---|
| Montana | Helena | November 8, 1889 | 41 |
| Nebraska | Lincoln | March 1, 1867 | 37 |
| Nevada | Carson City | October 31, 1864 | 36 |
| New Hampshire | Concord | June 21, 1788 | 9 |
| New Jersey | Trenton | December 18, 1787 | 3 |
| New Mexico | Santa Fe | January 6, 1912 | 47 |
| New York | Albany | July 26, 1788 | 11 |
| North Carolina | Raleigh | November 21, 1789 | 12 |
| North Dakota | Bismarck | November 2, 1889 | 39 |
| Ohio | Columbus | March 1, 1803 | 17 |
| Oklahoma | Oklahoma City | November 16, 1907 | 46 |
| Oregon | Salem | February 14, 1859 | 33 |
| Pennsylvania | Harrisburg | December 12, 1787 | 2 |
| Rhode Island | Providence | May 29, 1790 | 13 |
| South Carolina | Columbia | May 23, 1788 | 8 |
| South Dakota | Pierre | November 2, 1889 | 40 |
| Tennessee | Nashville | June 1, 1796 | 16 |
| Texas | Austin | December 29, 1845 | 28 |
| Utah | Salt Lake City | January 4, 1896 | 45 |
| Vermont | Montpelier | March 4, 1791 | 14 |
| Virginia | Richmond | June 25, 1788 | 10 |
| Washington | Olympia | November 11, 1889 | 42 |
| West Virginia | Charleston | June 20, 1863 | 35 |
| Wisconsin | Madison | May 29, 1848 | 30 |
| Wyoming | Cheyenne | July 10, 1890 | 44 |

# New England States Quiz

**A.** Write the letter of the capital city on the line provided beside each state.

**State**

_____ 1. Connecticut

_____ 2. Maine

_____ 3. Massachusetts

_____ 4. New Hampshire

_____ 5. Rhode Island

_____ 6. Vermont

**Capital**

a. Concord

b. Providence

c. Montpelier

d. Boston

e. Hartford

f. Augusta

**B.** Write the letter of the state nickname on the line provided beside each state.

**State**

_____ 7. Connecticut

_____ 8. Maine

_____ 9. Massachusetts

_____ 10. New Hampshire

_____ 11. Rhode Island

_____ 12. Vermont

**Nickname**

a. The Pine Tree State

b. The Granite State

c. The Ocean State

d. The Green Mountain State

e. The Constitution State

f. The Bay State

**C.** Write the letter of the state flag on the line provided beside each state.

**State**

_____ 13. Connecticut

_____ 14. Maine

_____ 15. Massachusetts

_____ 16. New Hampshire

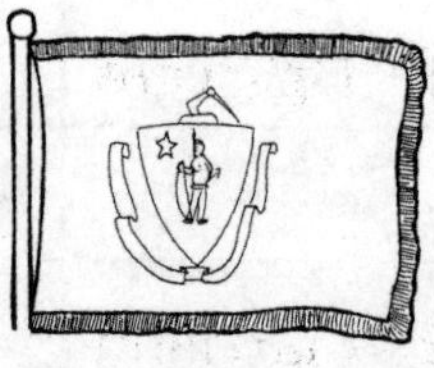

_____ 17. Rhode Island

_____ 18. Vermont

**Flag**

Appendix

# Mid-Atlantic States Quiz

**A.** Write the letter of the capital city on the line provided beside each state.

**State**

_____ 1. Delaware

_____ 2. Maryland

_____ 3. New Jersey

_____ 4. New York

_____ 5. Pennsylvania

**Capital**

a. Albany

b. Harrisburg

c. Annapolis

d. Trenton

e. Dover

**B.** Write the letter of the state nickname on the line provided beside each state.

**State**

_____ 6. Delaware

_____ 7. Maryland

_____ 8. New Jersey

_____ 9. New York

_____ 10. Pennsylvania

**Nickname**

a. The Garden State

b. The Empire State

c. The Old Line State

d. The First State

e. The Keystone State

**C.** Write the letter of the state flag on the line provided beside each state.

**State**

_____ 11. Delaware

_____ 12. Maryland

_____ 13. New Jersey

_____ 14. New York

_____ 15. Pennsylvania

**Flag**

a.

b.

c.

d.

e.

# Southern States Quiz

**A.** Write the letter of the capital city on the line provided beside each state.

**State**                                **Capital**

_____ 1. Alabama              a. Frankfort

_____ 2. Arkansas             b. Atlanta

_____ 3. Florida                c. Columbia

_____ 4. Georgia               d. Nashville

_____ 5. Kentucky             e. Little Rock

_____ 6. Louisiana            f. Charleston

_____ 7. Mississippi          g. Montgomery

_____ 8. North Carolina     h. Raleigh

_____ 9. South Carolina     i. Baton Rouge

_____ 10. Tennessee          j. Tallahassee

_____ 11. Virginia              k. Richmond

_____ 12. West Virginia      l. Jackson

**B.** Write the letter of the state nickname on the line provided beside each state.

**State**                                **Nickname**

_____ 13. Alabama             a. The Mountain State

_____ 14. Arkansas            b. The Bluegrass State

_____ 15. Florida               c. The Palmetto State

_____ 16. Georgia              d. The Old Dominion State

_____ 17. Kentucky            e. The Volunteer State

_____ 18. Louisiana           f. The Sunshine State

_____ 19. Mississippi         g. The Yellowhammer State

_____ 20. North Carolina    h. The Magnolia State

_____ 21. South Carolina    i. The Tar Heel State

_____ 22. Tennessee          j. The Natural State

_____ 23. Virginia              k. The Pelican State

_____ 24. West Virginia      l. The Peach State

# Southern States Quiz *(cont.)*

**C.**  **Write the letter of the flag on the line provided beside each state.**

### State

_____ 25. Alabama

_____ 26. Arkansas

_____ 27. Florida

_____ 28. Georgia

_____ 29. Kentucky

_____ 30. Louisiana

_____ 31. Mississippi

_____ 32. North Carolina

_____ 33. South Carolina

_____ 34. Tennessee

_____ 35. Virginia

_____ 36. West Virginia

### Flag

a.

b.

c.

d.

e.

f.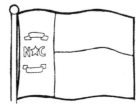

g.

h.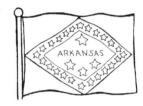

i.

j.

k.

l.

# Midwest States Quiz

**A.    Write the letter of the capital city on the line provided beside each state.**

**State**                                   **Capital**

_____  1. Illinois                 a.  Des Moines

_____  2. Indiana                 b.  St. Paul

_____  3. Iowa                    c.  Springfield

_____  4. Michigan               d.  Columbus

_____  5. Minnesota             e.  Madison

_____  6. Missouri                f.  Lansing

_____  7. Ohio                    g.  Indianapolis

_____  8. Wisconsin              h.  Jefferson City

**B.    Write the letter of the state nickname on the line provided beside each state.**

**State**                                   **Nickname**

_____  9. Illinois                 a.  The Great Lakes State

_____ 10. Indiana                 b.  The North Star State

_____ 11. Iowa                    c.  The Hoosier State

_____ 12. Michigan               d.  The Buckeye State

_____ 13. Minnesota             e.  The Badger State

_____ 14. Missouri                f.  The Hawkeye State

_____ 15. Ohio                    g.  Land of Lincoln

_____ 16. Wisconsin              h.  The Show Me State

# Midwest States Quiz *(cont.)*

**C.** **Write the letter of the state flag on the line provided beside each state.**

**State**                               **Flag**

_____ 17. Illinois

_____ 18. Indiana

_____ 19. Iowa

_____ 20. Michigan

_____ 21. Minnesota

_____ 22. Missouri

_____ 23. Ohio

_____ 24. Wisconsin

a.

e.

b.

f.

c.

g.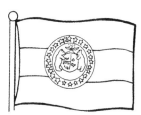

d.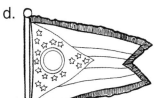

h.

# Great Plains States Quiz

**A.** Write the letter of the capital city on the line provided beside each state.

**State**                                          **Capital**

_____ 1. Kansas                                 a. Pierre

_____ 2. Nebraska                               b. Bismarck

_____ 3. North Dakota                           c. Topeka

_____ 4. South Dakota                           d. Lincoln

**B.** Write the letter of the state nickname on the line provided beside each state.

**State**                                          **Nickname**

_____ 5. Kansas                                 a. The Cornhusker State

_____ 6. Nebraska                               b. Mount Rushmore State

_____ 7. North Dakota                           c. The Sunflower State

_____ 8. South Dakota                           d. The Peace Garden State

**C.** Write the letter of the state flag on the line provided beside each state.

**State**                                          **Flag**

_____ 9. Kansas

_____ 10. Kansas

_____ 11. Kansas

_____ 12. Kansas

# Southwest States Quiz

**A.** **Write the letter of the capital city on the line provided beside each state.**

**State**

_____ 1. Arizona

_____ 2. New Mexico

_____ 3. Oklahoma

_____ 4. Texas

**Capital**

a. Austin

b. Oklahoma City

c. Phoenix

d. Santa Fe

**B.** **Write the letter of the state nickname on the line provided beside each state.**

**State**

_____ 5. Arizona

_____ 6. New Mexico

_____ 7. Oklahoma

_____ 8. Texas

**Nickname**

a. The Sooner State

b. The Lone Star State

c. The Land of Enchantment

d. The Grand Canyon State

**C.** **Write the letter of the state flag on the line provided beside each state.**

**State**

_____ 9. Arizona

_____ 10. New Mexico

_____ 11. Oklahoma

_____ 12. Texas

**Flag**

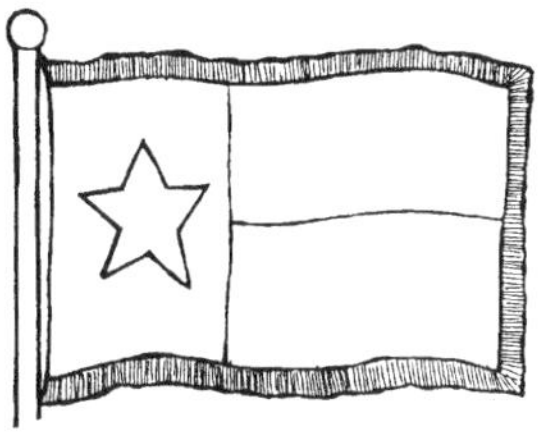

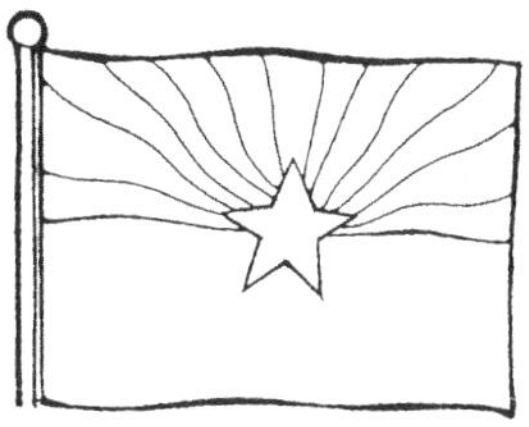

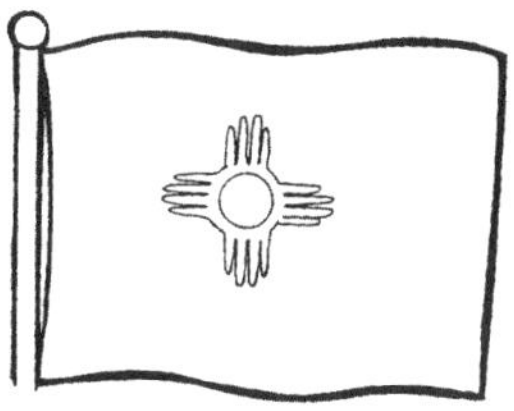

# Western States Quiz

**A.** **Write the letter of the capital on the line provided beside each state.**

**State**

_____ 1. California

_____ 2. Colorado

_____ 3. Hawaii

_____ 4. Idaho

_____ 5. Montana

_____ 6. Nevada

_____ 7. Utah

_____ 8. Wyoming

**Capital**

a. Helena

b. Salt Lake City

c. Boise

d. Carson City

e. Denver

f. Cheyenne

g. Sacramento

h. Honolulu

**B.** **Write the letter of the nickname on the line provided beside each state.**

**State**

_____ 9. California

_____ 10. Colorado

_____ 11. Hawaii

_____ 12. Idaho

_____ 13. Montana

_____ 14. Nevada

_____ 15. Utah

_____ 16. Wyoming

**Nickname**

a. The Gem State

b. The Golden State

c. The Equality or Cowboy State

d. The Beehive State

e. The Centennial State

f. The Aloha State

g. The Treasure State

h. The Silver State

# Western States Quiz *(cont.)*

**C.** **Write the letter of the state flag on the line provided beside each state.**

**State**                                    **Flag**

_____ 17. California

_____ 18. Colorado          a. 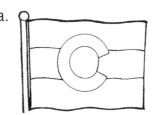          e.

_____ 19. Hawaii

_____ 20. Idaho             b.                                 f.

_____ 21. Montana

_____ 22. Nevada            c.                                 g.

_____ 23. Utah

_____ 24. Wyoming           d.                                 h.

# Pacific Northwest States

**A.** **Write the letter of the capital city on the line provided beside each state.**

**State**

**Capital**

_____ 1. Alaska

a. Olympia

_____ 2. Oregon

b. Juneau

_____ 3. Washington

c. Salem

**B.** **Write the letter of the state nickname on the line provided beside each state.**

**State**

**Nickname**

_____ 4. Alaska

a. The Evergreen State

_____ 5. Oregon

b. The Beaver State

_____ 6. Washington

c. The Last Frontier

**C.** **Write the letter of the state flag on the line provided beside each state.**

**State**

**Flag**

_____ 7. Alaska

a.

_____ 8. Oregon

c.

b.

_____ 9. Washington

# Answer Key

**Page 17—Connecticut**
**State song:** "Yankee Doodle"

**Page 22—Maine**
**State nickname:** Pine Tree State

**Page 27—Massachusetts**

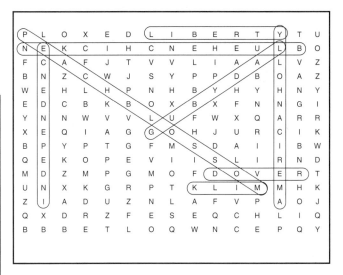

**Page 32—New Hampshire**
**Motto:** Live Free or Die

**Page 37—Rhode Island**

1. Pokanoket
2. Patuxet
3. Quadequina
4. Nauset
5. Wampanoag
6. Mohawks
7. Mahican
8. Sokokis
9. Wessaguscusset

**Wampanoag means:** People of the Dawn

**Page 42—Vermont**
**Across**

1. maple syrup
6. Montpelier
8. Monarch
9. Ethan Allen
10. Mansfield

**Down**

2. Unity
3. Freedom
4. Fourteen
5. Red Clover
7. Morgan

**Page 47—Delaware**

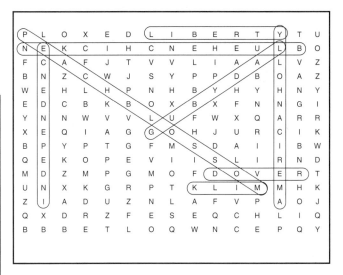

**Page 52—Maryland**
**Maryland's motto:** Manly Deeds, Womanly Words

**Page 57—New Jersey**
Answers will vary.

**Page 62—New York**

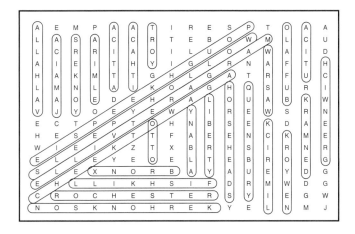

**New York Landmark:** Empire State Building

**Page 67—Pennsylvania**
Document #1: Declaration of Independence

Document #2: United States Constitution

# Answer Key *(cont.)*

**Page 72—Washington, D.C.**

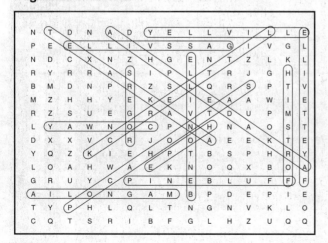

**Page 77—Alabama**

1. Hank Aaron
2. Harper Lee
3. Joe Louis
4. Coretta Scott King
5. Willie Mays
6. Helen Keller
7. Carl Lewis
8. George Wallace
9. Emmy Lou Harris
10. Jesse Owens

**Page 82—Arkansas**

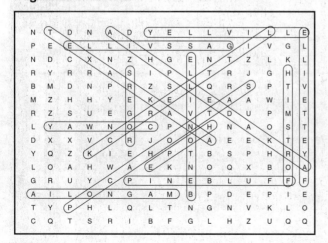

**Page 87—Florida**

**Coded phrase:** Alligators live in Florida.

**Page 92—Georgia**

1. American alligator
2. gopher tortoise
3. snapping turtle
4. snakes
5. black bear
6. river otter
7. raccoon
8. bobcat
9. great blue heron
10. belted kingfisher
11. great white egret

**Where they live:** Okefenokee Swamp

**Page 97—Kentucky**

**Coded phrase:** United we stand; Divided we fall

**Page 102—Louisiana**

1. Louisiana Purchase
2. Mardi Gras
3. Cajun
4. Evangeline
5. Baton Rouge
6. Alligator
7. New Orleans
8. Fat Tuesday

**Coded phrase:** Bayou State

**Page 107—Mississippi**

Answers will vary.

**Page 112—North Carolina**

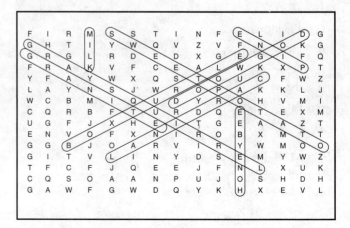

**Slogan in puzzle:** First in Flight

# Answer Key *(cont.)*

## Page 117—South Carolina

1. Rivers Bridge
2. Ft. Sumter
3. Charleston Harbor
4. Grimball's Landing
5. Simmons Bluff
6. Secessionville
7. Ft. Wagner
8. Honey Hill

**Coded phrase:** Civil War Battles in South Carolina

## Page 122—Tennessee

## Page 127—Virginia

D   Colonial Williamsburg

E   Jamestown

G   Yorktown

A   Mount Vernon

C   Richmond

F   Chesapeake Bay

B   Monticello

## Page 132—West Virginia

**Coded phrase:** Montani semper liberi *which means* Mountaineers are always free.

## Page 137—Illinois

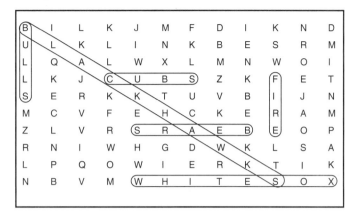

## Page 142—Indiana

**Coded phrase:** In 1854, the average length of the school term in Indiana was just two and one half months, possibly because at the time it was illegal to take a bath in the winter.

## Page 147—Iowa

**Coded phrase:** Our liberties we prize and our rights we will maintain.

## Page 152—Michigan

Lake Huron, Lake Ontario, Lake Michigan, Lake Erie, Lake Superior

## Page 157—Minnesota

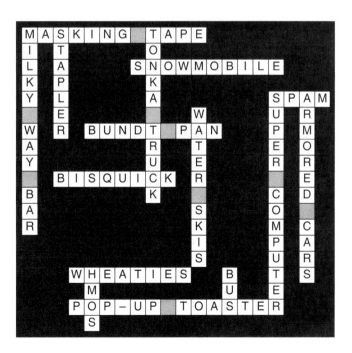

# Answer Key *(cont.)*

## Page 162—Missouri

1. Kansas City
2. Saint Louis
3. Springfield
4. Independence
5. Columbia
6. Saint Joseph
7. Saint Charles

## Page 167—Ohio

A Neil Alden Armstrong
Q Annie Oakley
G Arsenio Hall
M Benjamin Harrison
B Bill Boyd
Z Cy Young
D George Armstrong Custer
P Jack Nicklaus
F James Abram Garfield
R Jesse Owens
H John Herschel Glenn
S Judith Resnik
N Kenisaw Mountain Landis
C Nancy Cartwright
Y Orville Wright
L Rutherford Hayes
U Steven Spielberg
W Tecumseh
X Ted Turner
E Thomas Alva Edison
I Ulysses Simpson Grant
K Warren Gamaliel Harding
V William H. Taft
O William McKinley
T William Tecumseh Sherman
J Zane Grey

## Page 172—Wisconsin

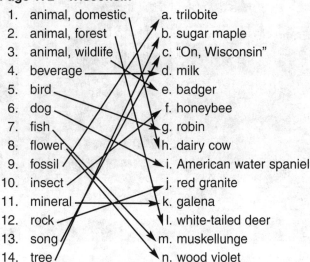

1. animal, domestic
2. animal, forest
3. animal, wildlife
4. beverage
5. bird
6. dog
7. fish
8. flower
9. fossil
10. insect
11. mineral
12. rock
13. song
14. tree

a. trilobite
b. sugar maple
c. "On, Wisconsin"
d. milk
e. badger
f. honeybee
g. robin
h. dairy cow
i. American water spaniel
j. red granite
k. galena
l. white-tailed deer
m. muskellunge
n. wood violet

## Page 177—Kansas

1. Abilene—*Greyhound* Capital
2. Cassoday—Prairie *Chicken* Capital
3. Chetopa—*Catfish* Capital
4. Cloud County—*Stained Glass* Capital
5. Dodge City—*Cowboy* Capital
6. Downs—*Storytelling* Capital
7. Geary County—*Fishing* Capital
8. Goodland—*Sunflower* Capital
9. Johnson County—*Bluebird* Capital
10. Kechi—*Antique* Capital
11. Kirwin—*Goose* Capital
12. LaCrosse—*Barbed Wire* Capital
13. Lenexa—*Spinach* Capital
14. McPherson—*Light* Capital
15. Phillips County—*Cow and Calf* Capital
16. Russell Springs—*Cow Chip* Capital
17. Thayer—*Watermelon* Capital
18. Wichita—*Air* Capital

## Page 182—Nebraska

1. Chimney
2. Omaha
3. Rock
4. Nebraska
5. Halsey
6. Unbelievable
7. State
8. Kearney
9. Express
10. Red
11. Series

**State nickname:** Cornhuskers

## Page 187—North Dakota

There once was a ranger from **Bismarck**
Who sought things North Dakotan in his park.
He smelled a **wild prairie rose**,
Saw a **flickertail** pose,
But alas, no Western **Meadowlark**

# Answer Key *(cont.)*

## Page 192—South Dakota

Black Hills spruce
coyote
"Great Faces, Great Places"
"Hail, South Dakota"
honeybee
kuchen
pasque
Pierre
Rose Quartz
triceratops
walleye
Chinese ring neck pheasant

mineral
capital
bird
flower
dessert
tree
fossil
animal
slogan
insect
song
fish

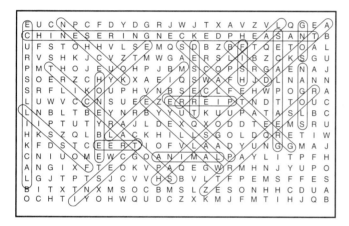

## Page 197—Arizona

1. Phoenix
2. PaloVerde
3. Grand Canyon
4. Petrified Forest
5. cactus wren
6. javelina

**Coded phrase:** Navajo Nation

## Page 202—New Mexico

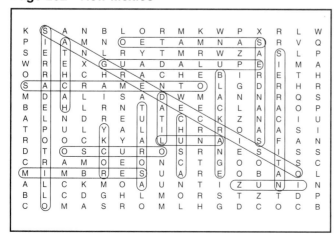

## Page 207—Oklahoma

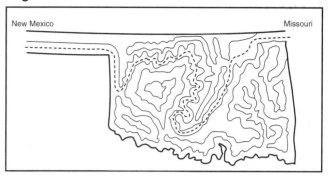

## Page 212—Texas

**Across**

4. Mockingbird
6. Houston
8. Austin

**Down**

1. Longhorn
2. Louisiana
3. Arkansas
5. Bluebonnet
7. New Mexico

## Page 217—California

1. The highest point in California is *Mount Whitney*. It is 173,940 inches above sea level.
2. The lowest point in California is *Bad Water*. It is 3,384 inches below sea level.
3. Fallbrook County grows more avocados than anywhere else in the world.
4. The largest county in the country is *San Bernardino County*.
5. The largest living tree is in *Sequoia National Park*. It measures 1,224 inches in circumference.
6. California raises the most *turkeys*.

**Bonus Questions:**

1. The young artichoke queen is better known by the name *Marilyn Monroe*.
2. Answers will vary.

## Page 222—Colorado

1. Sunshine
2. Leadville
3. Elevation
4. Incorporated
5. Rather
6. Very

**Capital:** Denver

# Answer Key *(cont.)*

**Page 227—Hawaii**

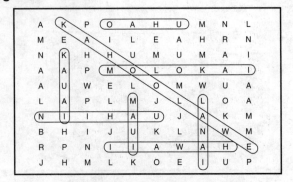

**Page 232—Idaho**

**Page 237—Montana**

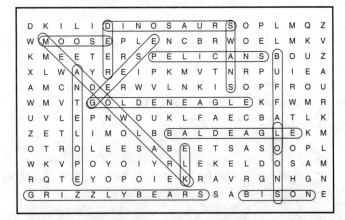

**Page 242—Nevada**

**Page 247—Utah**
**Coded phrase:** The Beehive State

**Page 252—Wyoming**

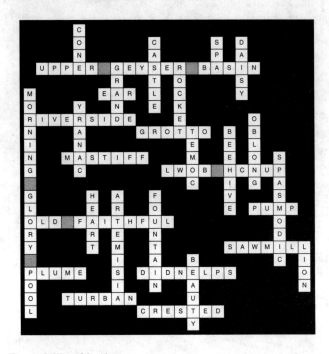

**Page 257—Alaska**
**Across**
1. Iliamna
3. Malaspina
5. Yukon
6. Ptarmigan
7. Juneau
8. Aurora Borealis

**Down**
1. Iditarod
2. McKinley
3. Mushing
4. Sitka Spruce

**Page 262—Oregon**

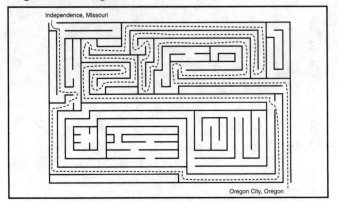

Independence, Missouri

Oregon City, Oregon

# Answer Key (cont.)

**Page 267—Washington**

```
L K F D S E Q P K L U W P
Q R L M M U T M U T T M U T
G H U M P T U L I P S R S
W E V B L U U N N F R S P
B G C L W K R S D O I L A
A R T U M W A T E R L L A
T O U M W I T E X K N B C
P E Q L M L N Q P S D O Y
E G A L L A W A L L A W N
O Y O P L U L A U R A N C
```

**Page 270—New England States Quiz**

1. e
2. f
3. d
4. a
5. b
6. c
7. e
8. a
9. f
10. b
11. c
12. d
13. b
14. c
15. d
16. f
17. a
18. e

**Page 271—Mid-Atlantic States Quiz**

1. e
2. c
3. d
4. a
5. b
6. d
7. c
8. a
9. b
10. e
11. b
12. d

13. e
14. a
15. c

**Pages 272–273—Southern States Quiz**

1. g
2. e
3. j
4. b
5. a
6. i
7. l
8. h
9. c
10. d
11. k
12. f
13. g
14. j
15. f
16. l
17. b
18. k
19. h
20. i
21. c
22. e
23. d
24. a
25. e
26. h
27. b
28. a
29. d
30. c
31. j
32. f
33. g
34. i
35. k
36. l

# Answer Key *(cont.)*

**Pages 274–275—Midwest States Quiz**

1. c
2. g
3. a
4. f
5. b
6. h
7. d
8. e
9. g
10. c
11. f
12. a
13. b
14. h
15. e
16. d
17. f
18. c
19. a
20. b
21. h
22. g
23. d
24. e

**Page 276—Great Plains States Quiz**

1. c
2. d
3. b
4. a
5. c
6. a
7. d
8. b
9. c
10. a
11. d
12. b

**Page 277—Southwest States Quiz**

1. c
2. d
3. b
4. a
5. d
6. c
7. a
8. b
9. c
10. d
11. b
12. a

**Pages 278–279—Western States Quiz**

1. g
2. e
3. h
4. c
5. a
6. d
7. b
8. f
9. b
10. e
11. f
12. a
13. g
14. h
15. d
16. c
17. g
18. a
19. h
20. e
21. b
22. d
23. c
24. f

**Page 280—Pacific Northwest**

1. b
2. c
3. a
4. c
5. b
6. a
7. a
8. c
9. b